Praise for Tracy K. Smith's

ORDINARY LIGHT

"*Ordinary Light* shines bright not because of extraordinary events that occurred in Smith's life but because of the warm glow the memoir casts on the simple everyday life of a young girl yearning to do great things. . . . Smith's spare yet beautiful prose transforms her story into a shining example of how one person's shared memories can brighten everyone's world."

—*Minneapolis Star Tribune*

"[A] forceful memoir . . . rendered indelibly."   —*The New Yorker*

"A riveting read. . . . Smith writes about her childhood with humor and acute insight."   —Terre Roche,
O, The Oprah Magazine

"[Smith's] self-scrutiny, her empathy, and her lifelong quest to figure things out—in particular our bedeviling national aches, religion and race—make for an indelible self-portrait: moving, utterly clear, and compulsively readable."

—Mark Doty, author of *Fire to Fire: New and Selected Poems*

"A lyrical reminiscence. . . . [*Ordinary Light*] overflows with memorable stories."   —*Pittsburgh Tribune-Review*

"Both precise and transcendent. . . . [Smith's] revelations about identity, religion, and family feel as momentous as anything Barack Obama once put between covers."   *Vulture*

Tracy K. Smith

ORDINARY LIGHT

Tracy K. Smith is the United States Poet Laureate. She is the author of four acclaimed books of poetry, including *Wade in the Water* and *Life on Mars*, winner of the 2012 Pulitzer Prize, a *New York Times* Notable Book, a *New York Times Book Review* Editors' Choice, and a *New Yorker*, *Library Journal*, and *Publishers Weekly* Best Book of the Year. A professor of creative writing at Princeton University, she lives in Princeton with her family.

ORDINARY LIGHT

ORDINARY LIGHT

a memoir

Tracy K. Smith

Vintage Books
A Division of Penguin Random House LLC
New York

FIRST VINTAGE BOOKS EDITION, MARCH 2016

The Library of Congress has cataloged the Knopf edition as follows:
Smith, Tracy K.
Ordinary light : a memoir / Tracy K. Smith. — First edition.
pages cm
1. Smith, Tracy K.   2. Smith, Tracy K.—Family.   3. African American women
authors—Biography.   4. Mothers—United States—Death.   5. Mothers and
daughters—United States.   6. Coming of age—United States.   7. Home—
Psychological aspects.   8. African Americans—Race identity.   9. Identity
(Psychology)—United States.   10. Poets—Psychology.   I. Title.
PS.M5955Z46 2015   818'.603—dc23   [B]   2014026185

Vintage Books Trade Paperback ISBN: 978-0-345-80407-5
eBook ISBN: 978-0-307-96267-6

Book design by Betty Lew

www.vintagebooks.com

Printed in the United States of America
10   9

FOR NAOMI

But something deep and watchful in the child knows that this is bound to end, is already ending. In a moment someone will get up and turn on the light.

—JAMES BALDWIN, "SONNY'S BLUES"

CONTENTS

CONTENTS

ORDINARY LIGHT

PROLOGUE: THE MIRACLE

SHE LEFT US AT NIGHT. IT HAD FELT LIKE NIGHT FOR A LONG time, the days at once short and ceaselessly long. November-dark. She'd been lifting her hand to signal for relief, a code we'd concocted once it became too much effort for her to speak and too difficult for us to understand her when she did. When it became clear that it was taking everything out of her just to lift the arm, we told her to blink, a movement that, when you're watching for it, becomes impossibly hard to discern. "Was that a blink?" we'd ask when her eyelids just seemed to ripple or twitch. "Are you blinking, Mom? Was that a blink?" until finally, she'd heave the lids up and let them thud back down to say, *Yes, the pain weighs that much, and I am lying here, pinned beneath it. Do something.*

Did we recognize the day when it arrived? A day with so much pain, a day when her patience had dissolved and she wanted nothing but to be outside of it. *Pain.* The word itself doesn't hurt enough, doesn't know how to tell us what it stands for. We gave her morphine. Each time she asked for it, we asked her if she was sure, and she found a way to tell us that she was, and so we were sure—weren't we?—that this was the end, this was when and how she would go.

I was grateful for my brother Conrad and his wife, both doctors. None of the rest of us would have known how to administer the drug in such a way as to say what we needed it to say—*Take this dose, measured out, controlled, a proven means of temporary relief—* rather than what we knew it actually meant. Grateful, and hopeful that the training might stand guard against the fact that the patient was our mother.

The nurse who came by each day was a cheerful person who knew not to be cheery. Calm, available, knowing, pleasant. But she stopped short of chipper. She must have been instructed not to bring that kind of feeling into a home that was preparing for death. Not to bring hope. Instead, she brought mild comfort, a commendable gentleness that helped to rebuild something inside us. The nurse cared for our mother the way we sought to care for our mother: with no signs of struggle, no stifled rage at God and the unfair world, no tears. In changing our mother's bandages and handling her flesh with such competence and ease, the nurse cared for us, too. Once a day for only an hour at a time, she came and eased our load just enough to get us to the next day when we knew she'd come again.

I had sat and read the hospice literature one morning at the dining room table. A binder with information about how to care for the dying at home. It said that as death approaches, the body becomes cool to the touch. The limbs lose their warmth as the body concentrates its energy on the essential functions. Sometimes when I was alone with my mother, I'd touch her feet and legs, checking to see how cool she had become. I was both frightened and reassured that the literature was correct, as if her body was saying goodbye to the world, preparing itself for a journey— though that's not it, exactly, for the body goes nowhere, merely shuts down in preparation for being left. I could sense my mother leaving, getting ready for some elsewhere I couldn't visit, and like the cool hands and feet I'd check for every day, it both crushed and heartened me. Every day, she spoke less, ate less, surrendered a little more of her presence in this world. Every day, she seemed to be more firmly aligned with a place or a state I believed in but couldn't decipher.

When the dark outside was real—not just the dark of approaching winter, and not just the dark of rain, which we'd had for days, too—her dying came on. We recognized it. We circled her bed, though we stopped short of holding hands, perhaps because that gesture would have meant we were holding on, and we were finally ready to let her go. Each of us took a turn saying "I love you" and "Goodbye." We made our promises. Then we heard a sound that seemed to carve a tunnel between our world and some other. It was an otherworldly breath, a vivid presence that blew past us without stopping, leaving us, the living, clamped in place by the silence that followed. I would come back to the sound and the presence of that breath again and again, thinking how miraculous it was that she had ridden off on that last exhalation, her life instantly whisked away, carried over into a place none of us will ever understand until perhaps we are there ourselves.

It's the kind of miracle we never let ourselves consider, the miracle of death. She followed that last breath wherever it led and left her body behind in the old four-poster Queen Anne bed, where for the first time in all of our lives it was a body and nothing more.

After it was clear that she was gone, my sister Wanda rose from the floor where she'd been sitting—we'd all gone from standing around her to sitting or huddling there on the rug around the bed; perhaps we had fallen to our knees in unconscious obedience to the largeness that had claimed our mother, the invisible power she had joined—and crawled into bed beside her, nestling next to her under the covers just as we'd all done when we were children. The act struck me then as futile. In those last many weeks, I'd grown used to looking at my mother, changed almost daily, it seemed, by the disease. And every day, I'd fought to find a way to see her as herself, as not so very far from whom she'd always been to me. But now she was something else altogether. Wasn't it obvious? The body already stiffening, the unnatural, regrettable set to the jaw, as if the spirit had exited through her mouth. Still, Wanda, the first-born, clung to her, crying, eyeing each of us as if to say, *She was mine first. Which of you is going to drag me away?* It was the type of gesture I'd have expected my father to chastise her for, though of course he didn't; none of us did. He was just as undone as any of us, though he'd done his best. In the moments after it was clear what had happened, when we found ourselves coming to in the bleak and unreal reality of her death, he'd said to my sisters and me, "You must be brave"—the thing fathers tell children in old wartime movies. I'd tried my best not to judge him as lacking in imagination, for I knew that while what he'd said was patently unoriginal, it was also true. I tried not to judge Wanda, either, but I admit that I took her invitation to even the possibility of struggle as in questionable taste. Perhaps, after a moment, she came to the same view herself, at which point she stood up and agreed to wait upstairs with the rest of us.

We all instinctively wanted the strangers who were already on their way to find our mother as presentable in death as she had always been in life, and so Conrad had agreed to stay behind to prepare the body, to change her clothes and the bed linens. He and his wife, Janet, the doctors, doing what nurses do in order to protect the shell, the empty shape, the idea of our mother from even the slightest tinge of scorn or even simply the rote disregard the attendants might have brought to their work. He'd cried doing it. Readying her to be taken away had been his moment of realization, his genuine goodbye.

There was a moment when I found myself alone with her in the room. Had I crept back down to steal a last look, or had we all agreed to give one another that much? It's been twenty years now. I've forgotten so much that I once forbade myself to forget, but I do remember this: snipping five or seven strands of her hair with a pair of nail scissors from her bureau. Just a few short hairs from the nape of her neck. Suddenly, those few strands, things I'd have once thought nothing of brushing off her shoulders or discarding from among the tines of a hairbrush, were consecrated, a host. For a moment, I contemplated eating them, but then they'd be gone and I'd have been left with nothing, so I placed them in a small plastic bag, the kind of bag in which spare threads or extra buttons are provided when you purchase a sweater or coat, and tucked that into the flap of my address book.

I

MY BOOK HOUSE

THE HALLWAY LEADING TO MY PARENTS' BEDROOM WAS lined with oak bookshelves my father built. Simple, sturdy work upon which stretched decades' worth of school-bus-yellow *National Geographic* magazines, and the stern brown spines of the *Encyclopedia Britannica* dating from before my birth. On a low shelf there was a frayed blue-and-green twelve-volume set of nursery rhymes and children's tales called *My Book House* in which my sister Jean had written her name over and over in large, teetering letters. It was an antique from the 1940s, and in one of the early volumes there was a story called "Little Black Sambo." Sambo was depicted as a dark-skinned pickaninny running around the bush of Africa. My parents laughed at the story in the way people laugh about something that was once incendiary but has since run out of force, and yet I gathered that that particular laughter also had something to do with why we never, ever ate at the restaurant in our town called Sambo's.

There were the books my father would forever push me to read: *Kidnapped, Gulliver's Travels, Ivanhoe,* and the ones I eventually came to discover on my own, books I'd disappear into for days at a time: *Black Beauty, Anne of Green Gables. To Be Young, Gifted and Black* stood beside *Yes I Can,* by Sammy Davis, Jr. (which I remember poring over one morning when I was eight; everyone else was still asleep, and I read it while eating plate after plate heaped with my mother's Alabama lemon cheese layer cake, with its lemon curd and fluffy coconut icing). There were dime-store mysteries and my father's science-fiction paperbacks and chaste 1950s teen romances alongside *The Sonnets of William Shakespeare* and *The Works of Ralph Waldo Emerson*. Joke books and cookbooks. Books whose titles appeared to be in the midst of conversation: *Manchild in the Promised Land* beside *Stranger in a Strange Land* beside *Be My Guest,* by hotelier Conrad Hilton. And right below them, a yard or so of Reader's Digest Abridged Classics, squat little books into which three hefty novels had been scaled down and squeezed together for quick consumption. All of them snugly in place and restful, having made their peace with one another in a past that predated me.

I always assumed that our father was responsible for gathering most of those volumes. He was the one I imagined sending stacks of perforated order forms off to the book clubs, the one who'd sit down in the evenings with the *Reader's Digest* or stretch out on the couch with a pipe and a science-fiction paperback. But our mother must have read them, too. She'd been a teacher once, before I was born. Mostly now what she seemed to read was her Bible or the palm-sized Christian devotional magazine that came once a month, *Our Daily Bread*. There were some of her books on the shelves, I'm sure of it, books on child rearing and theology, but the majority of what sat there spoke to my father's sense of the world—or the world as he'd like us to know it: a vast and varied place full of mystery and order, just those two forces working together and upon each other in ceaselessly fascinating ways. For our mother, those same two forces were sides of the one and only God, *I Am That I Am*. For our father, they were tied up in physical laws that could be located everywhere: in the animal kingdom, the human body, the endless darkness of space. Did he see them in the world of people, too, I wonder? Were they the laws that informed what one person did to another, be it hurtful or kind? When he'd enlisted in the service at eighteen and left the South, had he been fleeing a mystery that had gotten the better of him or seeking a new and better order?

Dad had become an engineer in the air force. He'd been to Europe and Asia on his tour of duty and had brought emblems of those places home for the rest of us to turn over in our hands or stow away in the china cabinet among the holiday dishes. He came back from Thailand six months after I was born with a reel-to-reel player and mahogany-encased hi-fi component set. On Saturdays after I was old enough to talk, I'd beg him to queue up the big machine and sit beside me listening to *Camelot* or *The King and I*, while the giant spools spun slowly around like the eyes on a robot. I wonder if those were the only recordings we had or if I simply liked being swept up in the fantasy that my father and I were members of the same royal court.

Most every faraway thing we knew of or possessed had been filtered to us through our father, and I, for one, came to think of him as a character from the books he collected—someone out of Dickens or Thackeray who had fled a humble past and made himself anew, led off by his curiosity and the wish for adventure and kept aloft by his wits, his innumerable gifts. The fact that he spent most of his days just a few miles away at the air force base and that he'd come home to us every night, never once picking up and taking off like the characters in books often do, didn't deter my sense of him as a citizen of the world. Whenever I came upon my father sitting alone with his head cocked up to that place where thoughts originate, I'd imagine he was retreading his steps through faraway cities or stitching himself into a dream of some other life in a place that didn't exist yet in words. As I got older, I'd sometimes puzzle over whether it was unrest that held him there in what seemed to be ponderous distraction, but never did I ask him. I preferred to keep the idea of him, at least for myself, as something of a mystery.

I felt large, coming from a man like that. I'd watch him move through our house, watch him arrange a pillow behind his back and stretch out his legs beside him on the couch like a king. "Catch me a glass of water," he'd call toward the kitchen, and when it appeared, I'd watch the liquid transformed into might as it disappeared down his throat. When he lay down on his back, his chest and abdomen rising and falling with rhythmic sleep, I remember reclining atop, weighting him to the world with my small body and listening to his great heart rumbling beneath my ear.

When the air force sent our father out of town on temporary duty, I'd crawl into bed at night beside my mother. My brothers and sisters had done the same thing until they got too big to do so, by which time I was just starting to toddle around underfoot. Sometimes, I'd wonder if my mother had had me so long after she'd given birth to the others simply because she'd wanted another baby around the house, someone to cuddle up with and coo to and carry around like a living doll. When she was mine like that, I'd sit up against the pillows beside her, wanting to chat and giggle, zooming through the details of my afternoon and my wishes for the days and weeks ahead. Or I'd lie beside her and listen while she talked on the phone with one of her sisters back East— conversations during which her voice took on a different timbre, where she'd suck her teeth or let out a quick guttural *hmph* or burst into throaty laughter at a comment that would have struck me as nonsense. When that other voice coaxed her to travel the distance back to the old days down South, she'd let slip a phrase like "ain't that a blip," and then, anticipating my reproach, cast me a look meant to say, *Don't worry; I know* ain't *isn't a word.* After she hung up, if I asked, she'd give me enough of a synopsis so that I could understand some of what they'd been talking about, even if my grasp of who was who in her enormous family remained loose. And then she'd lead me in a bedtime prayer for all of them in her great big raucous clan. Perhaps she wanted to make sure I learned all of their names, or perhaps she would have done so silently anyway: *Please bless Aunt Evelyn, Aunt Ursula, Aunt Gladys, and Aunt Lucille and Aunt June* and on and on until, eventually, their names became a kind of song.

All eight of her sisters, with their thick dark hair and their exquisite perfumes, were for the longest time only a vague collage of incomplete impressions in my mind. The smell of something cooking on a gas stove or the matching chintz drapes and sofa in someone's living room. A skinny, pull-down stairwell leading up into the attic where someone else had set up her sewing. Candy bowls and plates of cookies. An unguarded, gut-bucket laughter spilling over into the wee hours of night. They belonged to a world that felt almost completely foreign to me, though I also knew that I somehow belonged to it, that I could claim it as my heritage, that those men and women were people I carried inside me, too, even if I couldn't yet recognize them. What would it take for me to learn my way around in that labyrinth of voices and the knowledge they all seemed to rise up from, a knowledge that almost always rode in on laughter—even the dark, dry laughter a story like "Little Black Sambo" conjured?

Often before saying good night, my mother and I would read a chapter together from *Little Visits with God*, a book of stories about children put into situations in which something must be decided. Small decisions affecting girls in pedal pushers and Mary Janes or clean-cut boys with sharp creases down the fronts of their pants. I loved the ritual of lying beside my mother and working through the chapters with names like "How to Treat Mean People" or "Smile Before Sundown," thinking how truly simple it was, when it really came down to it, to do what is right. I remember being absorbed by one drawing of a girl holding a box of cookies, stuck in a quandary about whether to share them. I found it easy enough to race ahead and determine what should be done in most of the book's scenarios. Instead of suspense, *Little Visits* promised something different. The allure of that bounty of cookies—were they peanut butter? Chocolate chip? The protagonist's pressed jumper and shiny 1950s shoes, like emblems of a world in which perfection was the likeliest of all outcomes, a world in which children ran from house to house under the clear blue sky, listening, eventually if not at first, to a calm and clear voice telling them what to do, how to be, a voice that watched over them, guarding against harm. A world a child could grasp and parse and line up confidently in her mind before drifting off to sleep. "Stand perfectly still!" a father called out to his daughter in a different chapter. Obeying him, the girl averted being bitten by a snake hiding in tall grass. A world built to a child's scale, whose mysteries stood within a child's grasp, and revealed themselves at a child's request.

I doubt my mother believed the world was that simple, that transparently clear, but it strikes me as logical that she would have wanted me to see it that way, at least for a time. It strikes me as logical that she would have wanted me to obey the voice of my father and to equate it with the voice of God, commanding, "Stand perfectly still!" or "Come here this instant," with an infallible authority.

It strikes me as logical that she might have wanted me to live awhile in a world governed by such certainty and to take the confidence and the faith imparted by that world with me into the real world, once the time for such passage arrived.

Of course, I didn't make such a distinction then. I couldn't have. And so it seemed to me that God, who cared enough to nudge children to share with one another and who kept an eye out for danger lurking unseen, was the kind of person (for He did seem to me a person, someone to call on by name—a father with a son, no less, though it wasn't lost on me that He was certain to be much more than that, too) I wanted to have by my side.

As my mother read, I'd sometimes let my eyes drift across her face, taking her in out of habit, memorizing her, breathing in her smell, the way she held herself, the lilting cadence of her voice. Her eyes were wide-set and large, so large and clear they were the first thing anyone saw about her. When she smiled, which she did often, it started in those wide, clear, impossibly large eyes before spreading to span her entire face. I'd count her beauty marks: one near her nose, one on the cheek, the ones on the back of her arm and peeking out from the deep V of her nightgown's neckline (adding in the one near the bottom of her thigh, which I couldn't see because it sat beneath the blanket). Then I'd study her hair. Short hair she was always complaining wouldn't grow. Hair that had to be coaxed and coddled and conditioned and primped and permed or tucked up underneath a shiny wig before it would act right. Considering her body, I'd hear the echo of all the things she'd found to bemoan: she was full-hipped, dieting incessantly; her feet were too big; her nails were brittle, always fighting a losing battle to remain intact. But watching her warmed me. I was calm and safe beside her, right at home. I didn't think to call it beauty, but beside her, I felt what the presence of beauty makes a person feel. It smelled like her Mary Kay night cream and the Oil of Olay she'd let me smooth onto my face before bed. And it was warm and solid, like her sleeping back, which I'd burrow into when she flicked off the light and the room went black.

Did I ever wonder who my mother used to be, before she belonged to me? I have the recollection of her struggling once or twice to describe her younger self to me, and finding that girl unrecognizable. The phrase she used, that so much seemed to hang upon, was "I was searching." *What were you searching for?* I would ask, confused, eager to understand. Why couldn't she explain? "I was lonely," she offered. "I was looking for an answer." *Why? An answer to what?* My questions sought hard definites, when what it sounds like to me now is that she didn't know. Did it just make for an easy story to tell, or was what she found at the end of that search really the same voice the children in *Little Visits* learned to discern and obey? Having lived beside her, with the voice of God as close and as discernible, I was urged to believe, as that of my father, I had no idea what it could have meant to be "searching." What could have possibly been lost?

I grew up in Northern California, one town over from Travis Air Force Base, where my father was stationed. The town was Fairfield, a spot on the map smack in the middle between San Francisco and Sacramento, and for a long time, it seems now, I was still small enough to believe our house was enormous. My father filled the outside with trees, shrubs, flowers, and other plants he tended with devotion more scientific than aesthetic. He liked to watch how things grew, transformed, survived—the logical, natural world backed and set in motion by something that resisted explanation. My mother decorated the inside with antiques obtained and refinished over the years and drapes and pillows she sewed herself. It was a physical space that began to take on the features of her inner world: pleasing, tidy, functional, with slight nods to fantasy, like an ornate fireplace mantel my father built at her behest or a family of pewter quails that made a perpetual slow march across the living room coffee table. It was the life she assembled for us, I see now. A life that would tell us, and the world, if it cared to notice, that we bothered with ourselves, that we understood dignity, that we were worthy of everything that mattered. No matter what the world thought it knew about blacks, no matter what it tried to teach us to believe about ourselves, the home we returned to each night assured us that, no matter who was setting the bar, we could remain certain we measured up. When our teachers came for lunch, as they all eventually did, this is what she wanted them to see.

There were seven of us: Mom, Dad, Wanda, Jean, Conrad, Michael, and, after a lapse of about eight and a half years, me. "Seven is God's perfect number," my mother said sometimes, dragging one of the kitchen chairs to the dining room table before dinner. We might have been eight. They would have called the other child Ian if it had been a boy. "I guess it wasn't meant to be," my mother would offer whenever I'd ask why there was such a large gap between my older siblings and me. The doctor had wanted to use the minuscule body for research, but my mother refused. It would have seemed cruel to poke and prod and slice into the child who wasn't meant to be. Would that have been me, or was I always me, waiting to bring up the rear, to fall into place as the youngest, the baby, the kitten of the clan? (That was even what they called me, *Kitten*.) Seven meant that, for a long time, I always had someone willing to look away from the real action of what was happening in our house and with whom to exchange a significant glance: *Did you catch that?* or *Shhh—don't say a thing*. Seven meant that, for a long time, I could always hear the murmur of voices from my bedroom at night; I'd fall asleep in the knowledge that we were many, that we were all still here, that the world as we understood it to be was still on track.

Seven is God's favorite number, but in time our nuclear unit, like every other, would disband. In the now I'm remembering, however, we are steady, steadfast, happy, and whole. No one has yet left home and in so doing tripped the wire on a progression leading us all further into the future waiting to claim us. In the now I'm remembering, it is still only this: Michael and Conrad together in the room upstairs on the left, Wanda filling the big pitcher with water while Jean helps bring the food to the dining room. My father putting aside his book and calling us all to stand around the table with our heads bowed and then to sit down to hot rolls with butter and a meal promising that nothing bad would come for us for a long time.

WILD KINGDOM

I T WAS A SUNDAY AFTERNOON AND I WAS FOUR, RIDING BE-
tween my parents in the front seat of the wood-paneled Chevy
station wagon as my father guided us westward along Interstate 80.
The world outside the windows was hot and bright, caught up
in a gasoline shortage and a hostage crisis; on TV each night, we
watched the angry bearded faces chanting in faraway streets, shouting things against Americans like us. Everything was suddenly
costlier, more precious, cause to put on the brakes, to creep along
at a measly 55 mph. My two sisters shared the backseat and seemed
to be mirror opposites of one another in every way: they both had
bobbed hair, but Wanda's was curled so that the ends flipped up
exuberantly, while Jean's tucked shyly underneath. My brothers,
Michael, who wore a string of puka shells that accentuated the big
permanent teeth he'd still not quite fully grown into, and Conrad,
with his large, wise eyes and his afro that always, despite his efforts,
came to a slight point on the top of his head, shared the space we
referred to as the "far-far-back."

It must have been late summer, because we were on our way to
the Gustafssons' ranch to pick up ripe fruit for my mother's homemade preserves. Mr. and Mrs. Gus were friends from a place called
the Hospitality House, where military families spent occasional
evenings together in a thing called *fellowship*, which meant people
arrived near sundown to hold hands in a circle and pray. Afterward,
everyone ate lemon cream sandwich cookies, and the kids drank

punch out of the same small paper cups I used when I brushed my teeth at home. The adults would stand around with coffee, paid out like slot machine winnings from the giant percolator on the table. There must have been a lot of gatherings like this over the years, because the whole room had taken on the smell of stale coffee—a smell I'd forever associate with Jesus.

We were heading to Mr. Gus's ranch, because my father loved to eat two pieces of toast with his breakfast and to fold each slice around pears cooked to an impossible sweetness and spiced with cinnamon and cloves or two figs swimming in thick amber syrup. My father's love of breakfast had turned the morning meal, for all of us, into a ritual, a rite we enacted with joy every single day. To that end, every summer, I helped my mother stir vast pots of the summer's harvest into the thick magic we'd later ladle into the glass canning jars. And every morning, practically, I'd spoon some of the stuff from summers past onto my own toast or biscuit, hardly thinking that so much of what the jams and preserves were made of was her.

The Gustafssons lived in a modest red ranch house just over the hill on the other side of the interstate, but they had a whole hillside's worth of fig trees and orchards of pears, peaches, apricots (which we called "ape-ricots," though just about everyone I met later in life would say "app"), and bitter black walnuts, along with a few old work mules and some chickens and cows. And there were cats and dogs that wandered the acres in obedience to their own sense of purpose, barely interested in stopping to let you pat their thistle-ridden fur. When they got to be a little older, my brothers helped out at the Gustafssons' place to earn spending money in the summer months. Once, they watched in anxious disbelief as a bull scratched the dirt with his front legs and blew out a cloud of hot steam before charging straight for where they stood filling his water trough. They hopped the fence to safety in time, but even when they told the story years later, there remained the shadow of terror just beneath their laughter.

At the top of the Gustafssons' drive, there were bags of picked fruit waiting for us on the porch, but Mr. Gus took us on a tour of the ranch before packing them into our car. We'd just come from church. I was wearing one of my favorite outfits, a blue-and-white dress with a white cardigan and socks and brown Buster Brown shoes. Our ankles and feet got dusty following Mr. Gus through the parched grass and sun-baked dirt, but no one seemed bothered by it. Even my sisters and mother walking in high heels and pantyhose didn't seem to mind.

As we came to each different variety of tree, Mr. Gus would pull down a bough and offer everyone a piece of fruit. My mother split open an apricot with her thumbs and handed it to me. The flesh was warm and sweet, with a bright tang that reminded me of sunlight. Later, she gave me a bite of a small peach and bits of a walnut Mr. Gus had cracked between his bare hands. Mischief flashed on her face as she tore a fig in two and put half of it into my father's mouth. When she offered some to me, I said, "No, thank you," and shook my head, repulsed by the white pith and the pulpy flesh. It looked like a venomous sea creature, but when she lifted the fruit to her own lips, she practically swooned, like a woman on television who had just lowered herself into a bathtub full of bubbles.

When we approached a hen and her cluster of chicks, I instinctively began to reach out toward the downy babies, but Mr. Gus stopped me. Without speaking, he placed his hand near the chicks and held it there a moment. Immediately, the mother began to flap her wings in agitation and moved in angrily to peck him. She bobbed up and down, driving her beak into his bare hand like the needle in my mother's sewing machine. He didn't recoil right away, but when he finally did and gave me his hand to examine, there was a purpled and bloody patch of skin the diameter of a gobstopper. I pulled the sleeves of my cardigan down over my own hands and walked on.

We came to a clearing where a few cows and one calf stood grazing. The cows were unbothered and slow, larger than any other living thing I'd seen up close. Mr. Gus laid a hand on one, who didn't stop her jaws from their slow grind of a clump of grass, though her head swung around to face him. Her eyes were deep and kindly, rimmed in black and shaded by thick long lashes, like a lady's. I couldn't help it; her placid femininity backed by quiet strength—not like the frantic hen whose love had made her nervous but rather calm, grounded in a steadfast, sturdy certainty— reminded me of my mother. Instantly, I trusted her, would have lifted my own hand to the thick mottled wall of fur were it not for her calf, which was watching us from farther away. Small and brown, with new fur I could already imagine the plush of against my cheek, the calf saw me, too, and she (I decided it was a she) stood still, having also just grasped our shared affinity (at least it seemed that she had), eyeing me in a way I took to mean that my own feelings were mirrored in hers. I forgot all about the wicked chicken as I ran toward the calf, who took a few lively steps away, but coyly, as if to suggest we play a game of tag.

This is for me, I remember telling myself, meaning the sweet young calf and the strong, serene mother. I knew that I knew them, understood their bond, and that they knew me, too. I knew that I could slip in among them for a moment and revel in the love that spread out around them. It was all I knew, and so I dashed after the calf, laughing, wanting to show her, to step into their version of the language my mother and I spoke, and to carry that joy, that giddy out-of-breath knowing, back over into the human.

Then, before I could tell myself what had happened, the calf was lowering her two hind legs back to the ground and casting a quick look over her shoulder as she pranced off. And I was doubled into myself, clutching my stomach, which throbbed and burned where the calf's hooves had struck me, ashamed for the sobs that any second, I knew, would begin to issue from my throat.

I felt betrayed, stunned by this first taste of cruelty. It was my first collision with the world's solid fist.

On the ride home, my father said, "That calf wasn't being mean," looking down from the road. "It was only protecting itself." The straw-colored hills off to the side were dotted with cows and unsaddled horses that whirred past in what felt like a taunt.

"From what?" I asked, as another knot of tears inched higher in my throat.

"From *you!*" My father let out a quick laugh, and his laughter jostled loose the tears I had been struggling to swallow. I felt as though I'd been wronged, but I also knew that my father was right. How many times had we sat together after Sunday dinner watching one or another episode of *Mutual of Omaha's Wild Kingdom* with Marlon Perkins, in which a pride of lions or hyenas tore into the side of an unlucky zebra? And how many times had my father sought to silence my disapproval with some variation of the phrase "It's a necessary part of nature"? We'd go on to do the same thing that evening at home, except this time as I watched, I would feel myself implicated, as though I had stepped irreversibly into a strange and fearsome dominion. One in which I was capable of inciting panicked flight but vulnerable, too. Fragile as the creature that might soon feel the flash of contact.

SPIRITS AND DEMONS

M Y FIRST HALLOWEEN WAS THE YEAR I WAS FIVE. SOMEHOW
the others had gotten past without my catching on, my
brothers and sisters being too old for the spectacle, or merely less
intrigued by what it promised. But the year I was five, my best
friend planned to go trick-or-treating dressed as Raggedy Ann.
Once she'd explained to me what to expect—the costume, the
candy, the weeks-long pirate booty of sugary bliss—I cajoled my
parents to let me go along. From the moment they said yes, all I
could imagine was a bounty laid out like a road to infinity: Tootsie
Rolls, peanut butter cups, candy corn, lollipops, and more, offered
freely by stranger and friend alike on one night only.

I imagined going as a whole host of things: Bugs Bunny would
have been near the top of the list. I thought he was so clever and
debonair and quite nearly handsome, at least for a rabbit. I had a
stuffed fox named Rascal that I'd carried around dotingly since I
was three, and he would have made a nice model for a costume,
too. But the animal costumes would prove to be time-consuming
and expensive to make, with a discouragingly wide margin of
error. I wouldn't want to be mistaken for the Easter Bunny or a
red dog. My mother said she could sew up a ghost costume from
a white sheet in just an evening, and since the time was drawing
near, it seemed the most reasonable choice to make.

"When will my costume be done?" I asked for the tenth time
and with Halloween just a few days away.

"Don't worry," she replied again and again, though with increasingly less assurance than I was used to hearing in almost every other thing she said. I found it strange. Mom had sewn me dress after dress in no time at all, and she'd made curtains and bedspreads, quilts and pillows. There seemed to be nothing out there she hadn't made or couldn't learn to with the ease and skill of a true seamstress, but she was dragging her feet with the ghost costume. I couldn't help but worry.

Part of the bang of Halloween was bound to be muffled by the fact that October 31 was also my father's birthday. Instead of traipsing through the neighborhood in costumes, we usually gathered around the dining room table for roast beef or pork chops. After dinner, we'd adjourn to the family room for *Star Trek* reruns and slices of my mother's homemade pound cake, a staple in my family, which my father liked to place atop a bowl of vanilla ice cream that had just begun to melt. It was important to mark the occasion, even with something as simple, as unceremonious as this: a good meal followed by the silence that signals generalized contentment. Hugs and kisses. A pair of pajamas and a necktie or two. My mother would buy packages of white handkerchiefs as gifts from me to him, and I'd present him with a card I made myself: HAPPY BIRTHDAY DADDY floating above a drawing of him and our house. The year I was four, I drew our backyard and our dog, Sebastian.

"What is that?" he asked, pointing to something indistinct coming out of Sebastian's stomach.

"That's where he . . . defecates," I'd explained. "And that"— here, I'd pointed to a dark spot on the otherwise green lawn—"is dog mess." (I couldn't figure out just then how to get from a verb like *defecate* to whatever the product of such an act should be called. Our parents didn't believe in babyish nicknames for perfectly normal bodily functions. We never used words like *poop* or *pee*, and it would be years before I'd discover there were worse words out there in circulation, words like *shit* and *piss*.) My father thanked me, gently suggesting that in the future I didn't need to bother with "every last anatomical detail" in my art.

To ignore the occasion of my father's birthday, even if we only ever celebrated it modestly, would have been hurtful, not just to him but to the idea of us as an invincible unit, as something to cleave to even if it meant missing out on what everyone else in the world was doing. However, this year was different; it marked the moment when I'd asked for and been granted the opportunity to have both.

It may well have been that my mother was busy shopping for Dad's birthday dinner and had gotten temporarily sidetracked from working on my costume. Or maybe she was overwhelmed with plans for the party in my kindergarten class. She was, after all, the room mother, and on the day of the party, she planned to bring in cookies, punch, and a whole six-foot-long "snake" sandwich for all of us to eat. (She also informed me that bobbing for apples, which one of the other mothers had agreed to facilitate, was unhygienic and that I should put some serious thought into whether I really wanted to participate.) Nevertheless, I was beginning to suspect that something else altogether was holding up my costume.

"I don't believe in ghosts and monsters," she'd said when I asked her if such things were real.

"What about witches?"

"Witchcraft is real, but God doesn't like it." I'd heard the word *witchcraft* before but never given it much thought. I'd been under the impression that it was the made-up stuff of fiction, like the harmless bits of magic Samantha the witch performed in reruns of the old TV show *Bewitched* or the more wicked but equally unlikely feats that set fairy tales into motion.

"What about skeletons and jack-o'-lanterns?" My best friend's parents had toasted the pumpkin seeds after carving her jack-o'-lantern, and we sprinkled them with salt and ate them. They were so delicious I'd persuaded my mother to let us do the same at home. My father had even carved a smiling face into my pumpkin and put a nub of a candle inside.

"We're Christians," my mother reminded me. "We believe in God and Jesus." She made her face expressionless and relaxed in a manner that hinted something heavy might be on the way. "And, as a Christian, I don't think God is very happy on Halloween."

I wondered how one night of kids in costumes out trick-or-treating could bother God.

"I know dressing up and getting candy is fun," she continued, "but what Halloween celebrates, things like evil spirits and demons, are the things of the occult. They belong to the devil, and they can be dangerous."

I'd heard those words before, too—*spirits, demons, the occult.* They came up at church, in stories where one of God's followers must remind his foolish and forgetful people of God's commandments. Like Moses, when the Israelites went to such lengths in order to worship a golden calf. Or Jesus, casting out demons from the possessed. Though I had never personally come up against an evil spirit or a demon and doubted that I ever would, my mother was asking me to understand that such stories were warnings I ought to take seriously. *Be sober-minded; be watchful. Your adversary the devil prowls around like a roaring lion, seeking someone to devour.* The stakes my mother was hinting at were far higher than they appeared to be.

I sensed that she was torn. She wanted to make me understand the bigger picture, but she also wanted to make me happy. She was most concerned, I'd guess, with the symbolism of a night like Halloween, the things our costumes and make-believe fright seemed to glorify. But she also understood how excessive it would be to argue that a single night of trick-or-treating could have had heavy implications for my everlasting soul.

And I was torn, too. I knew she wanted me to make the right decisions in all things, just like the children in *Little Visits with God*, decisions that would glorify God. She would probably have been very glad if I had then and there decided to retract my request and skip Halloween altogether, but I couldn't get the candy out of my mind and the fun my friend Kim had assured me of. I wanted to push harder, to make her see that I understood the danger (I thought I did) and that I would be careful to keep my heart and spirit attuned to God and all that was good (I would certainly try). But I also sensed there was a good chance that if I questioned Halloween any further, her sense of moral duty might require her to put on the brakes, to shut down the Halloween machine entirely, so I nodded and forced myself to say nothing. She eyed me a moment, thinking but choosing not to speak, and the conversation dwindled away.

The thirty-first fell on a Monday. The snake sandwich was really just chicken salad on long submarine rolls, which had been cut and laid out so that the whole thing looked like a huge wriggling serpent with two big black olives for eyes and a mouth propped open as if about to strike. Everyone in my kindergarten class was thrilled, except for one girl who exploded into loud sobs that didn't subside even after my mother knelt down and explained to her how the sandwich was made. There were cookies in the shape of pumpkins and a punchbowl of 7Up in which floated a whole half gallon of orange sherbet. I was so proud that my mother had thought of everything—she'd even rigged the punchbowl with dry ice, so it seemed to fume like a witch's cauldron. Yet I was confused, too. It all seemed so scary, so real, yet she'd made it clear that none of this Halloween stuff met with her actual approval. Was it for me? Was it a way of telling me she understood that I understood and that we could do this for fun, without believing any of it and without fear that it bothered God? Or was she sad inside from all of it, sad in the way God would have been sad about the smoke and the snakes and all the ghoulish to-do? With my eyes, I kept trying to ask her what was going on, why she had given in so wholeheartedly to the spooky affair, but she was too busy making sure everyone had gotten enough to eat and drink.

After lunch, we lined up at the apple-bobbing basin. I stood behind Jimmy Higgins, who, when it was his turn to go under, splashed around like a cat someone had tossed into a well. Even after he came up for air, he was still slobbering, and a thick trail of yellow mucous slithered out from one of his nostrils (it took a moment before he noticed and sucked it back up into his head). Watching Jimmy had made me want to forfeit my turn, but backing out would have given credence to my mother's other admonitions, both uttered and implied. So I put on the plastic smock and stood peering into the cloudy water. I closed my eyes before descending into the murk. It was unpleasant and cold, and the apples shied away like darting fish. I'd been blowing bubbles out through my nose so as not to choke down there, but there came a time when I ran out of air. I opened my mouth, though I knew in my heart of hearts that it wouldn't land me an apple. It didn't. Instead, water rushed down my throat. When I came up, I tried not to look as punished as I felt, but I couldn't help sputtering. Someone came at me with an already-wet towel, untying the plastic apron and handing it to the next child in line. A long, dark hair that was not my own stuck to my tongue. Finally, after so much searching and waiting, my mother's eyes at last met mine, only now I was in no mind to reassert my question or risk reading *I told you so* in her gaze. I went and stood beside her, not looking up, only leaning my head into her side, watching as the number of children with dry hair and clothes dwindled down to none.

"The party was so nice," I beamed on the ride home. A popcorn ball and a caramel apple had long since taken my mind off the indignities of the bobbing pool. "I didn't know you knew how to do all that, Mommy." And watching her watch the road for the few blocks it took to get back to our house—watching her hands calm yet firm upon the wheel and the way she looked down at me from time to time, letting me smile up into her face and returning the smile with real warmth, with love I could see and feel—I could tell that no matter what she believed in, right at that very moment she and I were alone together, Kathy and Tracy, just our two souls in the car moving surely toward home, full and intact with something bigger and more real than any of the questions or beliefs we might struggle to fit into words. I knew, just at that very moment, that she was glad in the way every mother who makes her child happy is glad.

Before dinner, my mother sat down to finish stitching up my costume. It wasn't merely a sheet into which eyeholes had been cut but a two-piece affair with bell sleeves and a removable head. The holes for my eyes had stitching around the edges so the fabric wouldn't fray. At the top of the head, the mask wasn't as round as I'd envisioned it would be. In fact, it was rather pointy. I wouldn't look like Casper the Friendly Ghost at all, yet it did remind me of something I'd seen before but couldn't quite put my finger on. No matter. My heart raced at the prospect of venturing out into the night.

Conrad's eyes got bigger and rounder when he saw me in my costume. It seemed to remind him of something else, too, and because he was older—fifteen and already in high school by then—he surely must have known exactly what it was. He looked at my mother with what appeared to be bewildered disbelief. There must not have been too much riding on it, though, because she merely shrugged him off with a cryptic smile.

"Remember your manners," she told me as I stepped up onto the landing by the front door. "And don't wander off from Kim and her dad."

Outside, the evening was warm. I saw plenty of superheroes bought right off the shelf and packs of homemade *Star Wars* characters pieced together by all the kids whose parents had taken them to see the movie. (I recognized them from the lunchboxes and stickers my friends carried to school, though I didn't know them firsthand or why they'd caught most everyone else up in an intergalactic frenzy.) Older kids out on their own in hastily conceived costumes scared me, they were so riled up with freedom and lust for candy. One had thrown a paper bag on his head like the Unknown Comic; others were draped in makeshift togas or parents' bathrobes.

For every three or four times I shouted "Trick or treat," one person handing out candy would point at me and ask what I was supposed to be. When I answered that I was a ghost, most seemed relieved, though one or two appeared to remain skeptical. Once, looking up for an explanation of all this adult confusion, I caught Kim's dad shaking his head, an expression of mild exasperation plastered to his face. I knew this had to do with me and with the silent conversation that had taken place between Conrad and our mom, but I couldn't figure out what the precise terms were. What if I asked Kim's dad what the fuss was all about, and his answer was that I had done something wrong? Or what if my mother had made a mistake in her rush to be done with Halloween? Wouldn't it be worse if all the to-do revealed that the error was hers and not mine? It didn't even occur to me that no error had been committed, only a subtly calculated act, a trick instead of a treat, directed not so much at me but at the very ethos of the holiday itself. If I had, my child's mind could not have unraveled the convoluted logic that had driven a black woman from the Jim Crow–era South to dress her daughter, even only allusively, as one of the most despicable emblems of racial hatred, as someone worse than the devil himself.

I'm not sure I can claim a clear understanding even now. My mother was in her early forties that autumn, nearly the same age I am now. The KKK, with its flaming crosses and its lynching sprees and the ghastly apparition of those white hoods, would have been real to her—not merely symbols of an earlier era but artifacts of a time she had known, specters from the real-life stories that would have haunted her childhood. Was stitching up a mini Klan costume for her unsuspecting five-year-old a way of depleting the image of whatever lingering private terror it might have held for her? I suspect she wasn't fully conscious of what she'd done until she'd done it, at which point the only thing to do was remark to herself, "Ain't that a blip," and then get on with things. Of course, none of this occurred to me then. At the time, I did what any five-year-old would do. I continued along, holding out my bag, smiling my biggest, most exemplary smile, even though nobody could see it behind my great big pointed white hood.

"Is it okay if I take this off?" I finally thought to ask, lifting the top part of the costume off over my head as we turned into the last cul-de-sac of the evening.

"That sounds like a good idea," Kim's dad answered, sensing it might be easier that way for all of us.

At home, I wasn't given access to any of the loot until it had all been spread out on the family room floor and examined. We'd been hearing rumors of kids eating Halloween candy that had been spiked with hallucinogens. One child, the story went, had even been given a candied apple with a whole razor blade inside. (In one version of the tale, he'd sliced his tongue open biting into the treat. In another, he'd bitten into the apple just shy of the blade.) Anything that had come open in my trick-or-treat bag was relegated to the trash. A box of raisins was discarded, too, just in case. What was left was a confectionary spectacle: candy enough for all seven of us and then some. My parents laid claim to anything with coconut: Mounds and Almond Joy bars and the chewy tricolor Neapolitan squares wrapped in clear cellophane. My siblings cozied up to their own small share of the stash even as the last witches and robots of the season climbed up our stone-speckled front steps.

Where exactly was the occult? I wondered, staring out the storm door into the finally quiet evening. Was there really a place where spirits and demons—all the beings God disliked—came from or congregated? Who made them and what did they want? Had they been good at first and only turned bad, like the Klansmen still alive in my mother's memory, the ones who must have watched quizzically from the margins of her mind, not knowing whether, at the sight of me, to feel a sense of victory or defeat? They must have been far from God, but how could that be, if God was everywhere? Maybe they hovered between Him and us, though that, too, seemed wrong, for didn't God live in the hearts of those who believed? What was it like for God as we went about our lives, doing the things He loved and the things He hated, some-times without even knowing the difference between the two? And what was it like for the strange in-between beings, the ones we pre-tended to run from on Halloween? How many worlds were there, and what did they want from us, there, in our houses, under the low roofs of our lives?

KIN

WHENEVER MY FATHER TALKED ABOUT NEW YORK, HIS face pinched in and words like *filth* and *squalor* darted out of his mouth. "Why would anyone *choose* to live in New York?" he'd ask, and, not knowing any better, I'd figure it must be the kind of place where life was so relentlessly mean that people often came to blows with whatever object was closest at hand. If it was, what did it mean for my aunts and uncles—women with thick legs and strong arms who clapped their hands and threw back their heads when they laughed; men who called everyone by nicknames, kicked off their shoes, and ate sandwiches at midday made from biscuits and peach preserves and thick strips of leftover bacon that stuck out past the bread? What kind of lives were they, not to mention my innocent cousins, living in a place like New York?

When I was six years old, my cousin Nina visited from Manhattan. In one of our family photo albums, there is a picture of the two of us together as babies, sitting on the porch of our grandmother's house in white sun hats with elastic bands under our chins. I hadn't met her many more times than that, but just about every autumn, I'd inherit a large box full of Nina's outgrown dresses. Those two things, the photo and the dresses, always gave me the impression that Nina and I were the best of friends, but when she arrived, it dawned on me that I was greeting a stranger.

Nina was two years older than me, tall and thin, with long legs covered in mosquito bites, which she scratched with an exquisite vigor. When my mother told her that scraping away at her legs like that would leave scars, Nina said she knew, and then she scratched them anyway, grating her shins with her fingernails and sighing in pleasure. She scratched with such gusto that she made my legs itch, too, but I sat on my hands, remembering what I'd been taught. Nina further fascinated me in the first hours after her arrival by singing Rod Stewart's "Da Ya Think I'm Sexy?" over and over like her very own theme song. When she sang it, she shimmied her hips from side to side and smiled a smile that told me she was being deliberately provocative. If it was a stunt, it worked. I watched in breathless disbelief, timid and stunned, hotly curious about what else she was capable of.

The next morning, I looked on in wonder as Nina stirred a slice of American cheese into a bowl of piping hot grits. She didn't want the eggs my mother offered her, or the toast, and it had been her idea to ask for the cheese, which turned the white grits pale orange.

"Try it!" she urged me, lifting a forkful up to her mouth. The melted cheese dangled over the bowl like ticker tape.

At first I hesitated asking for my own slice of cheese—I liked putting the scrambled eggs and the grits side by side on a plate and then mixing the two discrete mounds together until they formed one lumpy porridge, just like my dad—but Nina's conviction intrigued me. I unwrapped a sheet of cheese from the pack of singles and lay it atop the grits, watching it wilt and wrinkle in surrender to the heat. It didn't quite look right to me, but it sure tasted right, especially once I'd shoveled my eggs onto the heap, and I wondered why I'd never been taught to do that before.

When my plate was empty, I stood up and called to my mom, "I enjoyed my breakfast," laying my napkin on the table and pushing in my chair, just like my dad always did.

"Thank you, Aunt Kathy," Nina chimed as she carried her own bowl all the way over to the sink.

That wasn't how we usually did things, but it struck me as polite, so I picked up my plate and utensils and followed suit. Then the two of us excused ourselves to the front yard to play.

When we got outside, after she had made certain that no one was watching, Nina licked her index finger and wrote MOTHERFUCK on the dirty window of my mom's car. I didn't know what it meant, but I knew it meant something, and my initial reaction was silence—the kind of silence a child feels when some new gear in the world begins to turn for the first time. MOTHERFUCK revolved slowly in my stomach and my head and my heart, pushing every other thing away.

There were kids who whispered or occasionally even yelled the word *fuck* on the playground at school, bigger kids who seemed to relish the shock and the weight of it. *Fuck* was mostly just that, a shock and a weight, pure inflection, a word without precise meaning. It signified something bad, worse than bad. The kind of thing that would cause a teacher to march out to whomever had launched it into the airspace and yank him (it was always a him) off the playground by his elbow or the neck of his shirt. Those boys wore happy, wicked smiles all the way to the principal's office, reveling in the thrill a word like that leaves in its wake. Still, no matter how much I'd thought I knew about *fuck*, I had never witnessed it buttressed against a word like *mother*. Was MOTHERFUCK a noun or a verb? Whatever it was asking me to imagine tugged me into an alien zone.

"That's not a word," I tried to insist.

"Yes it is," Nina countered, though she didn't need to; I knew in my heart she was probably right. She had picked up the word in barbarous New York and carried it with her all the way to sunny California. She wouldn't have done that if it had no value.

I must have struck my cousin as so traumatically perplexed—were my eyes really beginning to well up with tears?—that she felt obliged to lick her whole palm and wipe the word from view. It disappeared, but every time I saw the smudge where it had been, the dark feeling returned, a feeling like being out of my depth in water that, only a few yards back, had felt safe. I think it might have weighed upon Nina, too, to be disappointed so immediately by the cousin she'd traveled such a distance to see.

It was spring break. I wonder if Nina's mother, my aunt Ursula, searching for something to hold her daughter's attention during the string of unstructured afternoons, had had to convince Nina to leave her friends behind for a week or if my cousin had been eager to glimpse the fabled Golden State, that place with the wide sun-smacked streets, Disneyland, and its own cavalcade of television stars moving freely among ordinary mortals. Whatever her reasons were for coming, and whatever she had been expecting, what Nina found in Fairfield was a hot, dry, low-to-the-ground expanse of white-, yellow-, and olive-colored stucco houses set behind uniform rectangles of lawn. Disneyland was a whole eight hours away by car, though in me, perhaps she'd run up against what may have struck her as a Disney-like fantasy of the way the world worked: *if you're a good girl, everything will be okay.*

I couldn't help it. I was steeped in the wisdom of *Little Visits with God,* fearful of disappointing my heavenly Father—and worse, wounding my mother with anything less than exemplary behavior (or infuriating my actual father, whose eyes would redden when he was about to scold us with one of his go-to phrases, like "Stop that infernal racket," or if one of us had really done it, "Get out of my sight"). When I saw other boys or girls misbehaving, I was shocked, pained for their parents, who would have to take them aside and explain how things ought to be done. I'm not sure, now, why it is the parents with whom I identified. Perhaps having so many older siblings helping to reinforce our parents' wishes had made me hyperaware of what was expected of children and what kind of work went into showing them right from wrong. Once, sitting in the grocery store aisle in a metal shopping cart, I watched a boy my own age pump his legs back and forth as if he were on a playground swing. His mother had turned her back, comparing labels or price stickers on boxes of cereal, and in the few moments he had to himself, the boy worked up enough momentum to wheel himself several feet up the aisle. At one point, he and I made eye contact. He smiled recklessly, waiting to see if I was going to imitate him, but I was too dismayed by the thought of sending my mother scurrying after me to give it a try. Besides, what he was doing was naughty. If it wasn't, why had he waited until his mother's back was turned to try it?

My mother was proud of my decorum. She liked having a little girl who instinctively wanted to obey. She would give me instructions once, and I'd do just as she said, never considering the alternative. Obedience came so naturally to me that I am sometimes now perplexed by my own daughter's equally adamant belief in the primacy of her own free will. Sometimes, I catch myself feeling cheated out of what I had naturally expected would be my due: a child so willing to please me she'd be incapable of doing anything other than what I ask.

Nina struck me as my inverse, my photographic negative. She wasn't dangerous or bad—I see her behavior now as quite adorably spirited—but she knew how to test things, there on the sidewalk or in our living room shimmying to her own tune: *If you want my body, and you think I'm sexy, / Come on, sugar, let me know.*

"Why don't you tell Nina about Jesus," my mom suggested to me one morning before my cousin had ventured downstairs.

Anticipating the conversation that would ensue, the engine in my chest picked up speed. Not because I was embarrassed or because I was being asked to attest to something I didn't believe, but because I wanted to make a good case, to get it right and convince Nina of how happy she would be—as happy as the kempt boys and girls who clasped their hands in prayer or smiled up at firm but loving parents in the pages I studied every night before sleeping—if she opened her heart and asked Jesus to come inside. For if it wasn't belief that accounted for our differences, what could it have been?

I went upstairs and sat on the foot of Nina's bed. I held the copy of *Little Visits* in my lap, thinking it might be helpful to show her how all the children in the book had found use for God's word and His will in their lives.

"Have you ever invited Jesus into your heart?" I asked her.

Nina knew full well who Jesus was, of course—everyone did—but had she ever prayed for Him to help her when she needed help or to guide her to do good things when it would have been easier (and, I suspected she might believe, more fun) to do bad?

"Well," I continued, "if you ask Him, He'll never leave you. When you're afraid, you can call on Him, and when you need it, you can pray to Him for help."

Nina asked a sensible follow-up question. "He'll give me *whatever* I ask for?" And, not wanting to mislead her, I explained that there are three answers that God or Jesus will give you when you pray for something: *Yes, No,* or *Wait.* When it appeared that the odds of getting a *No* seemed to be giving Nina some pause, I tried to step up my pitch. I told her about guardian angels, making it sound like God would give her her own personal bodyguard, and about the many mansions and gold-paved streets in Heaven.

But Nina was shrewd. Her face held on to just the hint of a smile, and I couldn't quite tell what she was thinking. Was I getting through to her, or was she simply humoring me, letting me go through my spiel so that she could more carefully observe this strange breed of girl she had never before encountered? I sat at the foot of her bed, which was normally my bed, while she leaned back against a pillow, watching me talk. I felt like a guest, like someone brought in to amuse a queen, and when I ran out of things to say, I stood up and backed away. It strikes me that I must have been afraid, not of failing God or disappointing my mother so much as having to accept the fact that my cousin's understanding of the world was incontrovertible, nothing I would manage to rein in or tamp down in fifteen minutes on an April morning. Nothing I, in my limited set of experiences, was likely to comprehend. Her view of the world stood on sturdy block letters, just like the word she'd written on the windshield of my mother's car, and it cast shadows of doubt upon the hard-and-fast absolutes I'd been taught to accept.

Soon after that, Nina and I started bickering. Not constantly and not for very long, but there were moments each day when she would roll her eyes at my Pollyannaish outlook, and I would frown at some tidbit of the Big Bad City that had crept into our play. I was on edge, afraid that another ticking bomb (like MOTHERFUCK, which I couldn't stop remembering) would be held out for me to turn over in my hands.

My mother knew things were tense between us. "Nina is family," she reminded me, adding, "If you're having a hard time, pray about it."

So at night, I did. When my mother tucked me into the bed Wanda had left behind when she'd gone away to college, I asked Jesus to watch over Nina and show her how to be good. It was easy to close my eyes and believe that if I could show Nina Jesus's love, everything would be as bright and cheery between us as a bowlful of cheesy grits.

One afternoon, while we were outside hitting tennis balls against the garage door, Nina and I fell into another disagreement. If it had to do with tennis, the game was merely a pretext, a more acceptable instigator of anger than, say, the fact that we were fed up with one another's company. Instead of laying out her case (she knew it wouldn't have persuaded me) or agreeing to disagree (she'd already done that when she'd erased MOTHERFUCK from the windscreen of the car or sat patiently while I told her all about Heaven), Nina lifted her tennis racquet in the air and brought it down upon me as if it were the hammer of some pagan god.

When it hit, the racquet, which she had swung in an act of emphasis—emphasis and exasperation—hurt like a slap to my sensibility, a smack at my notion of all that mattered in the world. It hurt harder than an ordinary blow (at least I thought it must have; I'd never actually been struck by anyone but a calf before), and it made one thing clear: if I wanted to salvage things with my cousin—if I wanted to return to the easy rapport we'd had as babies posing for pictures in our white sun hats—I'd have to swing back.

The air was full of a stifling acrid smell from the Callery pear trees blossoming up and down our block. I drew in a deep breath. It was hard to do, but I gripped my racquet in both hands and raised it up near my ears like a bat. It was going to feel just awful bringing the racquet down on Nina's shoulder or her back, but I knew I had to. She wasn't going anywhere for several more days, and if I ran crying to my mom, it would only confirm that I was foolish and prim, a Goody Two-shoes and a bore. I closed my eyes and swung. I knew it was the kind of thing that Jesus would be miserable watching me do. Once I managed to get the image of Jesus out of my mind, I thought of my mother and of how, were she to catch sight of us, she would at first be confused, thinking it couldn't possibly be her daughter there beating the living devil out of Nina with a tennis racquet.

I was crying, which didn't surprise me, but when I saw that Nina's face was streaked with tears, too, I recognized that we had reached a kind of draw. We both must have sensed it, because we gave up with the racquets and went inside to sit on the couch. I felt those same gears, the ones set in motion by MOTHERFUCK, spinning freely in a space that had, less than a week ago, been difficult to clear. I was still too shaken to know whether that meant something in me had been broken or whether it had merely broken free. I had no idea what Nina felt. We sat beside one another on the family room couch, our arms just barely touching, neither of us bothering to move away from the other.

MAGGIE WAS PLUMP WITH A SCRATCHY VOICE, PERCUSSIVE AND quick. She wore military fatigues and shiny brogan boots. We'd met her in the meat aisle of the air force commissary, and in the few minutes it had taken for my mother to ask where she was from and how long she'd been stationed at Travis, Maggie dropped phrases like "aw, hell" and "my old man" that gave me the feeling

I knew things about her that I ought not to know. When she used a foul word, she glanced my way, then looked back at my mother and said " 'Scuse me," smiling.

On the day of Maggie's visit, my mother wore a beige shirt-dress with a brown leather belt and matching flats. She smelled good. The whole house smelled good. She made a Waldorf salad (which I secretly disliked), rice pilaf with chicken, and green beans amandine. She'd even gotten up early to make the dough for home-made rolls. I had been charged with buttering the pan, a task that had earned me bits of the raw, chewy dough for which I'd opened my mouth as wide as a baby bird's. Most important, there was a still-warm pound cake waiting under a domed cake saver for its turn on the table.

Maggie was nothing like the ladies from the church who came by in their floral dresses to drink coffee and pray, sitting straight as boards; nothing like the military wives we'd meet sometimes in restaurants to swap stories about one posting or another, the ones who disappeared from our lives as quickly as they came, trans-ferred to another base or just drifting along a different axis. Now, I wonder if that was at least part of the reason why my mother had invited Maggie over in the first place. Perhaps she herself was tired of the remoteness and self-control of her relations with other women. Maybe she hoped that Maggie's presence in our home might constitute an occasion to let her own voice climb up to the top or dive down to the bottom of its register, to slap her thighs in laughter, to stand up and imitate one person or another in the boisterous, free way she did with her husband and children or her own brothers and sisters.

When Maggie walked through our door, she looked quizzical, as if she'd been looking for a nightclub and had been led to a chapel instead. She followed my mother into the living room and sat down, face still frozen in a curious expression. I was sitting on the floor in front of the coffee table, working my way through a new coloring book and not quite fully listening to what they were saying, but the second or third time one of Maggie's *ain't*s landed in my ear, I managed to get in a quick "Don't say *ain't*, say *isn't*." I tried saying it gently, in case Maggie had forgotten or in case she never knew in the first place. After that, my mother asked me to go and make sure there were napkins on the table. I knew they were there, because I had just that morning rolled them up and threaded them through the pewter napkin rings, but I went to check anyway, taking the opportunity to steal a pat of butter from the dish and let it go to liquid on my tongue.

When the three of us sat down to lunch, I recalled the manners that had been instilled in me. Napkin in my lap, mouth closed while I chewed, no smacking, no elbows on the table, no reaching across for extra helpings. I took small, neat bites. If I needed to speak, I prefaced my comment with "Excuse me, Mommy." If there was a food I didn't like (like Waldorf salad), I ate it anyway, out of courtesy. Maggie was much easier on herself, heaping her plate and eating quickly, like a boy. During lunch, she looked around as if pulling her questions out of the different corners of the room. She asked my mother, "What do you *do* all day here in the house?" "Do you all go to church?" and "Do you play pinochle or whist?"

For my mother's part, she was friendly and smiling. She laughed when Maggie laughed and chuckled sometimes at the undertone of bewilderment in so much of what Maggie asked and observed. But she didn't ever stop being a hostess. She didn't take off her shoes or make any jokes. Instead, she comported herself in the same way as she did with the church ladies and the air force wives.

There was a line she could have crossed, a line she had allowed herself to cross before with women she'd met and invited over, women whose voices had become legendary in our family, thanks to the way my mother had narrated her encounters with them. One had been German, and she'd confided to my mother, "To German womens, black mens is *gold.*" Another said, "Aww, sookie sookie, now," and called my uncle Arthur "just as tender as a little lamb." I suspected that Mom would repeat one or two of Maggie's comments, mimicking her deep, raspy voice, once my father and siblings were home, but for the duration of their lunch, the side of my mother capable of clowning like that stayed tucked in tight. For whatever reason, Mom never showed Maggie the version of herself that Maggie was certain to have liked.

I think, now, about what my mother had meant when she'd told me, "I was searching." I imagine her a young woman alone with one or two or four children while her husband, my father, was overseas on duty. Had she reached out to God only after she'd exhausted the communities of women she hoped might keep her from feeling alone and unmoored? It must have been lonely, con-fiding in a sequence of people who came and went as if through a revolving door, there one day and transferred away the next. Had God become vital to her because, unlike the people in her life, people who moved according to the dictates of their military superiors, He was constant, always present? *I will never leave thee nor forsake thee.*

If there had been a particular motivation for inviting Maggie over, I must also acknowledge the possibility that it had to do with God. Mom did that from time to time, invited people over hoping our home might serve as a conduit for God's love. Once, a teenage girl named Faye, who lived in state-sponsored foster care, had spent the weekend with our family. I don't know how Mom had found

Faye, but she'd been put up in Wanda's empty bedroom and taken with us to church before being driven back to her foster parents on Sunday evening. Faye had been tight-lipped. She only smiled when my brothers went to lengths trying to make her laugh, and then only briefly. She projected a stoicism that made her seem much older than fourteen. It could be that she had been instructed to be on her best behavior or to be on guard against some ulterior motive, by whoever had given her permission to come with us in the first place. Or maybe the foster care system itself had made her wary. I don't know what our impression upon Faye had been, if we'd made her happy or uncomfortable or if anything in our lives had reached her as a model to be emulated. After she left, my mother spent some time trying to remove signs of water damage from the footboard of the bed where Faye had draped her wet towel.

After Mom and I cleared the lunch plates from the table, the look on Maggie's face said she had just about decided to collect her things and leave. She craned her neck looking around the room for one last clue. Maybe she caught sight of one of my father's ashtrays, clean as a whistle (one of my chores), or his pipe-stand on the governor's cabinet in the family room, because the next thing she came out with was "Do you smoke?"

My mother didn't smoke, and Maggie didn't seem inclined to light up all by herself.

"*Hmph*," Maggie said, twisting her mouth up into an off-kilter pout. "Well, do you *drank*?" It was a question asked, it seemed, to verify what she had already come to suspect: that there was nothing other than the coffee they had already drunk or the pitcher of ice water, beaded with condensation and still on the table within her reach.

Ah, but what if things had gone differently? What if my mother had reached under the kitchen sink to pull out a big green jug of Almaden Mountain Rhine, thunking it down on the table as if to say to Maggie, *I'll show you my hand if you show me yours?* What if, letting their glasses clink in the air, they'd let the conversation beeline away from small talk about hometowns or military postings to touch upon a topic with real meat and mass, like love? What if Maggie told my mother about the men she ran with and the places they went, the smoky air base lounges where songs like "Too Much, Too Little, Too Late" and "You'll Never Find Another Love Like Mine" were queued up on the jukebox? And what if my mother had inhaled deeply and then let it out, the long, slow breath of truth about what it really felt like to wait for her husband for months at a time, praying he was safe, praying he was worthy of her trust, while she was home looking after a small battalion of children? What might have transpired there between the two of them then?

My mother's poise was not an act, but there was something gleaming and spirited beneath it, something that instigated pranks and stunts that could bend the rest of us over in laughter. No matter how decorous she was and how much she lived by the grace and the humility of her faith, there was always this other thing we knew was there, this mirthsome, living thing that set her apart from the church ladies and the military wives and everyone else she knew. I loved when she brought it out and let it run around without reins, like a bareback horse. Like the time, cleaning out the kitchen pantry, she tossed my brothers Tupperware bowls and told them to put them on like crowns and gave them spatulas and turkey basters to hold up like scepters and then made the two of them pose for pictures in chairs perched atop the patio table as if they were a couple of insane Everglades kings. Or the evening when the topic of nicknames came up for discussion in the family. Everyone had a go at choosing a new moniker: Wanda chose Wani to replace her usual Sissy. My dad confided that, when the time came, he'd like for his grandchildren to refer to him as Papa, accented as in the French. I can't remember what I chose; I was happy with the nickname I already had: Kitten. When it was my mother's turn, she said that she didn't want to be called Mom, or Mama, and that we should cease calling her Mommy. She told us with a straight face, "Call me Sexy." She could be as giddy and unself-conscious as an actor heaving life into a new role or a child inventing a story, and her excitement and freedom ferried some of her exuberance of spirit over to us, but not everyone was lucky enough to know that side of her.

Maggie certainly wasn't. For whatever reasons on that day, my mother seemed incapable of calling it up or unwilling to let it out, and so our guest emptied her water glass and set it back down on the table, taking on the tone of someone who really must be getting back to work. Before I knew it, the three of us were standing by the front door, and my mother was thanking Maggie for having come.

"Well, ain't that a blip," my mother said after Maggie was gone, sighing.

"*Ain't* isn't a word," I reminded her.

"I know, Tracy. I know."

LEROY

HAD IT EVER STRUCK ME AS ODD THAT MY MOM, WHOM I called *Mom* or *Mommy*, should have referred to her own mother with such formality, as *Mother*, or that I should call my grandmother that, too? *Mother*? No matter that Mother was more likely than not to drop the *r* and more than a few *s*'s from most anything she said, she was invariably known as *Mother* to all thirteen of her children and all thirty or more of her grandchildren. I'd hardly thought to wonder why my mom, the eldest of a whole passel of Deep South farm kids, would have decided to call her *Mother* instead of *Mom* or *Mama* or even *Muh*, which is what our second cousins in Sacramento called my great-aunt Cora (we referred to that entire wing of the family as *Muh 'n 'em*). It did strike me as odd that I called my grandmother, whom I barely knew, something that sat so close to home—Mother—but I did. It was what everyone did.

My first fleshed-out memory of Mother comes from a two-week visit to Leroy, Alabama, that Mom and I took the summer after first grade. My brothers and sisters stayed home. They were in junior high and high school and even college by that point and had other things to do. Not to mention that it wasn't a simple matter of hopping in the car and driving, as the whole family had done in the years before I was born, when Dad was stationed in Texas or even as far north as New Hampshire. No, flying the seven of us out from California would have cost a fortune, so Mom and I made the trip by ourselves. I'd been to Alabama just one time before that I could remember, when I was three. But everything from that first visit is crowded out by the silent, gentle presence of my grandfather Daddy Herbert, who bought me crayons and comic books after I'd gashed my face trying to shave with his razor. It's a recollection tinted a pale pink from the drapes of the room where I convalesced.

The details of this summer, though, remain indelible. It had been my first time on an airplane. The stewardess gave me a set of pilot's wings and a pack of playing cards. At dinnertime, I ate a little square ramekin of lasagna and drank orange juice made watery and cold with squares of ice. It felt exotic, as if we had genuinely lifted off from our lives on the ground. Perhaps for that reason I had known to be quiet, to speak in the hushed tones of wonder or transgression. I stayed up late. My eyes were open for all of a Farrah Fawcett movie, and when it was over, I curled onto my mom's lap and finally slept.

When I woke up, we were there, and then we were in a car, on the road to Mother's house.

I'd been expecting the deep country, with pitch-black skies and insomniac owls, the kind of place that would have meant a leap through time back to the world my mother sometimes reminisced about, with its outhouses and smokehouses, its miles and miles of the cotton Daddy Herbert paid her and her siblings pennies a bushel to pick. Someone—was it my mother or her sister Evelyn?—used to laze at the ends of rows, daydreaming, letting the others take up her slack. At night they'd all sit down to a big country supper, with Daddy Herbert at the head of the table, proud of his army of boys and girls and of the land he'd worked hard to buy.

I'd expected to find a past like that still going about its business, flush with the present. Instead, there were Datsuns and Cadillacs parked on the streets and billboards and sprawling modern supermarkets that seemed to stand a whole world away from the version of Alabama my mother's stories had sketched in my mind's eye.

Once we pulled off the two-lane main road, we rolled onto a carpet of dense clay. There were tall oaks and pines on either side and houses that sat some distance from one another. A red clapboard house with white trim stood upon stilts; bits of daylight that had pierced through the trees and shrubs shone out from under it. We took a turn onto a smaller road—or was it, by then, a path?—which gave way to pebbly gravel. A bell of recognition chimed inside me when I saw Mother's house, a brick one-story that sat alongside a barn, a pond, and dense woods. Perhaps because I'd seen it in so many old photos of my grandparents standing together like a dark version of *American Gothic* and of my aunts and uncles, still just children, playing barefoot in the dirt.

The little house was my only respite from the blaring midday heat—humid, and relentless. Compared with the hot, dry afternoons and cool, breezy nights I was used to, Alabama weather seemed almost predatory. Inside, the place smelled of things I had trouble identifying: cooking gas, pork fat, tobacco juice, and cane syrup. Three generations lived there: Mother; her mother, Mama Lela, who, at nearly eighty, was smiling and chatty, chewing her snuff and spitting the dark sappy liquid into a Folger's coffee can; and Dinah, my mom's youngest sister, who was the same age as my sister Jean. (I could never get my mind around the fact that my mother and her mother had been pregnant at the same time, like sisters.) Within hours of our arrival, Dinah had taught me to plant my feet shoulder width apart and swing my hips back and forth while a forty-five of the disco hit "Le Freak" played over and over on the turntable. We danced together all morning, Dinah laughing and me reveling in the song's assurance that I was not so far from home—after all, it wasn't impossible to imagine my siblings listening to the same song just then on our stereo in California. "Le Freak" might have served as an anchor, a touchstone emboldening me to let go of some of my apprehension of that foreign place, had the record not melted onto the turntable the very next afternoon when the curtains were left open in hot sun.

As excited as I had been in the weeks leading up to our trip—*I'm going on an airplane! I'm going to my grandmother's house!*—Mother remained inscrutable to me, nothing like the kindhearted lady in my mom's stories, the one who turned out big fluffy cakes and sat laughing beside a lively, jocular Daddy Herbert. For one thing, my grandfather was gone. He died of a stroke the year I was four. Without him at her side, Mother seemed stern, watchful, almost feral. I felt scolded by her small staring eyes and the hardscrabble set of her mouth. Furthermore, the path of communication leading from her to me was a zigzag guaranteeing that anything set upon it would lose momentum, rolling to a standstill just shy of my feet. She'd ask, "Does that little gal want some water?" leaving my mom to look at me with an expression meant to reiterate the question, which I would then answer meekly, watching as it was repeated for Mother at an audible decibel level. When Mother did speak to me directly (often calling me by the name of my younger cousin Stacy), my ensuing silence—a result of confusion about her accent or her funny words for things—would prompt my mom to repeat it for me. It was like being stuck in a relentless game of telephone.

My brothers and sisters grew up spending summers in Leroy,

playing with a cadre of cousins; running around under the feet of Daddy Herbert and a younger, more easygoing Mother; racing up to the general store with the shiny coins they'd been given for sweeping the porch or folding laundry. But just when it should have been my turn for all that, the Mother everyone remembered seemed to disappear. Nobody said where she had gone or why she had left.

I admired the fact that my mom could stay afloat in this place that had me utterly confused, seeming as it did to rely upon a different language and currency. In her childhood home, Mom was herself and something more. She knew how to hold her own with Mother, how to put on an apron and become one of the women of the house, how to be silent without feeling chastised by the wordlessness of whole long segments of the day, even how to fetch Mama Lela her coffee can without wrinkling her nose at the dark funk of tobacco spittle. But that place—which had everything to do with the woman who'd made me (hadn't it?) and yet seemingly nothing to do with any version of me that I could recognize or even imagine—left me locked out, stuck to my knees in mud.

The two weeks were sweltering and long. When Mama Lela and my mom sat quilting together or when Mom rode with Mother to pay one of the old folks a visit, I'd nurse thoughts of what it would feel like if I could magically wake up and speak the language of this place—if I could move around in this kitchen, emptying a cup of this and a teaspoon of that into a shiny mixing bowl; if I could manage to coax a laugh or even a smile out of Mother; if Dinah's record were still around to catch the two of us up in its never-ending disco fantasy. I even sometimes imagined what I would sound like if I could borrow Dinah's voice for the remainder of my visit. She had a slight stammer—it didn't seem to cause her any embarrassment, and I quickly came to associate it with her sense of dominion, of authentic, uncontestable belonging not just to Alabama but to this big family stretching back for generations—and even that became emblematic of something I wanted. Other times, I fell into a deep longing for our real life, Mom's and mine, but not even crawling into bed beside her at night or folding myself in her arms during the day could make me feel less out of place here, less of a stranger.

One day, Mama Lela said something peculiar, something I couldn't quite understand. It made her laugh, and when I seemed confused, she said another thing that didn't make sense, and she laughed at that, too. Later, when I asked my mom what Mama Lela had meant, she told me that sometimes when people get to be very old they experience something called *senility*, which makes them do and say things that don't always make sense. Mom didn't say that Mama Lela *was* senile, only that older people sometimes brush up against senility from time to time, like it was a wall of wet paint. "Some folks call it the Second Childhood," Mom had said, and those words, in a single flash, made me trust Mama Lela. I felt comfortable around her, even when she said cryptic things that made her giggle to herself. It meant that from time to time she was a child, just like me.

I stayed indoors most days, sitting on the floor or reading in one of the chairs by the record player. I imagined my cousins playing in the woods on their visits to this place, but the woods were yet another unknown for me, so dark and alive. I worried that a wolf or a bear would find me there and carry me away. Even when Mom and Mother went out visiting or shopping, I stayed inside with Mama Lela, not bothering to decipher too much of what she said. I was afraid. Not for me but for my mom out there on those country roads. I can see very clearly now what my fear was built of, but I couldn't have put it into words easily then. Partly, I was afraid of the kinds of dangers I sensed must be lurking out there. The wolves and the bears that lived in my mind's woods, yes, but what I really feared were the dangers that had to do with people. I was afraid of having my mom pulled out of the car by an old country sheriff, the kind I'd seen in movies, who would call her *gal* instead of *ma'am,* and who'd tell her to *git along,* warning her not to go looking for trouble. The kinds of human harm that sat just outside of the frame of those stories of the long-ago days down south, just beyond the edges of Daddy Herbert's woods, just around the wrong bend. The terrible threats to people like us, threats of violence and scorn. Things people did to people they didn't view as people. Murders. Lynchings. Even just a few words spat out with the right kind of force. It's what the history I already knew had convinced me that our chapter of the past was built on, and what I tried to keep separate, for my own protection, from my view of my parents as children of the South, what I made an effort to avoid all reminder of, even if it forced me to steer clear of whole regions of the past for fear of catching a passing glimpse. Was all of that gone, along with the smokehouses and the acres of cotton, or had I just been lucky enough this trip to avoid it?

I was afraid of something else, too. Mother was sixty, and she still worked a little, cleaning for a family I surmised must have been white. The kids, one of them was named Butch, called her by her first name (or a version of it: *Ma-gree,* probably from Marguerite, which wasn't exactly her name but was close enough, he and his parents must have reckoned). She cleaned for them and looked after the kids, which I figured made her their servant. If Mother were to visit them and bring my mother along with her, I was afraid it would make my mother into a servant, too, in their eyes.

I didn't want that, didn't want anyone to think they could send her chasing after their children or tidying up their mess. I was scared, whenever she left, of this threat and the other, and in the long, still afternoons while she was out (afternoons that were dark, because the curtains were always drawn just as the day was getting hottest), I sat trying to play patiently beside Mama Lela, who rocked in her chair beside me, laughing and spitting into her Folger's can and talking to someone who may or may not have been me.

Because I never asked, I did not know if my mom knew how to steer completely clear of those kinds of dangers, if there was a woman inside the woman I knew who spoke the language of racial deference, or if she was, instead, fearless of standing her ground and staring down her opponent. I didn't even know if the word *opponent* set up the right way of thinking about it; was the South really, after all, just a simple matter of wrong versus right? I did know that my mom knew how to speak with the elderly black men and women who came out onto their porches to greet us or who asked us in for glasses of water or iced tea. She called them *sir* and *ma'am,* and she offered to attend to them, even in their own homes, fetching them pillows for their backs or stools for their feet. Being beside her when she was like that, I could make out a version of her young self, but I also saw how that respect for her elders was alive in the mom I knew at home in California, the one who took me with her on visits to the convalescent home, where we chatted with old ladies whose children were busy with other things.

One evening Mom and Mother came home with bags of groceries, fixings for a big meal and a fresh cake or two. My uncle Slade was on his way home from college for a visit, and we were going to sit up and listen to his stories. I was excited. My mother told me her brother was "crazy," but she said it in a way I knew meant he was funny, a jokester, like other of my uncles, someone who could rouse everyone to laughter. Slade, who was near Dinah in age, maybe a bit older, maybe a bit younger, was going to be successful; everyone knew it and said it and spoke about him with unfettered pride. I thought of him as someone I'd like, someone like my brothers, for whom I felt a similar admiration.

Slade was small, only about as tall as my mom. He had a big, strong voice and my mom's broad smile. That night after dinner, sitting on the couch that would unfold into his bed for the night, he'd told story after story about his life at school, stories about growing up in Leroy, stories I didn't understand but that I laughed at anyway, just glad for the chance to lean back into my mother's arms full of ease and mirth. His stories triggered other stories, too, even ones that were about his brothers and sisters who weren't there with us. It was as if this small group of siblings coming together— three of thirteen—had brought the whole family into being, just like Jesus said in the Bible, *Where two or three gather in my name, there am I with them.*

In one story, the schools had recently been integrated, and the black school that my aunts and uncles and mom had attended quite happily was disbanded. The teachers who knew them because they lived side by side as neighbors or even family were shuffled to other places, and the children were bused off to schools where for the first time they'd be learning alongside whites. It had meant buying one pair of shoes for each of the school-aged children, kids used to running around outdoors in bare feet, no matter the weather. Once, my uncle Carl made the mistake of leaving his oxfords on the heater overnight, and when he woke up in the morning, the rubber soles had melted. (I pictured them warped and liquidy, just like what had happened to Dinah's record of "Le Freak.") He'd had to squeeze his feet into a Sunday pair belonging to his sister Willa.

Uncle Slade remembered how, much later, after most of my aunts and some of my uncles had moved up North to New York, his brother Samuel had been threatened by an acquaintance. It probably had to do with money, but whatever the cause, my aunt Gladys caught wind of it and tried to set things straight for her brother by getting her hands on a pair of brass knuckles and showing up at the man's door wielding them.

Stories that, in another context, could have been viewed as sad or dangerous were occasions for joy on that night. And it was true that they somehow brought the rest of the family, even Daddy Herbert, back together.

"I saw me a pretty lady," Uncle Slade said once my eyes started growing heavy. He was mimicking a comedian on the circuit down in Louisiana, where he was in college. "I saw me a pretty lady," he continued, "and I said to myself, 'I'm gonna give that pretty lady a rose, and then I'm gonna *sock it to her.*'" It made no sense to me, but the music of it, the way those last four words kicked up in volume and dipped down in pitch, once again picked us all up and whisked us into laughter. My mom said it, too, later that night in reference to another story, "So why don't you go on and *sock it to her?*" And we'd laughed again. My laughter was built upon visceral bliss; I still had no idea what the joke meant or why it was funny. It just caught me up in the glee everybody else's understanding had tipped them into. It felt good to be awake and accompanied at this hour, an hour when I might otherwise have been lying in bed struggling to relax into sleep. I tried my hand at using the phrase, too, though I got mixed up along the way and said *"chuck it"* instead of *"sock it,"* and I suppose the error of what I'd said was funny in its own way, and it got everyone laughing all over again.

It was late when our laughter died down, after midnight,

though the sky had been pitch-dark with just the pinprick light of stars for hours. Waiting for Mom to brush her teeth and prepare for bed, I studied the pattern on the quilt in our room, trying to take it in as if my own story were stitched into its blocks. And as I breathed in the smells of the place, still strange, though less so by then, it struck me. There was so much I would never understand, so much that would never belong to me, not really. There were even parts of my mother that I might never fully get a handle on—aspects that had come to life upon her return here and that would go dormant again once we were back in California—but wasn't there a way to see all of that as a good thing, to take it as proof that we are, all of us, made up of near infinite facets? It wasn't a calming thought, but at that very moment, happy from the evening, and with my mother all to myself again for the night, I wasn't in need of assurances. *Chuck it to me.* We were one day closer to leaving, and I had one very small thing to carry away with me.

A HOME IN THE WORLD

SCHOOL DAYS, I'D WAKE UP TO EGGS AND TOAST, AND AFTER my mother had tied my hair in one or two or three ribboned pigtails, I'd walk the few blocks up Cement Hill Road with Benji and Bryan, neighbor boys in my second-grade class at Amy Blanc Elementary School. I was proud to be setting out on my own, but occasional rumors of far-off kidnappings—children who had been lured into strange cars and never seen again—made me cautious. "Walk straight to school," my parents would tell me. "Stay together and don't go off with anyone, no matter what they say." Once, when a city worker spreading a fresh layer of asphalt onto the pavement whistled in my direction, I challenged Benji and Bryan to an impromptu race, just in case the man was scheming to abduct us. I was jittery and out of breath when we made it to the playground but also relieved, as if a tremendous threat had been cleverly averted. It wasn't until I sat down at my desk that I realized the man had merely been trying to alert me to a bookmark that had fallen from my open schoolbag.

While I was at school, my mother taught basic reading, math, and a class called Life Skills to men and women at the local adult school two miles away in the old part of town. It was the first job I'd ever known her to have, and the idea of her as somebody else's teacher rendered her inscrutable, someone who no longer fit easily within the cage of my mind. She had held down a job teaching grade school years before I was born, but I only ever thought of her as mine, ours, snug in the center of our home, cooking for us, loving us, keeping us clothed and fed. It's not that I thought she was incapable of more; I'd just assumed that the world was of interest to her only when it crossed into our private sphere, a view that had likely been shaped by my own seven-year-old sense of what mattered most. Still, if Mom had been a teacher once upon a time, it meant that she had belonged to more than just us. It meant that she had held sway over classrooms of boys and girls, captivating them or leaving them feeling restless and bored. It meant that she had caused them to smile or struggle or groan at the prospect of some new challenge and that she was expert enough to sit over their work with a red pen, filling the margins with her praise and censure.

The very next thing that entered my mind, when I thought of her like this, was a feeling of alarm. Alarm mixed with the most futile kind of retroactive fear. What if the boys and girls all those years ago hadn't liked her? What if they'd called her names behind her back or defied her outright? I longed to protect my mother from whatever pranks and fits those kids had been capable of, but of course I was too late, and so it was a relief when my thoughts returned to the present. At least in the here and now, I'd be able to see for myself if she was happy or sad, proud or harried. My mind was also eased by the fact that her students this time around were grown-ups. A grown-up would never misbehave the way a kid would.

I tried to imagine my mother standing at the head of a classroom on her first day, writing her name—*Mrs. Smith*—on the blackboard as a way of saying, *Let's begin,* to the roomful of new faces. I envisioned her walking up and down the aisles of desks, making sure that each head was properly bowed over the task at hand. Of course she was a lovely teacher, gentle, kind, and playful just beneath the surface. I never knew exactly how to imagine her adult students then, those men and women hungry for reading and math, eager to grow and to change. I see them now as nervous but trying to seem merely hardened. I see them as men and women who were poor, wanting to stand up finally to their own past resignations and defeats, to get out from under the fact that they'd never been taught to claim a genuine space for themselves or envision a big enough goal. I can see them now in a way I couldn't then, and still I wonder how they saw her. Did she put them off, the way she'd put that woman named Maggie off, as impossibly upright? Or was there someone in whom she inspired devotion, someone for whom the sound of her voice or the smell of her perfume was all it took to make a problem go away?

Working gave my mom new stories to tell. She said that when her students didn't want to do the assignment, they leaned back in their seats, sucked their teeth, and said, "Mrs. Smith, I ain't stud'n you." During a mock job interview, a student named Ray had prefaced his response to the question "Tell me a little bit about yourself" by saying, "Well, I was recently locked up for a few years." Mom would come home grinning about one of her students almost every night. Some of them sounded like children in adult bodies. But there was tenderness in her voice when she talked about them, too. I suspect she knew that her job at its most fundamental was really about mothering those people whose place in life was tenuous, people like Ray, who had started to believe the voices telling them that they were no more than the sum of their failings. *That's not the most important thing about you, Ray,* I could imagine Mom saying, once the laughter in the classroom had died down.

In the afternoons when Mom was teaching, I was fetched from

school by a spry white lady named Mrs. Kureitza, who pulled up in an old blue Cadillac and drove me to her shipshape trailer in a retirement "village" in the middle of town. I wasn't sure where my mother had found Mrs. Kureitza. Maybe she bought her Mary Kay products from the same lady my mom used. That would have made sense, judging from the way Mrs. Kureitza was so tucked in and teased, with an alert expression that had partly been penciled in. She was skinny and wore close-fitting double-knit pants. She'd give me a plate of saltines spread with peanut butter, or a bowl of Jell-O, and I'd breeze through my homework at the coffee table in her living room. At the same hour every day, she and I would walk to her son's house so she could make his bed and put a chocolate mint on his pillow while he was at his job. Once or twice, she was dropped in on by one of her boyfriends, old men who visited for just a few minutes at a time, never staying, wearing shirtsleeves or cardigans and calling her Louise.

When Mom took the adult school students on field trips, she was reminded of their numerous anxieties ("I just got out of the Big House"; "I brought an extra pair of underpants with me, just in case"), and they got to see her as a person in the world, some-one who negotiated with strangers and moved smoothly through public space. Was it a mother they saw in the way she nudged them along, cautioning them here, cajoling them there, or was she simply their teacher, the figure in charge, a woman who existed for a few hours a day and then disappeared from thought? I wonder now if the hours when she was Mrs. Smith were a kind of respite for her, a chance to lapse from the figure her children required her to be and become someone who, like every teacher, exists just for her students, one at a time and in a different way for each, and then slips out of grasp into a place where a student's imagination cannot reach.

ONE RAINY DECEMBER AFTERNOON BEFORE CHRISTMAS vacation—the kind of day that means winter in California, when the air is cool and the sky sits wet and gray and close to the ground—my teacher showed us how to make paper snowflakes. We were given scissors, construction paper, crayons, glitter, and glue and urged to make any kind of design we wanted. I was sitting on the classroom floor with my supplies around me. I made round snowflakes and square ones, snowflakes in bold vivid colors and others in austere white. I even made a garland of mini-snowflakes by folding the sheet as if I were making paper dolls. Gradually, I found myself losing interest in the art project and thumbing through a tiny Hello Kitty notebook I'd persuaded my mother to buy me from the neighborhood stationery store. On one of the first pages, Conrad and Michael, who were two grades apart in high school, had made a list of the teachers I should seek out once I was their age. Several more years would have to pass before I could take their advice, but it seemed key to the kind of future I wanted to be moving toward, so I guarded the list carefully.

Mr. Potosnak: Chemistry

Mr. Brodkey or Mr. Sumner: U.S. History

Mr. Lederer: English

Ms. Nacey: Trig ("What's trig?" "A kind of math.")

At the top of the next blank page, I wrote *1980*. Under that, I wrote my full name:

Tracy Kathleen Smith

Soon, I mused, people all over the world would be living in a new decade. I looked at the zero, the fresh, round, empty hole of it, and I imagined that every life, lived every day, everywhere, would go into filling up that space. Farmers, politicians, babies all the way in Africa, the boys and girls in my class, people I'd never ever meet— all of us would do our share to mark the coming decade. It was a knowledge populated, in my mind, by the faces on the nightly news: Americans and our leaders but also refugees and hostages, boys and girls looking hungrily at the camera, unbothered by the flies buzzing at their mouths and eyes. It was a view of the world, a world I'd be a part of. I'd live in 1980, and my presence would matter. The things I'd do every day would matter, not because of *who* I was but rather *that* I was.

My classmates were busy with their scissors. Our teacher, Mrs. Alexander, had already begun to hang our finished snowflakes up in the windows and along the classroom walls. Along all the neighborhood streets, Christmas lights and holiday figures would soon begin flickering on. A family named the Hurleys kept a sleigh with Santa and reindeer up on their rooftop all year long. It had been lit up in the morning when I'd passed it on my way to school and would stay that way until at least Valentine's Day, glinting in the sun and the dark of night alike, as if Mrs. Hurley (the one, it was rumored, who oversaw the decorations) was trying to flag down passing aircrafts or satellites. I wondered if leaving those lights on and letting them transmit their message of *Here I am!* into the distance gave Mrs. Hurley the same feeling of anticipation I experienced in the months that followed, every time I wrote 1980 at the top of a page. An anticipation punctuated by silence, by my watching and participating in what was at hand but often with a sense that there was something further off that mattered

more, something I'd one day reach and recognize. *Here I am!* Was
it the same phrase that popped into my mother's head when she
was guiding her students from one place or idea to the next? A
phrase that blared out like a promise but that also marked whoever
uttered it as a target, someone susceptible to whomever and whatever was listening.

AT THE ADULT SCHOOL, MOM MADE FRIENDS WITH ANOTHER
teacher, a woman named Nella. Nella was tall and sturdy, the kind
of big woman other people describe as statuesque but who refers
to herself as fat. She had one of those musical laughs that told you
she could really sing. I knew my mother envied that voice; she
was always lamenting that she couldn't carry a tune. When Nella
came over to our house, she and Mom would laugh about the
things their students said and about the other teachers at school,
some of whom seemed to be merely hapless; others, from what I
now remember, were more cynically checked out, tired of trying.
When Nella and Mom were not laughing, sometimes their voices
dropped down to a whisper, and they looked very serious sitting
there together on the blue chairs in the living room, leaning in
toward a topic that might have escaped if they didn't keep it cor-
ralled between them. Sometimes, I would walk into the room to
find their eyes shut and hands clasped in prayer.

Unlike many of the friends we'd collected in Fairfield, Aunt
Nella, as I learned to call her, was black. If a thing was funny
because of how it related to blacks—if it reveled in the music of
what James Baldwin called "Black English," or underscored what
W. E. B. DuBois described as our "double consciousness" (terms
I didn't learn for many more years but that made an immediate,

familiar sense once I did)—Nella was one of the few friends who could join in, knowing exactly what our laughter was built of. And if it hurt or felt wrong for a similar reason, she felt saddened or angry just like us.

Once, Nella had shown up at our door with two long bricks of pasteurized, processed government cheese.

"There's no way I can eat through all of this," she'd said, bubbling over with that operatic laughter on her way to our kitchen. She and my mother had chuckled themselves silly about the off-brand Velveeta, which Nella had gotten from a friend, who'd gotten it from another friend, who'd learned it could be collected, "no questions asked, out behind the post office."

Nella had two kids, and they lived across the railroad tracks from us, in a house I visited just once or twice, a neat small house on an old street, with trees that'd had time to grow tall and stout in the front yards. Her daughter, Lisa, was a high school student close in age to my brothers. She didn't come around much. The few times I'd met her, she had been quiet, with a big openmouthed smile that appeared sometimes in place of laughter. Nella's son, Anthony, was in kindergarten at a different school and often came with his mother when she paid us visits. Other times, she'd drop him off on his own—but not just to play with me. I suspected that our mothers wanted him to get to know my brothers and dad because Anthony's father was gone. He wasn't dead; if he'd been dead, they'd have said he had *passed on*. I understood *gone* to mean that Anthony's dad should have been there with Nella and the kids but that he wasn't, that he'd chosen to leave, and that his leaving, rather than being something Nella had accepted and let go of worrying over, was a constant ache or irk. Sometimes when my mom and Nella were talking in hushed voices about a *he* who had done something hurtful or unthinking, I gathered they were talking about Anthony's dad.

Watching them together, it became clear that Aunt Nella allowed my mother to relax and revel in the presence of a thing called Home. Home started with the South, as a way of eating and talking and reminiscing, but it stretched out into more, too. Home was a different geographic place for Nella, whose people didn't come from Alabama like Mom's did. I wasn't quite sure where she was from, but wherever it was, my mother gave that place back to her, too. Home was a place and time that my mom and Nella and generations like theirs had lived in quite happily, even as they were defending themselves against its famous snares. Home was bliss, but it was also a thing they'd had to weather and withstand. If Home was a mood, it was like being caught up in joy and consternation at once, the kind of feeling that makes you glad for what you once had and glad, also, to have left it all behind.

I'd known for a long time that there was also something painful at the very root of Home. To me, that pain was best summed up by the bevy of things the South had done to people of my parents' generation: the civil rights activists hosed down by police, the young black men and women sitting stone-faced at all-white lunch counters or behind jailhouse bars. Whenever my parents made reference to what things were like when they were my age, even benign things, the images that rose up in my mind, just out of frame, were the fire hoses and the lunch counters. My heart clenched in my chest to think about it, and my way of dealing with that sadness and anger and shame was to steer shy of talking about it altogether, to close my eyes to things that glared too brightly to look at head-on. But Anthony and Aunt Nella brought me into contact with feelings that defied silence. When Anthony and I were riding around on our bikes or spread out on the family room floor folding origami paper into cootie catchers, I felt like he and I were part of something just as real as all the things that very subtly relegated us to their margins. It reminded me of a TV show called *Gettin' to Know Me*, the only show I'd ever seen that focused on a black girl—and not only on her, but on her parents and little brother and grandparents as well. It took her entire world into consideration instead of making her a satellite to more prominent white characters. In every episode, the girl, who would have been just a little older than me, with neat braids or bushy loose ponytails, learned about black history from her grandmother, Mama Violet. I liked that the show told me that certain things were not unusual, things most of my friends would have found odd or in need of explanation, like calling your grandmother *Mama*, or living in a house full of handed-down quilts, or having your scalp greased and hair braided by someone who sat telling stories about black life back in the old days.

The girl on *Gettin' to Know Me* never clammed up when she felt herself getting close to the pain of Home. She knew which questions to ask. She was brave, strong in her sense of what that heavy history added up to—at least she was scripted to be. She didn't even seem to feel the faintest glimmer of discomfort when Mama Violet told her about how this home remedy or that quilt pattern had been passed down from slave times. I liked her because she stood as proof that girls like us were central to certain stories. Riding around the neighborhood with Anthony, sitting across the table from him at lunch, or playing in the next room while our mothers went on about their jobs, helped to counteract the quiet negation of California, a place with low, bare hills and a history as blank and clear as the sky on a sunny day.

Why was it so much easier to call out to the future than the past? I still couldn't bring myself to actually talk with my parents about what it must have meant to grow up in an age of racial violence. Any time the conversation crept close to that reality, I shut down. Yet my view of 1980 was peopled with victims and refugees, with emblems of struggle I had gleaned from the nightly news. I can still see the children who seemed to watch me in those daydreams. They were tired, expressionless. Once, watching a TV telethon with me in her trailer after school, Mrs. Kureitza caught sight of one of those children's faces, and she looked at me and said, "Why do black people always have such white-white teeth?" Those faces hadn't made her feel a part of the wider world at all but more like a spectator, someone on safari, it seemed to me, watching from the kind of distance that facilitates judgment or fear. It didn't stop me from liking her or from thinking of her as an ally or a friend, but it did remind me that simply because of who we were, she and I had been equipped to see certain things differently.

Sometimes, the faces in my 1980 were old and white, just like Mrs. Kureitza's, which is to say that, one way or another, I knew them. They were familiar faces, but in my mind they were yelling for change, for some wrong to be undone. Where did that image come from, and why did I view it as something to anticipate with a hungry alacrity? I sometimes sat in my classroom just drifting from one image of this kind to another, telling myself that the world was a place I would get to one day, and that when I was there, my presence would mean something. It was a promise I felt comfortable making to myself, a promise that must have had to do with what I could see that Mrs. Kureitza couldn't. *It's not that our teeth are any whiter, just that our skin is a whole lot blacker.*

I NEVER THOUGHT TO WONDER WHAT MY MOTHER SPENT HER IN-between times dreaming about. I had no way of knowing then, as I do now, that when a woman delivers her children to a safe place, even for just a few hours, a part of her becomes free in a way that a child cannot understand, reverting in an almost physical way to the person she was before she had children, as if she is testing to determine whether that person is still there. Who was my mother with her students gathered around her? Who was she with her back to them, writing on the chalkboard at the front of the room? Who was she in her boots and winter clothes, with her makeup and jewelry that might have been chosen to say to the world what Mrs. Hurley's Christmas lights said night after night and day after day to the stars and the clouds alike? *Here I am! Here I am!*

"Has anything changed in Tracy's home life?" Mrs. Alexander finally asked my mother over the phone one evening toward the spring of that school year, adding that I'd been acting quiet and far-off for some time. My teacher had no way of knowing what was going on in my thoughts, no way of determining what my dreamy silence was a symptom of. Had she asked me about it, I doubt I'd have known how to say much more than, "I'm fine," which wouldn't have been a lie, but neither would it have done much to assuage her fears. So she did what teachers must do when their concern is piqued, just as my mother, on the receiving end of that question, did what parents must do in those kinds of situations. She worried. She dwelled upon the worst imaginable scenarios: *Had anyone tried to hurt me? Was there anything I needed to tell her, anything at all, no matter what someone else might have warned me not to say, and no matter how hard it might be to put into words?* My mother conjured a flood of dark possibilities from what was once merely a trickle of working-mom guilt. *If damage has been done,* she told herself, *it was done because I was elsewhere, otherwise occupied.* If her absence had been the cause of the problem, then her presence, she determined, would be its solution. Mom sometimes told her version of the story when I was older: "When Tracy's teacher called to ask if anything was wrong, I realized that my being at work every afternoon was affecting her. So I quit." In her view, the story was proof that some things matter more than others, that parents must make sacrifices to keep their children safe and happy.

Because I was never asked to weigh in on the topic, I never got the chance to bring into language what I had actually been feeling in the weeks before the new decade had arrived. I never told my mother or anyone else how the faces that had appeared in my mind brought with them the certainty that I, too, belonged to what contained them—and that I wanted it that way. I certainly didn't want to be like Mrs. Kureitza, watching from an innocuous distance, a tourist snapping pictures and making jokes. I wanted to be there on the ground, waiting to be caught up—by history? agony?—and claimed.

The last time Mom collected me from her house, Mrs. Kureitza said goodbye, adding that I should stay in touch. After that, it was Mom waiting for me outside the school every day.

"What happened to your job?" I finally asked, once it had sunk in that she was no longer gone in the afternoons, no longer telling us stories at night about Ray and his cohort.

"It wasn't important," she said. She said it like she meant it, like it was simple fact, but it was a statement resonant with silence. Not the fearful kind I knew but another sort that strikes me now as brave, that calls out to loss, or disappointment, or sacrifice, and without hesitating says, *Here I am!*

II

MGM

AT THE END OF MY SECOND-GRADE YEAR, MY MOTHER RE-ceived another phone call from my teacher, Mrs. Alexander. This time, the news was good. Along with a select group of children in my class and a few others, I had the opportunity to transfer to an elementary school across town and enroll in a program called MGM, for "Mentally Gifted Minors." The name sounded official, if strange. Not the "Gifted" part, which I liked the ring of, but the "Minors." It sounded about as natural, and illuminating, as "Earthlings." What elementary school kid isn't a minor?

"Will I know anyone there?" I asked.

"I'm not sure," Mom answered. "But you'll be learning a lot more. Go ahead and think about it. You don't need to make up your mind just yet."

My father's advice was "You should rise to the challenge."

Conrad, who was in his second year at Stanford, also thought it was a good idea. "It can mean the difference between getting into a good college or a mediocre one," he told me, and then he explained what *mediocre* meant.

Michael seconded Conrad's opinion, only less charitably, tolerating my presence for a few minutes before letting me know I was a bother. He and his friends were always pretending to beat up on my beloved stuffed animals, then disappearing upstairs, shutting the door behind them to keep me out of their hair.

If MGM had Conrad's endorsement and my parents', I suspected my answer would be yes, but I wanted it to be clear that I recognized the decision as the kind a person ought to take her time with.

When I considered what I'd lose by leaving my old school, I pictured the faces I'd known since I was five. I thought of Kerry, with the freckles, who was shy, and of Donna, who was short-tempered and bossy. I thought of Benji's sister Lee-Anne, who taught me a series of X-rated jokes that I innocently repeated one night before dinner. My best friend, Kim, moved away the summer after kindergarten, but I thought of her, too, and a girl named Kris, who moved after first grade. If I did go, this time I'd finally be the one leaving; it would be nice to know how that felt. I also wanted to know what a real summer vacation was like. All I'd experienced until then was my school's year-round cycle of "45-15": 45 days of class and then 15 days of vacation, a pattern that repeated itself from one grade to the next.

Still, there was the faint anticipatory nostalgia of impending departure: wistful recollections of the monkey bars I'd learned to cross two and sometimes three rungs at a time; the foursquare courts, like blueprints for tiny houses with rooms marked A, B, C, and D; Tuesday afternoons, when we bought Astro Pops and Creamsicles after school and ran down the halls chanting, *I scream, you scream, we all scream for ice cream!* I was visited by remembered bits and pieces, a mental scrapbook I hadn't known I was keeping: running across the blacktop one afternoon with my mouth absently open and being startled by the presence of a fly on my tongue; getting accidentally kicked in the face on the jungle gym by David Mavis, and the oddly familiar taste of his brown suede shoe; neglecting to tell Danny Alvarez about the "Wednesday Wedding Day" plans I'd made for us and being rebuked at the "altar"; paying two quarters for my first hot lunch of a corn dog and Tater Tots, then vomiting it all back up hours later at home. I'm not sure what those snapshots added up to. Nothing it shouldn't have been easy enough to walk away from. Still, the decision itself seemed significant. I lived with it, contemplative, heavy-headed, as if every moment was the last of its kind, the final scenes of a life I had found reason to hand back in exchange for another.

"Yes," I told my mother a few days later, "I want to go into MGM." It was a choice that pushed me into three whole months of slow, unchoreographed free fall.

More than anything else, the long summer felt like institutionalized introspection.

I read the Encyclopedia Brown books, about a child sleuth who solves local mysteries, and the Henry Reed, Inc. series, about a boy who spends the summer with his aunt and uncle in Grover's Corner, New Jersey, and has adventures with a neighbor girl named Midge. I even somehow got my hands on a copy of *Are You There God? It's Me, Margaret*, about an adolescent girl and all the strange changes her body and mind are undergoing, a book I knew perfectly well my mother would not have condoned for me at my age. I settled into the daytime TV schedule of reruns: *The Jeffersons, Alice, The Love Boat, One Day at a Time*. I played two-square against the garage door and walked our dog, Sebastian, around and around the neighborhood. Because my friends were in school all day, they gradually began to disappear from my mind altogether, though of course they were all home by three o'clock just the same as before. I guess what I was feeling was the strange zero-gravity hover of being in-between places, phases, of having said goodbye to one thing before laying eyes on its replacement.

Once, I overheard Conrad discussing what he perceived as my recent weight gain with my mother. "Tracy needs more activity," he told her. "She's too sedentary." My body seemed the same to me, but the next week I was enrolled in a three-week round of tennis lessons.

I liked tennis. I liked it when Wanda came home during college breaks and took me to hit balls back and forth on the high school courts. At that point in her studies, she was thinking about becoming a physical therapist and had a T-shirt that read, "If it's physical it's therapy"—or as Jean, who liked to antagonize her, preferred to say, "If it's PHYSICAL it's therapy," with an exaggerated shift in volume intended to mimic the way Wanda's large bust distorted the text. Wanda didn't much mind the teasing and wore the shirt when we lobbed balls across the net.

No, tennis was fun. I liked watching Jimmy Connors and John McEnroe throw fits on TV and hearing the clean, distant sounds of the ball touching down before being whacked back across the net. I liked understanding the strange score-keeping language of *love* and *advantage*, with its math that skipped wantonly from 15 to 30 to 40, but I didn't quite take to the lessons. I could hit the ball well enough using my forehand swing, but backhand always made me nervous. If I let the ball bounce on my left side rather than my right, I could never tell what was going to happen. Often enough my racquet managed to make contact with the ball, but I was rarely successful in getting a backhand shot to travel all the way back over the net. I developed a strategy of running around the ball and turning it into a forehand shot, though when I did that, the coach, a scraggly, suntanned pro, would scold me. It wasn't long before I started second-guessing my every move. Sometimes, I froze with the ball heading straight for me, leaving me with no choice but to squeeze my knees together and employ the racquet as a shield. The game became a match with my own previously unknown shortcomings and anxieties. And suddenly, yes, I was conscious of my thighs having begun to rub together when I crossed the court. By the time three weeks were over—six lessons in all—my head for the game was shot.

After tennis came T-ball. We were a peewee team of boys and girls, beginners who would presumably graduate to a version of the game where the balls were actually pitched instead of balanced before the batter on a two-and-a-half-foot-tall tee. We didn't have uniforms or even matching T-shirts. I suppose they didn't bother with any of that because T-ball wasn't a real sport. Along with the other girls, I was usually put in the outfield. I stood there where balls seldom came, tossing my mitt in the air and daydreaming about what it would be like to finally start at my new school with all the other MGM kids. Sometimes, I sat down and started up a conversation with another outfielder, though that earned us both the disdain of our coach, a disdain I only helped to justify once it was my turn to bat. It was harder than it looked to swing at a stationary ball, and I struck out to a humiliating degree. Again, the game migrated up into my head, which was so full of the fear of failure that I second-guessed myself into oblivion.

At our final game, with my mom in the bleachers, I did manage to hit the ball. It was a nice, solid shot that toppled the tee and sent the ball down between second and third base and on into the no-man's-land I happened to know quite well. I sprinted with all my might to first base, where I stopped, out of breath, huffing and puffing, momentarily elated, glad that my feat had not been wasted on mere practice.

"Go on! Keep running!" Coach yelled. "Get to third!"

It was then that I realized no one had taught me the rules of the game. That explanation must have come while I was distracted in the outfield, or else Coach just assumed I already knew how to play. I understood on a basic level that we scored points every time one of our batters made it to home base. And we got sent out to field after a certain number of our batters had struck out (struck out or been tagged out?). But I didn't know much more than that. My lungs and throat were burning raw from my dash to first, but I decided to make a go for third, bypassing second altogether and running straight through the center of the diamond.

"No!" Coach yelled, sawing at the air with both his arms. "Go back; hit second!"

Shouldn't I just try for home, see if I could bring in a run for the team? I was beginning to remember some of the language of the game.

"Second!" Coach was saying. "Go back!"

A home run would have been nice, but his emphasis was persuasive. Turning back, I jogged toward second. Someone was waiting for me there with the ball in hand, and then it was our team's turn to put on our gloves and return to the outfield.

It was a relief when the sports lessons were over, though it meant going back to the flat line of unstructured days. Sometimes, bored and lonely for company, I'd wander out into the front yard. Sooner or later, I'd walk around the corner with the notion of paying a visit to Mrs. Meeks, a black neighbor lady my mother's age, or so I guessed—she was so overweight it was hard to tell for sure how old she was. The first time I'd ever visited, I'd been playing with a girl who lived next door to the Meekses. When her older brother was ignoring her or when she ran out of ways to entertain herself, she called on Mrs. Meeks, who kept bowls of hard candy all over the living room: little purple globes wrapped in cellophane, golden butterscotches, and the striped peppermint discs my mom carried in her purse. Even after the girl and her family moved away, I'd think of Mrs. Meeks sometimes when I had nothing else to do. Sometimes, when I rang the bell, Mr. Meeks would answer and call, "Loretta!" to his wife in the back. She'd say, "Okay, Meeks. I'm coming!" It always took her a few minutes to make it up to the kitchen, enough time for Mr. Meeks to offer me a grape soda in a tall glass of crushed ice.

The Meekses had no children, or else their children were already grown. They lived on a corner lot behind a yard plotted with juniper bushes and red lava rocks. Some of the other kids in the neighborhood stole handfuls of the rocks to throw at one another (I did, too, at one time, before I learned better). I liked visiting there, and my mother never stopped me from going. It gave me a feeling of sophistication to have made friends with a grown-up. I'd bring Mrs. Meeks pictures and cards that I'd made, and she'd always clap her hands and say how clever I was:

> I wrote this letter to tell you
> I wrote this letter to say
> Happy Mother's Day, Mrs. Meeks
> Even though it's not Mother's Day!

My parents always waved to Mr. Meeks when we drove past him on the street. I think they sometimes even walked over and paid the couple visits, which Mr. Meeks repaid mostly by himself. "Loretta's a bit of a shut-in," my father told me when I asked him about it. "I don't know that I have *ever* seen her outside the house." His emphasis on the word *ever* told me he was scandalized by such an idea. When I'd see Mrs. Meeks, she'd give me a great big hug, toppling me into her bosom, which smelled like powdery perfume and, more vaguely, of cigarettes. She wore a silky nightgown and slippers and tied up her hair in a satin scarf. Sometimes, if I learned a new fact on TV or in one of my books, I'd run over to her, knowing she'd clap her hands and say, "Ooh, Tracy, baby, you are so *clever!*" Sometimes my mother would clip some roses from our yard and let me carry a bouquet over, and when I handed Mrs. Meeks the arrangement, stems wrapped in a wet paper towel and then covered with tinfoil, she'd say, "Oh, Tracy, baby, these are *beautiful!* You are so *sweet.*" Other times, I'd ring the bell two or three times before accepting that nobody would answer, though if Mrs. Meeks never left the house, how could nobody be home?

During the same ceaseless summer, my father received news that his next air force posting would be in West Germany and would begin, if he intended to accept it, in September.

Having already begun to cut mental ties to my old school life, the thought of going to a whole new country whipped my heart into a frenzy.

"If we move, will I become German?" I asked my parents.

"No," my father answered. "No matter where you are, geographically, you will still be American."

"But if I wanted to, *could* I become German?"

"Theoretically, you could renounce your American citizenship, but that would be foolish. You're fortunate to be American. This is the best country in the world."

My father showed the first signs of bristling. And I could feel a resistance mounting in my own core, some part of me that didn't like the blank sweep of what he was beginning to say. It struck me, even then, as dangerous to be so certain of a thing like that, though

I also knew from watching my brothers argue politics with him that if I pushed back, he'd tighten his mouth and harden his gaze. "Shoot," he'd eventually say, "if you don't like it here, then move to the Soviet Union. Or China. You'll see how valuable this kind of freedom is once you give it up."

Over the next weeks, Mom and Dad made a show of considering the possibility. "You know, Floyd," my mother said one morning while Dad was reading the paper and working his way through a pot of coffee, "Conrad and the girls would have to stay here and finish college." Her voice was full of its usual relaxed poise, and her point—that the family would be split up if we took the assignment—had the effect of tempering my own excitement about going away.

I don't know if they'd ever thought as hard about any of my father's previous military transfers; I would have been just a baby, if I was born at all. But it was clear that they'd never before turned one down. Every two or three years, my brothers and sisters had been made to pack up, say their goodbyes, and throw themselves into new schools with a sense of blind hope. I'd grown up envying them that kind of mobility. I was three years old when we moved to California, and I'd only ever known two places before it, though if I'd truly been capable of knowing a place at age one or two, it was a knowledge that had been swallowed up by the part of the brain responsible for forgetting.

Ultimately, it came down to my parents' decision that we couldn't go to Germany and leave my brother and sisters alone halfway across the world. And so, just like that, my father said goodbye to twenty-six years of military service. He was forty-five years old. He pushed the uniforms with all their chevrons and colorful decorations to the back of his closet and let a beard grow in.

One Friday afternoon, he brought home the nameplate from his desk and his Swingline stapler, and we became civilians.

In no time, my father found work as an electronics engineer about eighty miles from home in then sleepy Silicon Valley. This was the early 1980s, before the viral explosion of Internet start-ups—long before the Internet itself. Technology had not yet begun to dominate the realm of private life; it didn't fit so easily into a person's pocket. Technology was public. It made bombs or launched rockets into space or made sick people well, and so it wasn't terribly strange that my father ought to be doing some kind of work that the rest of us barely knew how to envision. All we knew was that, instead of the air force blues or fatigues he used to wear, he left the house in sport jackets and ties and made his way to the town of Sunnyvale. It was a long drive away from our maze of neighborhood subdivisions, along overpasses and freeways threading between low wheat-colored hills. Finally, he'd cross the bridges leading him over the San Francisco Bay and continue south along the highway choked with other cars doing the same. It was a slow crawl, morning and night, at least ninety minutes each way, through tollbooths and traffic cloverleaves, to a background of talk radio. I wonder now what he thought about in the car. Did he view this new daily journey and what it led to (more money, for one) as a blessing or something worse?

I felt relief, but I didn't know why. Not about Germany but something more nebulous. I was only eight years old. I didn't understand most of the political talk that went on around me, but I could tell when my father was heating up. Usually, that happened when my brothers or sisters sought to challenge his views on things America had done in the world. When Americans made news for refusing to pledge allegiance to the flag, he'd snort at the

TV screen, "If you don't like it here—" and in my head, without wanting to, I'd finish his sentence. I didn't know what went on in the Soviet Union, but I didn't like hearing my father grow gruff and stern, didn't like watching him screw up his mouth, flare his nostrils and stew. Instinctively, I must have figured that some of this defensiveness had to do with the fact that his job since the age of nineteen had been to protect the United States. I assumed that stepping into an easier kind of life, one where he didn't have to stand quite so straight or always be so well-shaved, so perfectly shined and exemplary, would help my father to relax some of his stubborn fidelity to Uncle Sam. I didn't think that his patriotism might have been a choice, something he adhered to out of intrinsic belief rather than duty, yet I can see now how a black man of his age—a man who had been raised in the segregated South and who'd lived to witness the victories of the Civil Rights Movement— might hold tight to the conviction that American democracy truly was remarkable. Still, the very freedoms—to self-criticism, to dissent—that allow democracy to thrive seemed to unsettle him after a point.

I never thought about the anxiety he might have felt leaving the only professional world he'd ever known for one full of people who had, for the most part, only ever known something else. I'm nearly the same age now that he was then, and I'd wager that his discipline and intelligence, like his patriotism, were not traits he acquired in the military but the natural characteristics that had led him to enlist in the first place. The air force must have appealed to his innate love of order and to his belief in hard work. "You just have to *apply* yourself," he'd always say, slicing the air with his hand. It was his way of encouraging us or chastening us; his version of our mother's constant "You can do anything you set your mind to." Even for a man like him—someone methodical, meticulous, and always reading, learning, *bettering* himself—there must have been times when the task of keeping a family of our size afloat threatened to overwhelm him. But he never showed it. He stood at the prow of our household, steering us through season after season, year after year. Any worries and any fears were kept from our view. "Your job is to go to school," he'd tell us sometimes. "Mine is to take care of everything else." He did it so well, and so invisibly, that it never occurred to me he might have done so at any personal cost, though now I think of him as a young black man coming of age during an era when it was necessary, in so many ways, to fight for his rights. That's no unique feat; thousands have done it, and yet my father emerged on the other side not wearing the kind of brittle dignity that is an act of the will or a mask covering a spirit that has been beaten down enough times to be broken. He came out on the other side intact, ever convinced of his self-worth.

A few weeks into his new job, when the daily drive back and forth to Sunnyvale got to be too much, Dad decided to rent an apartment in neighboring Mountain View. It was a simple one-bedroom on the second floor of a bare-bones apartment complex, the kind with exterior stairways leading to the apartments and a covered carport instead of a yard. He drove there on Monday mornings and drove back home to us after work on Fridays. It wasn't new for Mom to be lonely for her husband. He'd traveled plenty during his years in the service, though now that she was no longer part of a community of air force wives, being apart from her husband must have felt different—but not insurmountable.

In the weeks before my school year started, Mom would sometimes drive down to spend a few nights with Dad during the middle of the week, taking me with her. I got used to the quiet of the car, listening to FM radio together, watching all the landmarks go past: the Golden Gate Bridge shrouded in fog off to the west as we crossed over the bay, the Coca-Cola sign lit up on the north-bound side of the highway with lights that flashed off and on like effervescent soda bubbles once we hit Interstate 101; the It's-It ice-cream factory beckoning deliciously out beyond the San Francisco airport. We'd leave in the early afternoon and make it to Mountain View just before the commuters came out, bottlenecking the road with their cars and their impatience to be home.

While Dad was at work, Mom and I took walks in his neighbor-hood. Sometimes, we'd stop by a nearby playground in the after-noon so I could jump rope or climb up on the big tire swing. There was hardly ever another child in sight, though one day my mother pushed me to strike up conversation with another black girl there by herself. She probably wouldn't have pushed if the girl had been white, though I'd have likely ended up playing with her, regardless. When I walked up and said hello, the girl told me that her mother was Wonder Woman.

"What?" I asked.

"You know, Wonder Woman? Lynda Carter? She's my mom."

"Really?" I could tell from looking at her it was a lie. She was just as black as I was, and her pants were a few inches too short.

As if she heard my thoughts, the girl persisted, telling me she lived in a mansion, since her mother was a famous movie star.

"Want to play on the bars?" I asked, trying to change the sub-ject. It worked, and we ran over to the bars and dangled there for a while. I told her that my mother and I were in town visiting my father.

"Are your parents divorced?" she asked, brightening with hope.

"No, but we live far away. My dad lives here during the week. For work."

"You have two houses? Are you rich?" she asked. Then she

added, in case I'd forgotten, "I'm rich, because my mom is Wonder Woman."

Some version of that same dance went on the whole time while we played. I found myself wishing I had the playground to myself, so it was a relief when Mom walked over to say Dad would be home soon. I was excited to get back to the apartment, that new nook in our life that still felt like a vacation from reality. When the three of us were together there in the evenings, I felt like a girl in a different family. One where the father worked all day in an office and then, before dinner, loosened his collar and poured himself a glass of scotch. The kind of girl who was never bored, who didn't have to worry, as Conrad had taught me to worry, about being *too sedentary*. Maybe my father's new life, with its promise of business trips and company picnics, was trying to tell me something about what my life would be like come September, once I finally landed in MGM. But what was it, exactly?

"Hey!" the girl called out when Mom and I were almost to the edge of the playground. We waved goodbye from opposite ends of the park, and then she called out again.

"I was just pretending earlier!" Her voice danced across the distances in the park. If I'd wanted to, I could have seen it as the force behind the swings, which were still swaying in the wind. "I'm not Wonder Woman's daughter. I'm a little black girl!"

LITTLE FEATS OF DARING

OUR DESKS WERE ARRANGED IN TWO ROWS ON EITHER SIDE of an empty aisle, through which Ms. Dyer walked back and forth when she was teaching. Everyone's desk was touching one other person's desk, and that person was your partner. Your partner would check your spelling tests and math quizzes. You'd brainstorm with your partner and take down the assignment for him when he was absent. I suspect you were supposed to like your partner, or at least look out for him. My partner was Kenny Moffett, a chubby, freckle-faced kid with reddish hair. He looked like a cartoon to me, with his cowlick and the spaces where a couple of his permanent teeth were still coming in. Kenny wasn't the partner I'd have chosen for myself. Looking around the room on the first day, I could have imagined sitting next to almost anyone else with more enthusiasm. I'd been hoping to be paired off with Sara, a tall blonde who, in the few moments before the school day officially started, had walked up to me and said, "Wanna be friends?" Or Katie, who looked a little like Kenny but was at least a girl. Katie was the nickname my mother called me at home sometimes, because of my middle name. In the last few weeks before coming to MGM, I'd toyed with asking everyone to call me by that name, but I'd chickened out, not resolute enough to let go of Tracy in the exchange. Sitting next to a Katie would at least have cemented a bond between myself and that name and perhaps eased the pang of having missed out on an opportunity. I wouldn't have been surprised to be paired up with Chris, the other black kid. I could tell we each drew confidence from the fact that the other was there but didn't want to set ourselves apart from the rest of the class; on the first day, we hadn't done more than flash a perfunctory smile when our eyes first met. As for Kenny, I could tell he'd have been happy sitting next to a boy he seemed to know from before, a white-haired boy named Ellis who looked more than a little like Andrew Jackson.

Kenny's fingernails were dirty, and within a few weeks, his desk became a vortex of loose papers and crumpled Now and Later wrappers. He was cheerful and friendly, but for some reason, I felt I ought to exaggerate my vexation with every little thing he did. I worried that my being Kenny's partner might invite the impression that my habits were as slovenly as his, so just to be safe, I put on a show of disgust when he used his pencil to pick his nose. I rolled my eyes when he smeared Elmer's glue onto his palms and peeled it off in thin, dried layers that looked like skin. If he whispered questions or offhand remarks when we were supposed to be working silently, I'd huff audibly and turn my back. Kenny seemed to like bumping up against my indignation and made a consistent effort to incite it. It became our shtick: we bickered all day like a mini old-timey mom and pop.

Ms. Dyer was warm yet demanding. She could make us laugh and remind us to be serious with equal ease. She remembered what it was like to be a kid and occasionally told us stories about herself when she was in third grade. If one of us was discouraged, she'd say, "Come on now, shooga booga, it'll be okay." She wore gold-rimmed octagonal glasses that had a cursive *K,* for Karen, stenciled into the bottom corner of the left lens. We weren't permitted to call her by her first name, but the fact that she revealed it to us conveyed goodwill, the way my father had lately started urging Conrad's college friends to call him Floyd rather than Mr. Smith. Ms. Dyer made us feel valuable, as if our ideas were currency, and we grew to love her rather quickly. The other children might even have stopped noticing that their teacher was black, but I didn't; it made me feel as though some piece of myself was up there with her, walking the aisle, clouding the chalkboard with questions and facts.

I felt pushed. I acquired new skills: playing clarinet in the school band. And discovered my weaknesses: times tables, procrastination. I was learning to love the feeling of sitting in the blue Queen Anne chair in the living room at home, leaning my head against its velvet-covered wings, and disappearing into the pages of books like *Little Women, All Creatures Great and Small,* or the several titles making up the Chronicles of Narnia. My reading list that year was long, and one book, by association or direct reference, led me to another. Other times, it would be mere whim that caused a book with an appealing picture on the cover or a familiar phrase as its title to garner my attention. Once I was settled in, I thrilled at the way simple words on a page could lift me up and carry me away from myself, away from being a nine-year-old black girl in Northern California in the 1980s and set me down in any kind of elsewhere. I could be Jo March, writing plays for her sisters to perform in, but at the turn of a page, I could just as easily become her sister Amy, declaring, "I want to be great or nothing." I liked the residue books left me with, the way that, washing my hands for lunch, I would be tugged back into the barn where James Herriot struggled to work up a useful lather from a tiny gray sliver of old soap.

The things I was conscious of learning made me think of Conrad and how wise college was making him and of how grateful I was for the bits and pieces of knowledge he dispensed to me, small morsels of the ideas his mind was churning through day by day. He'd told me about Plato's shadowy figures flickering on a cave wall that represented our limited view of the real and about Socrates's belief that a problem could be solved through the asking of questions. Thanks to Conrad, I wanted to find my way to the things that were powerful and puzzling and substantive—at least I told myself I did. I trusted my brother's judgment and coveted his approval. I knew my parents had instilled important things in me, things like belief in myself and respect for others, but moving forward, I wanted to be made in my brother's image.

One afternoon, Conrad and I were walking through the neighborhood when a bus full of friends from my old school drove past. Conrad was home for a long weekend and had just retrieved me from the spot where my new school's bus had dropped me off. When I made out a few familiar faces, I waved. They waved back through the windows. Then I stuck out my tongue. They returned the gesture, and, seeing that I was beginning to get a good rise, I stepped things up even more, doing a silly chicken dance, then flailing my arms and shaking my head like a lunatic until the bus was out of sight. That evening, Conrad said to our mother while the three of us stood putting away the dinner dishes, "I don't want Tracy to become the kind of kid who'll do anything for a laugh." I no longer recall Mom's reaction, but Conrad's assessment stuck with me. Why should I act like a clown if what I really wanted was to be gifted, someone with the ability to discern important things?

At recess, the kids in the regular classes would unleash their resentment over the many perks we got for being in MGM. Every Wednesday was a "minimum day" when we got sent home at noon so our teachers could discuss our special curriculum. Added to that were field trips, a yearly weeklong camping excursion, and elaborate special units on topics ranging from nuclear war to women's history. We even had our own unofficial region of the playground, an oblong bay of blacktop that sat between the monkey bars and the four MGM classroom doors. None of the regular kids set foot there, and when one of us left that area for the basketball courts or the tetherball poles, we'd be greeted by chants of *Mentally Gifted Monkeys!* and *Mother's Greatest Mistake!* I found the slurs mildly clever. So did Wanda. When I told her about them during one of her long-distance calls from LA, she laughed and took to referring to me as Mom's Greatest Mistake from time to time. But the kids who threw around such epithets did so in earnest. It was easy to see where their resentment was coming from. I had just crossed over myself from being a regular kid, and I knew that MGM felt a lot nicer; I was never bored or idle, and I was suddenly conscious that someone somewhere had decided I was special. I wasn't much concerned with the fairness of the system. Even if we MGM kids didn't really deserve so much more—even if we'd arbitrarily been given a special standing and all the privileges that went with it; even if it was wrong to acquiesce to the notion that we were the smarter ones and to let smarter become a synonym for better—I liked the way it felt getting the things we got, and doubt I ever saw myself back then as anything but deserving.

Still, even in our elect subset, there were gradations that my eyes eventually learned to see. Kathy lived in a big house and her mom drove a brand new Cadillac, but she was rougher around the edges than K.C., whose sweaters were monogrammed and who wore a fresh pair of Calvin Klein jeans (worn *in* but not anywhere close to *out*) every day. Some kids seemed to genuinely breeze through our schoolwork, while others dawdled, struggled, fell behind. One day, I overheard a boy in my class saying, "Well, everyone here is supposed to have an IQ of at least one hundred and thirty-six, but some people's parents just *got* them in."

There were so many occasions that autumn where I found myself running down the columns of a strange new social math. I watched the parents of my friends closely, intrigued by those who gave off an air of sophistication or alluring worldliness. They may well have possessed some kind of faith, but they didn't come off as expressly godly people. On Sundays, they went shopping or to the movies or drove home from Tahoe, where they'd gone to ski. My day-to-day life wasn't completely saturated with the ceremony of religion, but belief in God was a kind of bedrock; He was under our feet and in our hearts, always quietly present. Every Sunday started at church and ended with a big dinner we'd pray over together before eating, sometimes alongside our pastor or fellow members of First Baptist, where we were members. It intrigued me that hardly any of my classmates, let alone their parents, ever appeared concerned about whether God would be pleased with what they said or did. Even fewer seemed to find themselves conflicted by what science told them was true. None of them, I was sure of it, felt a pang of cowardice when they agreed, as they all did, that prayer did not belong in school. I envied them that freedom, the freedom to decide things based on what struck them as logical or just rather than what they reckoned God was counting on them to do or not to do.

I also found myself, for reasons that were entirely different, envying kids at school whose parents were doctors or dentists and who lived enshrouded by redwoods in the hills known as Green Valley. When I visited their houses, I looked longingly out their floor-to-ceiling windows onto the hillsides that sloped down into a maze of trees. I'd been perfectly comfortable my whole life, lacking in nothing, but rolling up their long winding drives in Mom's Plymouth Volaré, I'd sometimes try to see if I could trick myself into believing I was stepping out of a Mercedes. What did real wealth feel like, I'd wonder, knocking on the massive doors of the rich, doors that stretched up, it seemed, to a cathedral-like height. Did Conrad ever feel this way, too? Stanford was a place so full of wealth that my father had felt it necessary to remind my brother, almost sternly, that we weren't rich. He said, "Don't let this place put strange ideas into your head."

Sometimes my mother reminded me, "We are a peculiar people." She was quoting the Bible. Other times, she'd caution me. "Be in the world but not of the world." I think she meant for me to cleave to the differences between myself and the people who surrounded me, those who were rich, or white, or who lacked faith in God. Spotting those differences was easy. Even when the people in question were black—like Dr. Murray's girls, who invited my brothers to a white-tie cotillion but whom my mother seemed to distrust as overly high-toned; or Michelle, the daughter of one of my father's air force friends in Sacramento, who wore pink lipstick and nail polish and flipped her hair like a white girl—the distinction was easy enough to tease out, if difficult to name. Why, exactly, did my mother want me to stand apart? And why was it so important to her that I guard myself against too much sameness with everyone? When, if ever, was I supposed to relax? What, exactly, was my vigilance supposed to be protecting me from or guiding me toward?

The year before, on Conrad's first day of college, my parents and I had caravanned down to Palo Alto with both my brothers, who had ridden ahead in Dad's blue Toyota station wagon. Already, the hand-me-down car, with Conrad at its wheel and Michael in the seat beside him, seemed to know its way around the campus. Whenever the boys would sail through a yellow traffic light that turned red before my parents and I could get across, part of me would worry that we'd be separated from my brothers forever. The blue Toyota found shortcuts that weren't on our father's map, and whenever Dad complained that the boys didn't know what they were doing, a turn or two later, it would become clear that they did. It was as if Conrad had already learned to fit in even before he'd arrived. It wasn't long before Michael, who was only sixteen, started paying weekend visits to Stanford, designating himself a citizen of that place, too. Conrad's friends even learned Michael's nickname, which he'd earned for the way his long arms and legs spindled out from a compact torso. "Hey, Spider," they'd call out in greeting. At times like those, I wondered if Michael and Conrad had been given the same admonitions from our mother to remain peculiar, apart.

When Mom and Dad and I paid visits to Conrad on campus (it was easy enough to drop in when we were just up the road at Dad's apartment in Mountain View), my brother didn't make an effort to keep his college life from us or hide his home-self from his friends, many of whom had already come to our house in Fairfield with him over long weekends. The Christmas he was a freshman, our entire family had been invited to a holiday party hosted by the aunt and uncle of one of his new friends. We'd brought along our eighty-year-old great-uncle Ike, who was visiting at the time from Cleveland. Uncle Ike had mortified me with his country ways—he flung litter out of the car onto the highway, flirted unabashedly with girls less than a quarter his age, and was always *fixin'* to do this or *fi'n* to do that. But Conrad hadn't seemed worried. He'd introduced Uncle Ike to his friends and their parents, not bothering over what they made of the old man in the flannel shirt and pin-striped dress pants, just as he didn't seem overly concerned with what they thought of his kid sister setting up camp alongside a platter of crackers and port-wine cheese.

Over Christmas break his sophomore year, Conrad brought home one of his roommates, a kid named Dwight from Maryland. On the afternoon they arrived, I was looking through a big box my mother had come across in the attic, full of papers and projects from first and second grade, things I'd forgotten about, stories and rhymes, worksheets and drawings. Right away, Dwight asked me what it all was.

"It's just some stuff from when I was little."

"Can I see?" Anyone would have asked that, but Dwight sat crouching over the coffee table, his long arms and legs folded up in what may have been an attempt to make himself closer to my size. He sifted through the box with me, scrutinizing the pages and commenting on what I'd written. I knew there was nothing overly interesting among the things, but his interest didn't feel like the interest of someone who was just trying to be polite.

Later, in the evening after I was already tucked into my mom's bed (it was still my habit to sleep there when Dad was away during the week, and neither Mom nor I seemed eager for me to outgrow it), I heard the blurred murmurings of Dwight and my mother speaking together in the hall. She must have been giving him the towels and all the extra bedding he might need for the night. I should have been asleep, but I was being nosy. Dwight had been so friendly, so solicitous, as if I weren't just a little kid getting in the way of his time with my brother but a person worth listening to. He made me feel the way Conrad made me feel, perhaps even a little better, because he wasn't my brother and didn't have any obligation to love or even to like me. He made me feel just a hint of what I hoped a young man might make me feel when I was in college myself. As I lay awake listening to the rhythm of his conversation with my mother, imagining the words they were exchanging, I strained to catch just one comment devoted to me, one quick affirmation that I was a person of interest to a person of such interest to me.

I couldn't make out much, but I did hear the inflection of "Good night" in each of their voices, and then my mom's footsteps as she made her way to her bed.

The next morning, Dwight had a flight to catch. I was disappointed to see him go, but at least I could count on more of Conrad's attention once his roommate had left. On his way out the door, Mom handed Dwight something. I knew right away from the size and shape of it that it was one of the advertisements for God she always had in the bottom of her purse. I winced inside, hoping it wouldn't turn Dwight off from all of us and that it wouldn't undo the good feelings that had been accruing since his arrival. What if he were to judge Mom or Conrad or me for the things printed inside the booklet?

"I'll think about it," he said in the way people speak when they don't want to sound like they've already made up their minds. Suddenly, I realized that this was the continuation of their conversation from the night before in the hall—a conversation that had been about more than just linens and towels or how to find the bathroom in the dark.

The next time we saw Dwight was in the days after New Year's. He hugged my mother. He had a curious expression in his eyes.

"I read the booklet you gave me on the plane," he told her. It was a hook meant to draw her out somewhat, though I wasn't sure yet for what. He stood there smiling. I worried it was just a polite smile or, worse, that it was the predatory smile of someone about to take aim and fire. That was what people tended to do, wasn't it, who didn't like being reminded of God and His son Jesus, who didn't believe in them in the first place?

I'd forgotten just how tall Dwight was. Michael, Conrad, Mom, and I all stood looking up at him, waiting.

A long time seemed to pass before I heard my mother ask, "And? What did you think?" She sounded like a parent fishing for information but also like someone readying herself to defend her God against an attack.

Michael and Conrad and I watched, still waiting.

The cartoon tract, which had a cover that read, "Hi There!" took, Dwight said, a mere eight frames to get to a two-page color spread of the raging fires of Hell. "Well," he continued, "it wasn't exactly . . . subtle." Dwight couldn't help it. A few beats of laughter got past him. It wasn't the kind of laugh that pelted us like hail. It pattered out and bounced around our ankles.

"Mom!" Conrad said, drawing the word out into two syllables. But Dwight's manner told Conrad it was all right to relax and join the laughter. He did, though beneath it was a surge of embarrassment. Michael and I followed suit. Ours was an ashamed laughter that pointed to how right Dwight was, but it was grateful laughter, too, signaling our relief that he hadn't been angered or dismayed by the gesture. I scrutinized the sound. It had something else in it—something unresolved that might not have known how to make its way out into the open air otherwise. Something like the discomfort of knowing we lived straddling an awkward divide: the divide between belief in the realness and the comfort of God and the need to be at ease in the world of our friends. Was that what our mother's laughter, which she'd finally been coaxed to loose, said, too?

Mom must have known full well how bluntly simplistic the booklet she'd given Dwight was. Was it only just then, with Dwight standing jocular and unfazed before her, that she recognized how outrageous such a tactic had been? Or was sending Dwight home to Bethesda with a pocket-sized lake of fire something she felt obliged to do, something she'd decided upon quickly, before her courage floundered, out of obedience to God's admonition to *Lead my sheep*?

Already I could feel myself wishing it were easier to stand up *to* some of the things I'd been taught I ought to stand up *for*. Yes, I believed what my mother believed, that God was real and that we were better off with Him in our lives than out of them, but if God's love was worth having, why did Bible tracts have to resort to such ham-fisted tactics? Wasn't it silly to try to scare a person into God's arms? Wasn't God a choice to be arrived at with calm assurance?

"HOW MANY OF YOU HAVE EVER BEEN TO CAMP BEFORE?" Ms. Dyer asked.

A few hands went up into the air, but mine continued to rest on my desk.

"You'll need to bring your own toiletries, like soap and lotion and toothpaste." I used lotion every day, like most other black people I knew, to ward off "ashy" skin; I wondered to myself if a white teacher would have been concerned enough to mention it. "And flip-flops for the showers. Oh—and the showers are communal, which means you'll be in there with other campers, boys with boys and girls with girls."

Did she hear my heart thumping up against my ribs? She must have, because the next thing she said was that if you didn't feel comfortable showering in front of other people, you could always shower in your bathing suit.

My cheeks were hot. This sounded to me like a lose-lose situation. Either I'd be forced to stand naked in front of my peers or else let everyone know how frightened I was to do so.

The camp would be held at a place called Whiskeytown and would last a week for all the MGM kids—except, as of then, we were no longer known as MGM but rather GATE, for Gifted and Talented Education, an acronym that proved more difficult for the regular kids to sabotage. Ms. Dyer told us about camp songs and s'mores. She explained how we'd be bunking and that we'd be hiking past beaver dams and waterfalls. There were a lot of other details she rattled off, things that whizzed past me because I was still in a panic about the showers.

Despite my trepidation, at home, I lobbied for the trip. "I really want to go," I assured my mom. I even convinced myself to panic over the possibility that she and my father might find reason to say no.

"What about your hair?" my mother asked. "You're not a little white girl who can just shake her head and go."

We agreed that a dozen cornrows should keep me from having to struggle too much on my own. Cornrows were a big compromise for me. The last time I'd worn them, they'd lasted only one day because I'd insisted on taking them out as soon as my friend next door told me, "Your hair looks funny."

Whiskeytown was a three-hour bus ride northward into mountainous forest. It was a California I'd never before seen, north past cities and suburban sprawl. There were winding roads and rivers and lakes where gold prospectors—the state's original forty-niners—had sought their fortunes. It was beautiful and astounding. I'd never been farther north than Sacramento and so had no idea that I lived this near to a place that remained so untouched, bare open fields that appeared more free and alive somehow than the hillsides closer to home. Perhaps it was the utter quiet, and the relative absence of traffic, that seemed to account for the landscape's autonomy. I wondered whom it belonged to. Wealthy ranchers? Doctors and dentists? In my heart, I hoped it was nobody's, that it belonged to itself. It struck me as the kind of place where God might come in order to take stock of His creation: eagles, foxes, centuries-old redwoods. I felt nervous and lucky, sensing this north country as the kind of place that, if there was any truth to fairy tales or pagan legends, housed the potential for some sort of magic.

We spent the evening of our arrival singing "Up in the Air, Junior Birdman" and "On Top of Old Smokey" after dinner. It was cold that far north, so we sang our camp songs indoors, in a huge cafeteria with a stone fireplace. We slept four to a cabin, where the sheets and blanket were thin and had a chalky smell about them. One of the counselors, Jill, was the younger sister of Conrad's high school girlfriend. She was like many of my classmates, a white girl from Green Valley, with long caramel-colored hair that she managed quite easily enough all by herself. I wondered if she had asked to have me in her group or if it had just been the luck of the draw.

Waking on the first morning to the bugle cry, I showered in my bathing suit, but it didn't take long for me to realize that it didn't make sense to wash only the areas that my bathing suit didn't cover. After that, I decided to just wait it out and do a proper job when I got home. The same went for what I still could only refer to as *defecating*, which I couldn't bring myself to do in the too-public-for-my-liking toilet stalls. A few days into the trip, at breakfast with a friend who was in the same boat as me, shower-wise, Jill said, "You guys haven't been showering, have you?" When our eyes bulged and we demanded to know who had told her, she looked at us, with her eyes the green and brown of glistening jasper, and smiled. "Oh, I can just tell."

Our campground sat at the center of more wide-open space than I'd ever before seen, all of it framed by forests of oaks and pines. Each morning, the whole group of us played soccer and red rover in a field. Thick fog hovered out across the horizon while the sun was still low. There were gophers popping up from their tunnels and beavers swimming the river, their oily wet fur glistening in the sun. As the day progressed to a cloudless clear blue, small groups of us were led on hikes up and down mountain trails. At our guide's instruction, we tasted wild green onions; they grew in bunches and were just as thin as blades of grass, only taller. We crossed running streams stepping rock to rock. I was frightened to near paralysis by things like walking across logs or climbing down steep muddy grades and fell into step in the rear of the pack, hoping to amass the courage while my classmates ahead of me made their way. More than once, my apprehension caused our guide to have to backtrack and help me over whatever small hurdle had gotten the better of me. It was a humiliation, but its sting was still less than the fear I felt at nearly every turn. When my feet got wet and I spent a good part of the day uncomfortably cold, I tried to remind myself that it was nothing short of a miracle that I was there in the first place, nothing shy of an act of God to have been allowed to throw my sleeping bag in with the rest of my class and ride off into a week of more or less self-supervision. Were my parents worried about me up there on my own?

Two days before our time at Whiskeytown was over, our four teachers and the camp director stood before us in the cafeteria. It was dark out and the fire was crackling, reinvigorating the woodsmoke smell that had seeped into the molecules of my hair, clothes, and unwashed skin.

"We have a very serious announcement to make," Mr. Samuels said. He was bearded, with ruddy cheeks and a round face, which he just then was keeping perfectly free of expression. "You may already have heard some rumors, but we wanted to be the ones to tell you that one of your classmates, Kenny Moffett, died this morning."

Mr. Samuels paused a moment to give our gasps and murmurs time to sound out, though for the most part the room remained silent. My thoughts froze and sped up at the same time. Kenny, the boy I sat beside every day in class, bickering with and making mischief? The boy with the dirty fingernails and the freckle-spattered face? I'd barely seen him since we arrived. It was almost as though I'd expected him still to be sitting there in the darkened classroom, waiting beside my empty desk, though of course class, with its chalkboards and corkboards and windows looking out onto the harbor of our schoolyard, now seemed a million miles away. I didn't know what to think or do, so I sat there willing my ears to listen.

"Kenny had a mild heart condition," Mr. Samuels continued. He said it like this was knowledge he had had for a long time. "He suffered a heart attack this morning while he and a classmate were out jogging."

I could gather who the classmate had been. Ellis, the kid who resembled Andrew Jackson, was Kenny's best friend. The two of them were funny together, working up little comic bits worthy of the Marx Brothers or Bob Hope and Bing Crosby, whom they had studied enough to imitate with a fair degree of accuracy, at least for nine-year-olds. (I liked those movies, too, for what it was worth. Conrad and I sometimes watched them together on TV when he visited for the weekend.) Both Kenny and Ellis had older parents, gray-haired mothers with wrinkles like grandmothers and old-man fathers we rarely saw, which might have explained why both boys had such an affinity for black-and-white movies. Whenever Kenny and Ellis performed one of their funny back-and-forths, and just as everyone else's laughter was dying down, one boy would ask the other who wrote his material. The answer, no matter the joke, was always "Bob Hope," and every time, it caused the two of them to grin with a private kind of pride.

Mr. Samuels went on to explain that the "accident" hadn't been anybody's fault and that Kenny probably hadn't felt a lot in those final moments. He and the other teachers stood together looking out into what must have seemed, just then, like a sea of some of the youngest, most vulnerable faces in the world. The teachers asked if any of us had questions. They encouraged us to talk about our feelings, "to get things out in the open," so that nobody had to feel alone in sorting through a classmate's death.

I didn't ask anything. And I didn't cry, the way some of the other campers were beginning to. For a moment, I thought that I should, that it would be the decent thing for Kenny's class partner to do, but I couldn't manage it. I felt a strange detachment from myself, unable to feel what such a thing was supposed to feel like. Reality raced back at me. Hadn't Kenny sat next to me less than a week ago? Hadn't we just argued about a broken pencil and about the mess of papers threatening to spill out from his desk? How could he have been in the seat beside me one day, smelling like peanut butter or Now and Laters, and then simply be gone, disappeared, a world away? I wasn't crying, but I felt for the first time that underneath our show of not liking one another Kenny and I had actually been friends, and it hurt.

Where did death take Kenny? Did he believe, as I did, in God and Heaven, or would death have carried him, out of obligation, somewhere else? (My mother would have wanted me to witness to Kenny, to tell him about Jesus and to behave as an emblem of Christ, but I hadn't.) What had it felt like, just before he was gone? Did he feel it coming? Had he called out for his mother? What would I do if I knew I was about to be gone? Would I see Jesus there waiting for me, just across a stream like the Baptist hymns say, or would everything have gone dark? And what about the blaze of warm white light people talked about, people like the man and woman I'd once seen on the episode of *The Phil Donahue Show* about near-death experiences? I didn't let myself think about Kenny's body lying lifeless in the grass or how it would be transported home to his parents. I didn't think about whether his desk would still be there beside mine, only empty, when we returned to school. Something that wasn't any of those things sat upon my mind, making it heavy and dull, sleepy and slow.

On the ride home a few days later, I was aware of not sharing in the same feeling that some of the other campers seemed to share, a feeling that lent them an air of uncomplicated belonging and ease. Some sang camp songs. Others shouted to one another across the bus rows. All week long, those same kids had bathed and used the toilet without shame or anxiety, falling into perfect step with just about everyone else at Whiskeytown. They'd hiked up and down mountains without getting too worked up about it, and at the end of the week, they'd found perfectly natural ways of talking about what had happened to Kenny, things I'd failed to fit into words or even coherent thoughts. Happy as I was to have run back and forth across the enormous field each morning and for the moments of awe at the beauty and the bounty of nature, I found myself stuck in a place that defied expression. My worries about tumbling into a stream or down a mountain path and about being seen in the shower or sleuthed out in the toilet had rendered me lonely, had sent me scuttling about so much of the time desperate to get things over with and to keep everyone from noticing me, hoping that would help to keep them from noticing all the ways in which I was so starkly different.

Watching the landscape revert to the familiar as we traveled back to Fairfield with one less child in tow, the voice in my mind muttered to itself, *At least I was there*. It was a variation of the mantra with which I'd once heralded the New Year: *Here I am!* At least I wouldn't be in quite the same position on Monday as the one or two kids who had opted out of camp altogether, deciding instead to spend the week at home.

"How was Vodka Village?" Wanda asked when I walked through our front door.

"Oh, it was fine," I managed, rushing past her to the bathroom.

That night a lot of it came back to me. The wide grassy field surrounded by oaks and pines. And how, once you stepped foot into the forest, it rang with a startling, living presence. The gophers and mountain beavers. The enormous bald eagles and flocks of honking geese, the rushing water of the creeks. I told my family about how challenging it had been to do some things, like crossing streams by walking across a path of stones or a log balanced between one side and the other, but in the end I'd done what had been asked of me and had been safe. None of the little feats of daring I'd been put up to in the woods had brought me to any harm.

When I told my family about Kenny, it was clear from their faces that they already knew. It helped take my mind off the terrible realness of his dying by imagining that he'd probably been happy when he died, completely unconcerned, just running around in the tall grass with his friend. It helped, too, to decide that he must finally know, if he hadn't known before, how alike the two of us really were.

I liked what the survivors of near-death experiences, at least the ones I'd seen that time on TV, had to say: that there was a tremendous light, warm and incomprehensibly bright, calling to them without words and that they had raced out of their bodies and down a dark tunnel without fear, eager to be absorbed by the light that summoned. The light was alive, they'd said, and it put their minds or their hearts, whatever was left of them, at peace. The ones who had gotten closest to it before being sent back said it had felt like they were going home.

TOTAL ADVENTURE

ON VALENTINE'S DAY, MOM PICKED ME UP FROM THE SCHOOL
nurse's office, where I sat begging my upset stomach to settle back down. Then she came home to finish getting ready for her
luncheon. Usually when she had company for lunch, she baked a
quiche (I'd often be enlisted to grate the cheese and poke holes into
the bottom of the crust so it didn't puff up with air) or assembled a
rice pilaf with chicken, slivered almonds, and chopped vegetables.
I was too out of sorts to keep track of what her Valentine's menu
was, but I knew she was expecting a visit from Mrs. Nussbaum,
another air force wife she'd met years earlier at the Hospitality
House. Mrs. Nussbaum was one of my favorite guests because she
always arrived with a gift for me, usually books or toys from the
Christian bookstore where she worked. Her life was devoted to
spreading the word of Christ, and she carried pocket-sized leather-
ette editions of the New Testament to hand out to the people
she met from day to day. Sometimes, she returned her entire pay-
check to the bookstore because she'd given away so many Bibles.
Mrs. Nussbaum was certain that I already knew Jesus, but as a
special Valentine's gift, she brought me a New International Version Children's Bible and a heart-shaped box of assorted chocolates. When I thanked her, instead of saying "You're welcome," she
pinched me on my cheeks a bit too hard and for a few seconds too
long, saying what a sweet girl I was.

Mrs. Nussbaum was from England. As a young woman during World War II, she had worked in an ammunitions factory. It was during the war that she met Mr. Nussbaum, an American GI, a very earnest, very animated man whose face, when he was talking about the many wars and disasters across the globe, would take on an expression of exhilaration and anger. For the longest time, I thought Mr. Nussbaum was from England, too; after so many years of living with his wife, he had begun to emulate her British accent. He'd also adopted her faith. He was born a Jew, and Mrs. Nussbaum had grown up a not-very-devout Protestant, but after the war, the two of them had been baptized together as Christians.

What little I knew about Jews came from a book of my mom's called *The Hiding Place,* about Dutch sisters named Corrie and Betsie ten Boom, who had hidden Jews in their home in the Netherlands during the Holocaust. They were Christians who sought to share God's love with others. When the ten Booms were discovered by the Nazis and eventually taken to a German concentration camp, they continued to try to spread the word of God with the other prisoners and even with the Nazi guards. It didn't occur to me until many years later that the subjects in *The Hiding Place* were the Christians and the Nazis and the objects were the Jews. At the time, I was taken with every coincidence—or miracle, as the book described each of them—that prevented the sisters from being killed or separated from one another. During the war, Mrs. Nussbaum had been on the receiving end of a miracle, too, when she traded shifts with a coworker in the ammunitions factory on the very day that the factory was bombed. Such coincidences gave me a giddy, otherworldly feeling, though when I thought about it later, of course I realized that a great many other miracles that might have been performed during the war were not.

The Nussbaums were a good twenty years older than my parents. Whenever my mother and father brought me along on visits to their home—a white stucco one-story with hedges and shutters that gave the impression of a gingerbread house—I was offered a seat at the kitchen table where a plate of cookies and a Bible storybook awaited. The adults would settle into the living room, drinking coffee and making conversation. They'd touch upon topics from the news or swap stories about life in the air force, but most of their conversations were about God. Even their discussions of current events tended to loop around to the Lord; either He wouldn't like what was going on, or He had foretold it someplace in the Bible, if you stacked up all the details in just the right way.

Mr. Nussbaum was an expert on Bible prophecy. When he began to explain how an event happening in the world lined up with one or another Bible reference, his eyes lit up, as though he were furious with humanity, but eager, too, to see God's promises fulfilled. He wasn't the only person trying to match up current events with biblical prophecy; I suppose it was a compelling pastime, like a heavenly scavenger hunt, for someone with the right command of the Bible. In the mornings, Mom watched *The 700 Club* on TV while I got ready for school. More than once, Pat Robertson, the host, promised viewers that the end of the world was coming in just a couple of years. When he tried to tell the future like that, Mom would reprimand him, saying to the TV screen, "No one knows the day or the hour," but she didn't change the channel, and every morning the show was on again while I got dressed or ate my breakfast. Sunday evenings, there was an old white-haired man we'd sometimes flip past on our way to *Hee Haw* or *The Muppet Show*. He waved a Bible in the air promising the End of Days was nigh and casting curses on evildoers and disbelievers. Once, he asked God to cover all the wicked people's bodies with pus-filled boils. His haunted, bloodshot eyes and mop of thick white hair terrified me. I was always relieved to hear my father snicker and call him an "old fool." Our God struck me as different from that man's God, though we called Him "Heavenly Father" just the same. It was confusing to me, especially because such men seemed to find so much to hate in the world, a world that, no matter all the rampant sin, still managed to hold a great deal of interest for me.

On Valentine's Day, while my mother and Mrs. Nussbaum sat in the dining room having lunch, I lay stretched out on the couch. My classmates still had two hours left of squirming at their desks, though they'd surely be rewarded with palm-sized boxes of sweet tarts and conversation hearts before the day was over. My mother had already told me that if I ate the chocolates before my stomach had a chance to recover, they'd only make me feel worse, so I was distracting myself by looking through the Bible. It was square and squat, with a hard cover and tissue-paper pages that crinkled between my fingers. My parents each had their own Bible printed on the same onionskin, with gold edging and columns of Christ's words in red ink. Holding one of my very own made me suspect that I might be capable of hearing God's word and taking on its wisdom, which was perhaps part of the reason for the next thing I decided to do. *I am eight years old*, I might just as well have said to myself, *and since I have been afforded this day, this book, this absence of anything better to pass the time, why not read for myself about God's plan for the Second Coming?*

It was a sunny afternoon, and daylight barged in through the window at my back, casting a blinding square of light on the TV screen. I heard birds calling to one another outside and wind in the leaves. Farther off, there were cars moving along the streets of our neighborhood, a traffic I knew how to convince myself sounded just like the tide. A room away, I heard my mother and Mrs. Nussbaum talking above the sounds of knives and forks. But in the lines and pages before me, I soon found myself lost in a labyrinth of strange tidings that, added to whatever rumbled through my intestines, pitched me into a bizarre and unsettled state. To call it nightmarish would be to discount the extreme foreignness of the imagery; the demons and plagues and fiery scrolls were like nothing my imagination could have fashioned on its own. Neither did it sound much like the moment of glory all the church hymns foretold: the homecoming of Christ on a cloudburst and a golden chariot. No, this was worse even than the mad Christians foretelling doom on TV. It was even more punitive, with an added measure of all the ghastly Halloween stuff my mother had sought to steer me clear of. My heart raced and my mouth filled with fear, just like it did when whoever was flipping channels would linger for a moment on the white-haired man casting aspersions from his television pulpit. Was my mind playing tricks on me? Had intestinal unrest distorted all sense of what my eyes were reading? I kept shaking my head, trying to snap things back into proper focus. *But why?* I asked almost aloud. The God who'd set a thing like that in motion probably would cover people in boils. It couldn't be right. Perhaps it was the kind of thing I ought to have been able to arrest, like a headache or fever, by shutting my eyes and going to sleep. Only I couldn't put the book down.

Already I was having dreams that seemed to bring me up close to that eerie inevitability. In one that recurred from time to time, it is that dark hour between hours when the night seems to hang perfectly still while dawn watches from just beyond the horizon. The hour when anxiety sits up in the bed, wanting company; when the phone rings with the kind of news that would cause my parents to make preparations for attending some faraway funeral. In the dream, we are all of us awake, standing around the kitchen table, dressed for church or a funeral, silent and waiting. Even the empty spaces in the house are fraught, the air palpably charged. When I move, the fine hairs on my arms feel the presence of something invisible passing through.

My father remembers there is something he must collect from the garage, and adrenaline spikes my chest. It is important that all of us remain together. My mother looks at him with a message in her eyes. And then I remember what has come over us: we are waiting for God.

Of course! God will be there soon, very soon, just as He promised, and so my father has to rush if he doesn't want to be left behind. Or else it is one of my brothers who needs to race upstairs and change clothes or my mother who has to step away for a moment to peel one or two more potatoes for the meal none of us will ever sit down to eat.

I was raised to believe in a moment when the earth would literally reject the laws of science, and the dead would spring from the grave to join Christ, who would be visible in a cluster of low-lying clouds. I certainly never heard any Christian offer up an alternate take on the Second Coming, never heard it rationalized into something plainer, easier to comprehend. It was not a metaphor but rather the moment when metaphor itself would fall away, laying all the many mysteries of God's kingdom naked before us, fully revealed. Not even my father, whose sense of faith was flexible enough to coexist with his equally ardent devotion to science, had managed to soften the Second Coming into anything penetrable by reason or logic. No Christian I'd ever met had consented to so much as blink an eye at the notion of the Rapture, at least not publicly. Did they wrestle with it privately? Were they as appalled by what the Bible foretold as I was, reading it verbatim for the very first time? Nobody said anything about it. Time and again throughout my life, I'd heard other Christians talk about how *soon and very soon* Christ would reappear, and how glorious the day would be when we found ourselves standing before Him at the Final Judgment. Having happened upon no alternative, I'd accepted it as one of the nonnegotiable elements of my faith, resigning myself to the possibility that one minute, I might be reading a book or talking to a friend or even sitting on the toilet, and the next, the whole planet could be standing there watching as the sky opened like a cracked egg. It could be anything: a flash of light as if from a nuclear blast (like the terrible blast I'd seen in documentary footage from the hydrogen bomb at Hiroshima, only infinitely bigger) followed by a weightless silence into which we'd simply lift off and drift. Whatever it was, it would happen in the blink of an eye during which every second or third person the world over would vanish into thin air. Even though such images repelled me, I couldn't not believe; it wasn't an option. Belief was stitched into me, soldered to my bones. It was almost as though I was born believing, as though I had believed even before I was born. Even if I had wanted to, even if I could have found a way to erase all the believing that lay beneath the things I could discern with my eyes and ears and beneath the things I could pick apart with my mind, how pigheaded and piddling would I feel on that final day, anchored to the earth while my mother and father and brothers and sisters all filed up to Heaven on an escalator to the clouds?

My stomach had felt so bad that morning at school that I'd had to run down the hallway to the bathroom more than once, but that biological drama seemed far-off suddenly; it was paltry in comparison to the upheaval the Bible was now telling me would and must come to pass: the plagues God was waiting to unleash, the suffering He had planned for us. Seeing it in what almost read as recipe form, I felt newly queasy, fearful for the world that would one day begin to ripple and churn under the necessity of such a strange, cruel destiny. I lay on the sofa, stuck in place, panicked but still, understanding there was nowhere to run. I couldn't get off the planet, couldn't escape God. I felt like one of the people in the old black-and-white Godzilla movie, the ones who look so tiny and frenzied as the giant lizard tromps through their city.

I let the sounds in the dining room come into focus. Teacups and saucers. The lid being lifted off the big metal cake saver. Quietly, tentatively, I took the cellophane off the box of chocolates and opened the lid. There was a thick brown sheet of pillowy waxed paper protecting the top layer (there were two layers!) from molestation. I lifted it off and looked at the smooth candies, each guarding the secret of its contents. I breathed in the air from the box: a medley of dark, sweet notes, but then, remembering the sternness of my mother's warning, I replaced the waxy blanket and the heart-shaped lid and returned my attention to the book. Mom was right. If I ate a chocolate while my stomach was still out of kilter, it would only stir up more trouble; the candy would taste good for a few moments before landing in my stomach like a grenade.

I felt uneasy around the Christians who claimed to long for Judgment Day, the ones who professed their faith in God too vehemently. Not the Nussbaums, who talked about God as if they were His fans, as if He were someone incredibly famous whom they'd met just once. No, my distrust was reserved for the people who made an exaggerated effort to flaunt their godliness. The ones who went out of their way to join hands and pray aloud in busy restaurants, as if doing so would shame others into giving their lives over to God. And, worse, the ones who worried to the point of distraction about the sin going on in other people's houses, the hate-filled men on TV, and the pious, grim-faced people in real life who sowed guilt every chance they got. And here suddenly was the Bible itself, giving me reason to feel not just discomfort but outright fear at the prospect of humankind being stomped to pulp like grapes, of beautiful cities being made to crumble despite the fact that they, too, were full of God's handiwork. It was maddening, crushing, bespeaking a God of fury rather than love. Was it fool talk? I didn't dare go so far as to call it that. Instead, I tried consoling myself with the odds that it would likely happen in a future so distant I'd already be gone.

I wasn't alone in wanting to reject a portion of Christendom. Sometimes, when my father heard tell of what another Christian had said or done, he'd blurt out a word like *asinine*. And whenever the usual debate between creation and evolution came up in conversation, he seemed rather relaxed, suggesting there must be more to the question than meets the eye. "Couldn't seven days in God's realm be the equivalent of millions of years in ours?" he'd ask, smiling and leaning into the conversation, which with luck might then be permitted to drift toward some bit of *Popular Science* or *Nature* magazine. With that single gesture, he'd opened up a whole range of ecstatic possibility in my mind. He'd given me a combat-free zone, a space where contradictions—like a spectacular Big Bang and God's originating *Let there be light*—might coexist, an access to the world of faith that did not require me to relinquish access to my faith in the world.

That Valentine's Day afternoon, with the darkly hallucinatory book of Revelation open in my lap, I longed to arrive at my own kind of hybrid understanding, a view capable of assuring me that faith—an amplitude and generosity of spirit—might somehow be compatible with the vision of the future unfolding before me in line after horrific line. But, with my stomach roiling and my eyes racing back and forth across the text, wanting to squint shut but also ravenous to see where it all led, I didn't as yet know how to get there.

I suppose I could've scrambled to my feet and interrupted my mother's lunch: "Excuse me, Mommy, but . . ." Then what would I have said? How would I have fit my fear into words? Even if I could have, my mother would probably have sought to soothe my distress by quoting a hymn: *Trust and obey, for there's no other way to be happy in Jesus, but to trust and obey,* a refrain that sometimes replayed in my head without my seeming to summon it. If he'd been home to ask, my father might've been able to appease me by saying a thing like: "Imagine how strange it would feel to visit a future two or three thousand years away. What words could you use to describe something that doesn't yet exist in the world you know?" But it wouldn't have been enough. I was as knotted and tied up in my heart and my head as I was in my stomach, only with nowhere to run.

After her lunch with my mother was over, I thanked Mrs. Nussbaum again for the gift, and I tried smiling more demurely so she wouldn't be able to catch quite as firm a hold on my cheeks, though she managed to get in a good, long squeeze despite my efforts.

That evening, I said nothing about what was on my mind. I didn't want my mother to take the book away from me, nor did I want reassurance of what it said. I wanted something I didn't yet know how to name—something I instinctively knew I ought not try to put into words. Some kind of crawl space that might provide me with an out, an alternate ending, a gentler version of God that didn't make Him seem like He'd decided to turn on us so emphatically. What alarmed me most was sensing that it was a single "us" that the book of Revelation described, that Christians like me and Christians like the ones I instinctively disliked were thrown into the same unholy soup with people who denied God's existence outright or who acknowledged it only with cool apathy.

Later that night, Wanda called from LA to wish Mom, Dad, Michael, and me a happy Valentine's Day (Jean and Conrad were already away at school by then). When the receiver got handed to me, I told her about my fears. I must have chosen her because she was good at making light of things, was always just a movement away from laughter. Often her irreverence was frustrating. When I'd been littler, sometimes she'd held me on her lap and then, without warning, opened her knees wide and let me almost drop onto the floor, laughing at the shock and betrayal on my face. Sometimes she'd pinched me with her toes, giggling when my eyes filled up with water. But I also remember turning to her one night, when, despite eating my fill at dinner, I woke up hungry. I might have gotten scolded for coming back into the kitchen and asking to be fed; I knew better than to get up after I'd already been put to bed. So I'd found a way of getting Wanda's attention, and she'd sat with me as I ate a packet of smoked almonds she'd dug out of her purse. I knew that Wanda was on my side, and I knew she believed in the Bible. She'd sought out a church to attend when she left for college. When she came back home for weekend visits, she helped out in the Sunday school classes at our church. Confronted with such an onerous text, Jean might have felt much like I did: afraid and put off. Michael would likely have wanted to take advantage of my fears, turning my confidence into a prank he and his high school friends could capitalize upon. Even Conrad, whose college studies were aimed at staking out a place for himself in medicine, wouldn't have had our eldest sister's determination to quell my fears while also affirming God's word.

So I told Wanda about the book of Revelation and about how anxious and afraid it made me. It was dark outside. The window gave back my own reflection in the kitchen light. Her voice was buoyant, bouncy. She said, "Don't worry, Kitten. If it happens, it'll be a total adventure." That *it* meant everything, the whole apocalyptic chain of events. *It* was a lumping together of the good and the ghastly, a breezy, offhand dismissal of nuance. *It* lightened things for me, told me to let go of trying to plan for something so far-off and far-out. Not only did her *it* begin to yank me out of the spin cycle my thoughts had sucked me into, but her emphasis on the word *total,* and the drawn-out valley-girl inflection she'd adopted, also helped drain my thoughts of their dark hysteria. Wanda, the first of us to leave home, must have known about adventure. Sometimes, she brought girls home with her from college who told stories about hitchhikers or skiing accidents—girls with alcoholic sisters or dead parents. Girls who were kind and happy but who had also survived perilous things. Girls who had lived. "Wanda is my wanderer," Mom would sometimes say. And that was what Wanda seemed to be striving for, with her sense of broad wonder, her appetite for anything. Perhaps she was right. Why shouldn't I look forward to a chance at *total* adventure?

Hanging up the phone, I could feel my body begin to unclench in relief, and the first thing I remembered was the chocolates. I walked back over to the box, which I'd left on the coffee table atop the *TV Guide,* and picked out a smooth round piece from the top layer. I bit down, expecting affirmation of my new, easier state of mind. To my intense disappointment, the candy was a cherry cordial, so hyperbolically sweet I sat there for a moment with the half-eaten morsel in one hand and the other hand cupped under my chin, trying to decide whether to spit the thing out.

No one else ever appears in my recurring dream about God and my family. The seven of us move around quietly, with a kind of nervous purpose, like the Jews hidden in the secret annex of the ten Boom sisters' house. I'd always awaken before we could be found, before God could come to collect us and transport us to Heaven. In the dark center of night, hours from dawn, I'd lie still in bed, stranded, caught between competing currents of feeling: disbelief that salvation could really be as literal as all that and a strange, powerful nostalgia for the very years I was in the process of living, when the world of my family was the only heaven I needed to believe in.

BOOK A BIG BAND

"DON'T YOU WISH YOU WERE WHITE?"

She was older than me. Tall and blond, with short hair like Julie Andrews's. Her parents were downstairs talking to my parents, and when she asked me the question, which no one else had ever posed to me, she said it as if it was my chance to finally come clean. She was standing at the foot of my bed holding the Tuesday Taylor doll whose head spun around so that sometimes she could be a blonde and other times a brunette.

I knew instinctively that the answer must be "No," which is what I told her.

"*Really?*" she asked back. "Not even *some*times?" Her insistence told me she thought I was lying.

I didn't give myself time to reflect because I had some sense of what was riding on my answer, but before I spoke, I let out a quick laugh intended to prove how silly, how utterly foolish she was to even ask.

"No. Never." I picked up Christie, the black Barbie, and without trying to make a show of things, directed my most loving attention to her.

My friend was different suddenly in my eyes, meaner and brutish, though she meant as little harm as any of the other girls who, over the years, would relax enough to expose similar assumptions: *You're not like other black people, are you? Can I touch your hair? If you could change one thing about yourself, what would it be?*

When I told the story to my family over dinner, no one was surprised.

"*Do* you wish you were white?" my mother asked, and I told her that I didn't, by then sure that I never had, that it would be foolish to wish myself into one of those girls with so little sense she thought she knew me better than I knew myself.

There were myriad versions of such girls, and I quickly learned to dread the moment when another friend would sign up for membership in the club. "Why don't black girls like to get their hair wet?" someone would ask, and I'd beg her with all my silent might not to take another step down that path. Over time, I'd learn to insert my own ellipses into such conversations, letting things trail off before I had the chance to be held up like a specimen for examination.

In fourth grade, a boy named Archie Murdoch interpreted a necklace I was wearing as indication that I was open for business as an object of curiosity. The necklace was a hand-me-down from Conrad's girlfriend, a string of ivory-colored beads made of carved Bakelite. It was the first time I'd worn anything so showy and ornamental, and I felt daintily refined. I carried that feeling with me onto the school bus, where I sat involuntarily straighter, elongating my neck to showcase my newly acquired beauty.

Archie must have caught some whiff of my pride as he boarded the bus, and it quickened him. Smiling or simply baring his teeth, he reached out to yank the necklace from my throat. "Who do you think you are?" he asked, laughing as the beads scattered across the school bus floor.

My chest clamped shut, and a few tears bolted out before I had a chance to will them back. I was crushed. I didn't even have the wherewithal to lash out with one of the insults in current circulation, and perhaps it was just as well; surely the situation would have called for something stronger. In my head, though I didn't notice right away, he became a cruel version of one of those girls, the ones with all the questions, with the blinders they required someone's fastidious help to remove, the ones who wittingly or not think it must be awful—quietly or glaringly or, in Archie's case, criminally awful—being anything but what they are, anything but white.

Was that the kind of thing that happens whenever you're black? Was it a mild, diluted version of what roamed about more brazenly in generations past? What about the other black kids at my school? Did they feel it? And if they did, why didn't we ever talk about it? Were we afraid? Maybe it seemed shameful to admit that we lived in a world whose terms were defined by the people least like us. Was that a condition we in our silence had chosen? Was there even a choice to be made?

And what about my family? In making a choice to live where and how we did, had the seven of us split ourselves off from some key part of black reality? If not, why did it feel like a revelation every time Nella came through our door? And why should one black girl in a TV program that had been off the air for some time still stand out in my mind as distant kin, someone I longed to see again?

There was another thing complicating my sense of race. The best way I can name it is to relate a story my sister Jean used to tell sometimes about a black girl who used to bully her during seventh grade. This was back when my father was stationed at Langley Air Force Base, so let's call the girl Virginia. I was only a baby when the story took place, but I'd heard it told so vividly in subsequent years that it had come to life for me, become one of my own stories.

"How come you talk so white?" Virginia would always ask,

bumping up wantonly against shy Jean, who hurried from her locker to her classrooms and back. What's the right answer to a question like that? If Jean had asked our father, he'd have scoffed, saying there is no such thing as "talking white," that speaking properly has nothing to do with race or even class but rather drive, intelligence, effort. He called people like Virginia *shiftless*. Perhaps one or two of my white friends, upon overhearing a question like that, would have thought a moment before replying, *Yeah, why do you talk like us?*

"Shoot," my father said sometimes, "those same people who fault you for speaking proper English are the first to complain, *'Ooh, it's because we black,'* whenever something doesn't go their way." There, he'd pause a moment in visible vexation, then huff aloud and spit out a word like *jokers*—or better yet *suckers,* with its lurid sibilants—in undisguised contempt. Our dad would have called Virginia *sorry*. He'd have said she was *sorry, up to no good, squandering her potential.*

But what made him so certain? He was raised in Sunflower, Alabama. Farm country. A speck on the map with its red clay roads, with its kids who'd have to take canoes to school when rain waters rose too high. His father and older brothers fought in France in World War II. Afternoons in the early 1940s, he used to spend time in his grandfather's blacksmith shop, watching him forge tools out of molten iron. As a boy, my dad was entranced by the same books he later encouraged us to love, books by Poe, Stevenson, Sir Walter Scott. He drew and wrote poems. Once, he made county headlines for whittling a perfectly lifelike squirrel out of basswood. "Boy Carves Squirrel," the rural paper had proclaimed. I never heard him complain about Jim Crow; it's not that he hadn't been affected by it, only that he refused to make it the cause of any significant development in his life. When he left home to join the military, he said it was because he was "sick of the weather down south." Even when he and my mother were turned away from the hotel where they'd planned to spend their honeymoon ("We had a reservation, but when the clerk saw us, he said they didn't serve *Negroes*"), his frustration was derailed by his delight in being with his new bride. At least that's the story he stood by for his children.

Looking at my father, with his handsome grace and his preternatural competence, I didn't know how to argue with him, but then I'd think of Jean narrating the story of Virginia, the trauma not yet fully gone from her voice, and I knew there was more to it than that.

Jean never did anything to Virginia, but Virginia sensed something about Jean that she couldn't let go of. Every time she'd accuse Jean of talking white, acting white, believing she was white, all Jean could do was whisper in her own defense, "No I don't."

One day, Virginia shoved up against Jean in the hall and challenged her to a fight. Wanda was already across town in high school, and Conrad was still in elementary, so Jean found herself completely alone. "Okay," she said, finally owning up to the inevitability of the situation. "Today after school."

Once the word got out, everyone started whispering about the fight, which left Jean sick with dread. Virginia was the kind of girl who could really do damage. She kept a jar of Vaseline in her locker, and when she fought, she would smear it over her face to keep from being scratched by her opponent. But what choice did my sister have? Wouldn't running away or telling only make things worse?

Our father was not what you'd call a race man. The vocabulary of social justice didn't fit naturally in his mouth. Growing up when and where he did, he wasn't blind to the subtle or glaring evidence of racial prejudice, but as far as he was concerned, the antidote was excellence, plain and simple: showing the world we were just as good, as smart, as adept, as brave, as *necessary* as anyone else. If the image we blacks projected got too nuanced, became threatening, began to make aggressive demands, then the message of excellence was lost, and he believed we went back to being the problem. When black athletes Tommie Smith and John Carlos brought the symbolism of racial protest to the 1968 Olympics in Mexico City, my father disapproved. Whenever that image of them with their black gloves and fists in the air flashed on the TV screen (I'd seen it over and over, even though it happened four years before I was born), my father would shake his head. Even if he didn't say the word, he thought they were *jokers* for discrediting themselves in the world's eyes. They'd won, hadn't they? Wasn't their victory statement enough? But no, they had to go and get *militant*, another word that sometimes fell out of his mouth like an epithet.

In the wake of the 1970s, that decade when a lot of black families had opted to give their children Swahili names, to live to the extent possible within a bubble of race pride and consciousness, we were different. We lived in suburban Northern California. My siblings and I were used to moving through a sea of white faces every day. We turned on the television and saw few examples of blacks and felt a certain relief when they were poised rather than clownish. We told ourselves that we didn't need foreign-sounding names or African garb to know that we were black; we needed only look in the mirror. And day after day, our mother and father were working to ensure that the person each of us saw there was prepared, kempt, and confident. Beyond this, we were encouraged simply to succeed: "You have to be twice as good as they are at everything you do," where the *they* in question was whites. The less frequently heard corollary to this was: "Sometimes we can be harder on one another than they are on us."

Still, I'd seen my dad put a white man in his place for offering an uninvited "soul brother" shake. It was like watching the end of an arm-wrestling match as my father wordlessly redirected the other man's grasp into a conventional handshake, the undeniable message being, *You don't know me like that.*

But what happens when a line gets drawn between us and ourselves? I try to imagine how Jean felt that year in junior high, trapped by the need to be *twice as good,* opening her mouth and knowing what Virginia and her friends would say. Perhaps Jean— and anyone like her—did constitute a threat. Perhaps she seemed to stand as proof of what the world must have been telling Virginia: *You must change.* Perhaps Jean's every word reached Virginia like a telegram from some inescapable future: *Renounce yourself. Agree that you're worth nothing. Learn how to talk, act, think white—or watch everything you've ever wanted in life get handed to someone who does.* Fighting words.

On the day of their big fight, Jean tried to make her peace with the task at hand. When the dismissal bell rang at three o'clock, she stood putting her books in her locker, collecting her wits. Then, like some preposterous deus ex machina, someone ran into the hall shouting "Fight! Fight!" about a much bigger brawl that had just broken out on campus. Suddenly, the entire school, including Virginia, was running out the doors, hungry for a glimpse of the action. For Jean, this was nothing short of a miracle. It was like being preempted by breaking news in prime time: a posse of boys was duking it out in back of the school. Everyone ran to catch a glimpse before things got broken up. My sweet sister walked home unmolested. Virginia never said a thing to her again.

Over and over, our parents told us the best stand we could take was to be our best, do the best. Nothing was too hard, nothing insurmountable. But was it wrong to wonder if we might also have been turning our backs on something vital in embracing such a task? Were we announcing to the world with our can-do attitude that we were willing to bear the burden of convincing whites not to judge blacks too quickly? Were we buying into the fallacy that racial prejudice is based on logic, reason, anything other than fear and lies? Or were we proving quietly, stealthily, that race is not what others—white and black alike—were content in understanding it to be?

"Don't you wish you were white?"

The sun came in through the eyelet curtains in my bedroom window. She didn't know it, but she meant, *Is it hard being black?* Even as a child I understood that the awareness that comes from living in a white world is complicated. I didn't know the girl terribly well, but I had an idea of what she felt, or wondered, or thought without realizing she thought it. My mind had learned to see both ways at once; hers had not yet come up against the need for such acrobatics. Did I wish I were white? No. I was quite sure I didn't. But sometimes I was made uncomfortable by my own ability to empathize so easily with whites, to submit to their scrutiny, to go out of my way to prove I—and, by extension, *we*—didn't pose a threat. It would have been nice sometimes to forget how such thinking felt.

Once I'd told my family the story, after the silence of it sinking in had passed, someone remembered a joke:

A man who has worked hard all his life never to sin, never to think bad thoughts, never to take the Lord's name in vain, dies one night in his sleep. He wakes up in Heaven, in his own beautiful mansion right across the street from where God Himself lives.

On his first night in Heaven, the man lies awake staring at the ceiling. Slowly, he begins to make out the sounds of a distant party: music pumping, people hooting and hollering, police sirens approaching. He puts on his robe and goes across the street to God's house to ask what is going on.

Greeting him, God explains, "Oh, that must just be all the folks down in Hell."

"So Hell is real," the man remarks to himself. Then, "May I see it?" he asks God.

God is not surprised by the request. Nothing surprises God. In the twinkling of an eye, He transports the man to Hell, where he sees a twelve-piece band and half-naked women and drunk men getting down on the dance floor. The man lingers there a moment before God transports him back up to Heaven.

"Lord," he says, "I don't understand. I served you faithfully my whole life on earth, but now, while I'm lying here bored to death in Heaven, all those sinners are having the time of their lives down in Hell. What's going on?"

God looks at the man for a moment without speaking. (It was at this point that whoever was telling the joke would purse his lips and cock an eyebrow, embodying a version of God we'd quickly recognize as black.) "You think I'ma book a big band for just *two* people?"

The joke could have been about anything. What was important was our laughter—our ability to laugh, to shake free our minds from everything else that defied such ready resolution.

I don't think we ever truly forgot about whites, even when we were alone among ourselves in the thick of family. I doubt any blacks do. There's always a place in the mind that feels different, distinct; not worse off or envious but simply aware of an extra thing that living in a world that loathes and fears us has necessitated we develop. Perhaps that thing is the counterbalance to the history of loss I often tried to block out with silence: a riotous upswing that, quickly, painlessly, allows the mind to unravel from all the knowing and wondering it has been taught to do; a simple tickle of recognition capable of catching us up in a feeling—no matter how very fleeting—of hysterical joy.

A NECESSARY RITE

ONE DAY DURING THE SUMMER, A BOX ARRIVED CONTAINING what resembled a miniature flying saucer. My father removed it from its packaging and held it up for me to look at. "It's an incubator," he told me triumphantly. "We're going to see how eggs hatch into birds." When he said the word *birds,* the *r* made an open-throated windy sound, as if it had taken flight, refusing to be tame. His movements were lively and crisp as he unfolded the instruction sheet and spread it on the table. "It'll be an experiment." At *experiment,* he rolled over the *r* like something solid, an object to be held up to the light and examined.

"Of course, we won't keep them," he'd explained that afternoon, driving back from the farm supply and feed store where we'd purchased quail eggs. "Once they're old enough to survive on their own, we'll set them free." Indeed, in the encyclopedia entry he sent me to reference, the bobwhite quail did resemble the dun-colored finches that nested in our trees and hopped along scouring the lawn for worms—the ones that scattered like buckshot whenever any of us set foot in the yard.

It was the kind of proposition I was used to. When my brother Michael had brought home ducklings one Easter, we'd kept them until they grew to be full-sized and dirty white. We'd even set up a kiddie pool filled with fresh water for them to bathe and preen in, though they seemed to require more grooming than that. They stank. They soiled the patio. Every five or six days, Mom would give them a good shower with the garden hose. Eventually, our dog learned to help her round them up. By the following Easter, we'd surrendered them to the duck pond by the public library, where we hoped they'd take to life in the suburban wild. The next animal endeavor had been a warren of Dutch rabbits, the offspring of two "brothers" I'd been given for Christmas when I was eight. (I wonder now if the store assured everyone that the rabbits they sold in pairs were brothers.) My father built a hutch with a private sleeping den and a pen I could easily reach into. Each time a new litter was born, my father would sequester the mother and the baby bunnies. "Otherwise," he'd told me matter-of-factly, "the male might eat the young." Our attempts at animal rearing always eventually gave way to disillusionment. When the rabbits stopped feeling like pets, we passed them on to a family for whom they seemed to offer a more worthwhile promise. Still, my father was always game for one more experiment, one more run-in with the contradictions—science vs. mystery, order vs. chaos—that never ceased to captivate him.

The incubator sat on a shelf in my room. There was a clear Christmas tree bulb that fit into the device to provide the requisite heat. The instruction booklet said I was also to rotate the eggs three times a day, just like the mother quail would have done. Beyond that, my father assured me, nature would do the rest.

It was summer vacation, a time of few distractions. There were books I was supposed to be reading before the start of fifth grade, but even that took only a small portion of each day to complete. I was invited to a birthday party for a friend from school, a girl named Amber, who all year had captivated me with the stories of *Giselle, Coppélia,* and *Swan Lake.* Together, Amber and I would scour the school library for all the books and records having to do with ballet. Her mother was an ex-ballerina and taught at a local dance studio where Amber and all her sisters took classes. Amber loved to dream of herself laced into the costumes and transformed into a queen or sylph. I'd taken ballet classes, too, as a little girl. I'd even been praised for my ability, but I'd decided rather abruptly to quit after my teacher one afternoon chided me, "Ballerinas don't eat peanut butter sandwiches!" After a lapse of five years, I found myself newly eager to get to the place all the ballet books promised to take me: to a world of glamour and magical transformations but also of drama, strife, and loss. Ballet: that rarefied form with its religion of beauty and grace. The slender, strong bodies, almost always white. A world so remote, so inaccessible, that I felt inconspicuous hiding my thoughts there, projecting my own nascent desire for emphatic feelings upon it. Is this what any little girl is doing when she first learns to swoon over fairy princesses? Is it an instinct she is responding to, an involuntary urge to be swept up in the torrent of romantic feeling, when a little girl prays that the prince in the story will be the right kind of prince and will drop down to one knee and ask for the maiden's hand? I'd pore over a photograph—the dancer beautiful, bereft, her very body pushed beyond the limits of the bearable—and feel perfectly undetectable in rehearsing my fantasy of what my own future might feel like: *One day I will house a tremendous heartache. One day I will reel with a singular ecstasy.* No one was the wiser. No one, myself included, knew that the ballet bodies were merely targets upon which to project appetites I didn't yet know that I housed: for passion or love, perhaps even for physical desire, which the starved, sinewy bodies must have told me looked like hunger itself.

Amber had visited my house just once before, at the end of

the school year. She'd been dropped off by her mother and two of her sisters and retrieved by her stepfather, a man in an air force uniform who had struck up a conversation about the service with my dad. This was my first time visiting her, and the otherworldliness of ballet had so inflected my perception of Amber that I was shocked to find her home so perfectly normal. It sat on a street similar to my own, where every house was the mirror image of one of its neighbors. The rooms were plain and tidy, even a little shabby. I don't know if it was the ordinariness of Amber's life that caused me to feel a slight sinking sensation or if it was the fact that our entire fourth-grade class had been invited indiscriminately to the party. I felt dejected. The whole group of us sat outside around a swimming pool into which had been tossed several colored rings, but none of us swam. We ate hot dogs and potato chips. We sang "Happy Birthday" over a big snowy sheet cake, and though I had wanted it to be more elaborate and to taste more exquisite than every other birthday cake bought in the grocery store bakery section, it had clearly been picked up that morning from Raley's or Albertsons and personalized with a hasty thread of pink piping. After the gifts were open, Amber announced that her father was being transferred overseas to Japan. This was the last time she'd see any of us.

We didn't live on the air base, and I didn't have many friends with fathers in the service. My brothers and sisters sometimes still complained about the ways our father's serial assignments in the military had marred their childhoods, forcing them to surrender friendships at the drop of a hat and put down roots over and over again, knowing they'd just be yanked up later. I'd never before been able to empathize with their frustration, but Amber's announcement put me in touch with a feeling of deep betrayal.

Finally, I could understand how such constant upheaval must have felt to my siblings. Amber appeared at once disappointed by the news but also mostly inured to it; perhaps she was already severing ties to all of us in her mind, preparing herself for the act of assimilation she'd be forced to attempt. I said a disbelieving goodbye and left the party feeling heartsick. The pastime we'd shared, for me at least, had been an urgent one, and I was left unsure as to whether our fantasies were being taken from me or whether I was to become their sole possessor.

The summer ticked past. After the entire third week with the incubator had come and gone with no baby chicks, I allowed myself to accept that something was wrong.

On a Saturday, after my father had been home a whole night and had had the chance to wake up at his leisure and eat one of Mom's breakfasts that he liked, I delivered the news to him with a leaden guilt. He frowned, following me upstairs. There was no visible evidence that the chicks inside were dead, but as we gazed at the eggs, it seemed oddly clear that we were in the presence of nothing alive. The plastic Chick-U-Bator glared at us, flimsy as a toy. My father offered a few conciliatory words. His rural upbringing had taught him that such losses were not unusual. He understood that life, while meaningful, was also fragile. But I felt like a failure.

On the day, a few weeks later, that an even larger box arrived in the mail, I watched the eager energy return to my father's every movement. He set it down on the floor and fished out his pocketknife. Lifting the contraption from the box, he assured me, "This is *foolproof!*" The very word seemed to chasten and sting. I had been a fool, hadn't I? I'd been lax in my responsibility, mooning about, bored or distracted, and as a result, the chicks had died.

They would never get the chance to stand on their feet and scour the grass for seeds; they'd never scatter into the distance out of instinctive distrust at my approach.

The new incubator was easily five times larger than the first, and it had its own heater and automatic egg turner. Inside, there were compartments for more than a dozen eggs, which we drove once more out to the feed store to collect, and then placed one by one into their cradles. We parked it near the upstairs linen closet, where it wouldn't see a lot of commotion. All in all, it seemed a far more elaborate setup than nature itself—all lockstep order, an authoritative array of knobs and displays—but it seemed wiser, too; I wouldn't have to do anything but wait the requisite number of weeks for the chicks to peck their way out. The enterprise was no longer a matter of faith but of science.

The job that kept my father away from home all week involved a thing called the Hubble Space Telescope. I didn't know much about it or what he and the other engineers did each day, but every now and then, he'd explain to one of us, or one of our guests, that they were contributing to a device that would look farther into space than ever before, a machine that would tell us how the universe itself was born. An unbounded hope, like that of a child, broke into his voice at the word *born*, and it sometimes caught me up, but only briefly. I was conflicted. For if the universe had been born at God's hand, and if no one had ever seen God—didn't the Bible say that none can or will or should seek to?—wasn't a project like the Hubble doomed? I didn't think about the astounding discoveries the horde of scientists and engineers might bring into relief in examining the vast span between the present moment and the dawn of everything, only that it would surely be hard to get to the very bottom of something God had seen fit to enshroud in mystery. Still, it was a job my father performed with the utmost scrutiny and, from what I could tell, an unflagging faith.

If I could have fashioned a model of my own imagination, perhaps it would have resembled the telescope my father was working on: heavy, made of steel and glass, and run through with lenses and wires whose work I could only half decipher, pointing off into a distance that had no shape. Perhaps there would sit, at the outer edges of that distance, something I was afraid to bring into focus, some knowledge or presence, the power or verity of which might cause the rest of me to cower. It felt like that sometimes, like there were limits to what I would let myself understand, limits to the whole to which I'd give myself access. I was ten years old, living with a vague knowledge that pain was part of my birthright, part of what was meant by a word like *Home*. It was not the kind of beautified self-inflicted angst that can transform a girl into a swan or a doll or an ice princess in the ballet. Not even the kind of grief that, in art, can bring back the dead. No, what I felt, what I feared and discerned, even from my rather far remove, was the very particular pain that was tied up in blood, in race, in laws and war. The pain we hate most because we know it has been borne by the people we love. The slurs and slights I knew were part and parcel of my parents' and grandparents' and all my aunts' and uncles' lives in the South. The laws that had sought to make people like them—like us, like *me*—subordinate. It was a pain that could be triggered at the slightest hint that the residue of those laws still lingered, even unconsciously, in the minds and imaginations and the deepest assumptions of all the people I knew who didn't have access to a pain like that of their own. *Who do you think you are? Don't you wish you were white?*

Almost three weeks from when we brought them home, the

first few eggs began to shake and rattle as the oldest or most intrepid chicks pecked through their shells. It caught me off guard; my fear of failing a second time had convinced me they'd turn out to be duds, like the first batch, but that afternoon, the incubator was teeming with life. The tiny birds were a wet mottled brown, dark as burnt toast in some places, sandy in others. Their markings resembled those of a tabby cat. They worked their way out of the eggs with a particular insistence, struggling, pausing, then resuming work until each egg had been scored with what looked like a lid. Then they stretched their small downy bodies and wriggled out. My father was right. It was remarkable to watch. I remembered my excitement, years before, at the yellow chicks and the baby calf at Mr. Gustafsson's ranch, but never before had I witnessed another thing being born. They were mine, in a way, but I knew they weren't, and I knew it was a little cruel that the birth of all these chicks should be attended solely by someone whose interest in them was at most fleeting and who could offer them little in the way of love or warmth or even safety, if those are indeed things that a chick is born seeking.

After all the other birds had hatched, I noticed there was one who had gotten most-way out of the shell but had fallen short of shaking the thing free. He struck me as stuck, exhausted, in need of help. I had succeeded at keeping all the others alive, or at staying out of the way of their surviving, and thought only that if this one last chick came through, I'd have a perfect record. If every last chick could hatch, perhaps the other eggs' not hatching could be blamed on something other than me. I didn't think of that last step—the chick shaking off the shell and stepping finally out of it—as a necessary rite of passage; it was merely something to be gotten past, the final obstacle to my own relief at having hatched every last egg. My father would be pleased, and I'd feel redeemed. So I reached in to lift the cap of shell from the chick's head. I would not be an alien observer but rather a mother, a protector. I'd carry the chick over the threshold and into life.

The shell stuck at first, as if what was left of the yolk had already started to harden. I was able to detach it with just a slight tug, but when I did, the chick slumped. Immediately, I felt a nervous unease. I wanted to watch what the chick did next, but I couldn't bear to. So I did what I should have done in the first place, which was nothing. I stood up and walked down the stairs. Hurried, actually, wanting to get away from the feeling of what I'd done. I tried to busy myself beside my mother in the kitchen, but waves of guilt kept me from relaxing. I'd just committed a crime, and I couldn't help wondering if anyone had seen me or if there was telltale blood on my hands.

That evening, I saw that the last chick had finally risen to its feet. The incubator was a flurry of activity, with the little birds hopping around and peeping at one another, but the bird I'd helped was hunched over, contorted, and the others ignored him. My father was home. When I showed him what had happened, he lifted the chick from the incubator and cupped him in his hands. There was something merciful but inevitable to the set of his shoulders as he carried the small thing away.

HUMOR

GOING BACK TO SCHOOL HAPPENED THE SAME WAY EVERY year. Two weeks before the end of summer vacation, Mom would take me shopping for new clothes and a new pair of shoes, and then, on the first day, I'd make an initial assessment of the classroom in an attempt to get the lay of the land. In Mr. Samuels's class, our desks were arranged in six-person clusters, like cans of soda.

Fifth grade was the year I started squinting at the chalkboard and getting headaches after school—like a white-hot ball stuck behind my eyes that sent me to my bed for hours at a time. The glasses I was eventually prescribed solved both problems, a pair with wire frames and plastic nose pads that kept me from having to push them up continually.

Fifth grade was also the year of Edgar Allan Poe's "The Tell-Tale Heart" and Farley Mowat's *Never Cry Wolf,* of O. Henry's "The Ransom of Red Chief" and Shirley Jackson's "The Lottery." We configured ourselves, cross-legged, into a big oval on the rug at the head of the classroom and answered Mr. Samuels's questions about the previous night's reading. Sometimes, we'd take turns reading passages aloud, so the story reached us as a chorus of familiar voices.

From the moment I saw it, sitting toward the bottom of a page in our reader, I couldn't help but memorize a poem whose meter had worked upon me quickly and in a way I didn't quite yet understand. Its rhyme scheme cemented, for me, a new sense of inevitability, allowing the lines to slip easily into my ear and stay there:

> *I'm Nobody! Who are you?*
> *Are you—Nobody—too?*
> *Then there's a pair of us!*
> *Don't tell! They'd banish us, you know!*
>
> *How dreary—to be—Somebody!*
> *How public—like a Frog—*
> *To tell one's name—the livelong June—*
> *To an admiring Bog!*

Every now and then, when I was thinking about something altogether different, the first stanza of this poem, by Emily Dickinson, would pop into the front of my mind, drawing me into mischievous collusion with the speaker: *Then there's a pair of us! / Don't tell!* I liked the sense of privacy the poem seemed to urge, as if there is some part of everyone—like the imagination, the spirit, or whatever it is that gravitates toward the language of poetry— worth protecting from the world. It made me feel special, privy to magic, as if whoever was speaking had sought me out, discerning an affinity.

When I came across *The Diaries of Adam and Eve*, a slim paperback with Mark Twain's photo on the cover, I spent most of an afternoon in my bedroom reading. It was funny. I laughed in several places (mostly Adam's complaints about Eve), but in a great many others (moments where Eve's beautiful, childlike explanations of the world emerge), I felt a satisfaction that surpassed laughter. I loved that Twain gave the characters of Adam and Eve such modern sensibilities; I was amused by the light in which each saw the other. In a way that was completely distinct from Dickinson, Twain had also led me into a realm that felt deeply private and yet inhabited by someone with whom I recognized instant kinship. Was it words that made such a thing happen or the person behind the words? I didn't know much about either writer, but it wasn't at all a curiosity about them as people that their work had awakened in me. Rather, I wanted to become a part of the thing Twain and Dickinson had found a way of tapping into. Like them, I wanted to be able to say things that were moving and funny and true—things so original that they might even keep on being said and being heard.

The first thing I wrote in the wake of that feeling was a poem called "Humor." It was short and deliberately unfunny, what I later learned to call a *persona poem,* in which humor itself was speaking. As far as I was concerned, what it had to say was no laughing matter. After all, humor was what helped us get through the parts of life that hurt, something we ought to revere, respect. I hadn't known I felt that way until my own poem—the first one I'd ever written that wasn't just a silly singsongy rhyme—showed me that I did, and that made me feel wise, as if my message was important for all of mankind. The poem ended with a high-handed directive to the reader: *Treat me with respect, for I shall do you good / in years to come.* I put down my pencil, satisfied with what I had just written. Sensing that the poem marked a personal milestone, I decided to place it inside the front cover of an oversized illustrated Bible (another of Mrs. Nussbaum's gifts to me) for safekeeping. Thinking again, I pulled it back out and wrote out a second copy, one I could bring with me to school the next day.

"Hmm," said Mr. Samuels when he read "Humor," adding that he found it "very interesting." He told me I should keep writing poems. That little nod of encouragement bolstered my own sense of having found the weight of my talent. Often after school, I'd finish my homework and then work on filling the pages of an old green stenographer's notebook with poems, certain that what guided me was nothing short of genuine Calling. Sometimes, I sat still, gaze tilted up toward the ceiling as if awaiting an audible voice. I was one of them, I told myself. A writer. *Then there's a pair of us! / Don't tell!*

My ease in that interior realm arrived just in time to offset some of the less-welcome external changes that had crept upon me. Jean, now twenty-three, had moved back home from Sacramento, where she'd been in college. She'd never fully warmed to life away from our mother. Her return was a thrill for me, and I think it was a relief for her. It brought her back into the habit of soaking up Mom's company, talking and laughing like friends instead of like mother and child. I liked being caught up in their closeness. One evening, when the three of us sat talking in the family room after dinner, I demonstrated how another girl and I had learned to hold our forearms close to our chests in order not to bounce too much while we ran. It was shortly afterward that the three of us went to J.C. Penney and picked out several white training bras, packaged in discreet cardboard boxes, like Old Maid cards or individual-sized portions of breakfast cereal.

In the fitting room, Jean showed me how to put the bra on. "Hook it in the front, then spin it around and put your arms through the straps," she told me. She added that eventually I might need to lean over and "situate" myself fully into the cups. That last bit of advice didn't make much difference just then, but I filed it away for future reference.

The bras did make a difference at school. I could run around again without feeling conspicuous. Before, I'd felt envious of the girls who still had flat chests and didn't have to think about what was going on up top while they jumped rope or ran laps during PE, but the bras reined in both my chest and my envy. Apart from noticing which girls were still wearing undershirts and which had followed suit in "taking the first step into womanhood," as Jean had said with mock decorum, my concern over breasts (my own and everyone else's) faded.

One morning before school, Mom regarded me differently than usual, sizing me up and then nodding to herself. Just the two of us were at home. Jean was already on her way to Walnut Creek, where she worked in the human resources division of a bank.

"Remind me that I need to talk to you about something tonight," Mom said.

I froze. I had an idea of what she might be about to tell me—I'd picked up bits and pieces here and there and had not liked the sound of them—and all morning I found myself bowled over by a leaden dread. The Talk. What else could it have been?

From what I'd already heard, The Talk spelled out a whole series of disturbing but necessary actions that, eventually, led to babies being born. It sickened me to think of men and women— my parents and neighbors and teachers—allowing themselves to do such things to one another. Sometimes, during early-morning band practice in the auditorium, I'd be playing along contentedly enough with the other woodwinds when the thought of it would surprise me. Suddenly, the reed in my mouth seemed to go all fleshy, and I'd find myself thinking, *Is this what it's like?* And then, because I knew I ought not to be thinking such things let alone trying to imagine how they felt, I got embarrassed and terrified that one day I'd be a woman with no choice but to want to do such things with some man. That was the worst of it. The fact that one day I would likely *choose* to do a thing like that. It made me feel like I didn't know myself at all.

During a several-measure rest in the theme song to *Superman,* I whispered to my friend Kira what my mom had said. "Just don't bring it up again," she suggested. "Forget to remind her."

I didn't bring it up. Not that night or the next morning, and neither did my mother. We went on like that for the better part of a week, before she finally sat down with me at the table. "I've been meaning to tell you that if you should start to bleed"—at that point, she made it clear that she meant *down there*—"sometime in the next few months or in the next year, you shouldn't be worried."

She explained the ins and outs of menstruation, which I'd mostly heard about already (I had, after all, read through that contraband copy of *Are You There God? It's Me, Margaret* in the second grade), but the thought of all that going on inside *my* body was another matter. Detecting the horror in my eyes, Mom tried to offer assurance: "You aren't the first person it'll happen to, and you surely won't be the last." I did find a certain balm in the sentiment.

Kira was relieved for me. She also felt pity, since the worst part of The Talk still loomed out there in the distance, inevitable as the earthquake that we'd grown up hearing would either make California an island or send it toppling into the sea.

At Christmastime, Mom enlisted Conrad to bring home some of his premed anatomy books and take me through the ins and outs of human reproduction the way a doctor would. In all the photos, the men and women stood with their arms at their sides and their palms facing the camera just beside their hips, as if their bodies were prizes being demonstrated to game show contestants. It was funny. When I felt myself getting flushed or embarrassed, I focused on the subjects' hands, and it relaxed me.

We sat on two chairs next to the sliding glass door in the family room. Outside, it was sunny and cool but not cold, a bright California December morning, with dewdrops still on the grass and trees that clung to their leaves. Conrad did a good job of explaining how the sperm and egg meet without eliciting too much embarrassment. But he told me more than I wanted to know about a thing called *foreplay*.

"Why would anyone want to do that?" I asked, no longer able to suppress the question.

He thought a moment. Out of discomfort, I focused on the collar of his polo shirt sticking up out of the neck of a wool sweater. I stared until the tiny loops of thread woven together to make the fabric of the shirt came into focus.

He paused, his large eyes widening. He must not have been taught the answer to that question in medical school. Then he shrugged his shoulders and, nodding his head only slightly, answered, "Because it feels . . . really good."

After that, the lesson was over.

But a few afternoons later, while Mom and I were driving down Cherry Glen Road on our way back from the grocery store, she asked, "Did you understand everything from your talk with Conrad?"

There was tall wheat-colored grass on either side of the road, and cows grazed in oblivious clusters behind a low barbed wire fence that stretched on for miles.

"Yes." The old anxiety returned.

Doing her part to pick up from where the biological facts left off, she told me that God created sex as a gift to mankind. She told me that Mary, the mother of Jesus, was a virgin, which meant she had never had sex, and that she was chosen by God to be Jesus's mother precisely because she was pure.

"Do you understand?"

"Yes." I'd heard of the Virgin Birth all my life, but this was the first time the phrase succeeded in disconcerting me.

"And do you know what it means to be able to wear white on your wedding day?"

"No."

"It means you are pure," she told me, adding that she hoped I'd be able to wear white when that day came.

She looked away from the road to lock eyes with me and smiled. I smiled back uncomfortably. I was sure my mother believed what she was saying. I knew she believed convincing me of this might ensure that life would reserve good things for me. But there was something with us in the car that hadn't been there just a few turns ago. The backseat was full of groceries for the holiday meal. A turkey and a ham. Pecans and lemons and jars of mincemeat for pies. Green beans and collard greens. Dozens of eggs and bacon and loaves of bread. Cardboard cylinders of orange juice concentrate. All the things we'd gobble up in our togetherness as a family. I stared into my lap, letting the road outside fade into the periphery. I could tell where we were by the different stops and turns the car made. It was lunchtime. There were potato chips in one of the bags, and sandwich fixings, but I wasn't hungry. And I had no appetite that I knew of for sex, though if Conrad was as credible as I believed him to be, I understood that my body would eventually give me no choice but to develop one.

As the pasture gave way to houses and lawns, it dawned on me that there might come a time when, to protect my mother, I would learn to keep some things secret.

❧

ONE FEBRUARY MORNING DURING BAND PRACTICE, I DEVELOPED a discomfort in my stomach so excruciating I had to put away my instrument and lie down on some of the vacant chairs in the woodwinds section. I stopped short of going to the nurse because I hadn't gotten sick at school since third grade, and I was certain whatever the feeling was would soon pass. It felt digestive, like I must have eaten some morsel of food that was about to send me rushing to the bathroom, but the urge didn't come. When the bell rang, I walked to class, not feeling great, but hopeful that the worst of it was over.

In Mr. Samuels's classroom, seated in our circle on the big rug beneath the chalkboard for reading, I felt noticeably better. My main concern was whether the rug itself was clean, because I was wearing a brand-new pair of white corduroy pants. I held my book in my lap and hoped for the best, and soon enough, I was lost in our conversation about the assigned reading, so much so that when the pain came back, it caught me off guard. And this time, it was stronger, a surge in my lower abdomen that felt as if something was trying to take root there.

"May I go to the bathroom?" I asked, thinking I could escape the feeling by fleeing the room.

The walk down the corridor felt ceaseless. I hugged myself, instinctively clenching my knees together. I was sure that when I got to the bathroom, I'd sit down and soon enough whatever had tied me up in knots would be gone. Only, when I got there, I didn't have the wherewithal even to unfasten my pants or to sit in the stall or to do anything but lean over the sink for a moment and think. Was I sweating? I faced myself in the mirror trying to discern who this new person was and what her body wanted from her. From the stalls behind me came the sound of some other girl straining to relieve herself. Soon enough, she went silent, and the smell that filled the room chased me back into the hall.

The feeling came and went in waves. Sometimes I forgot to notice it. I played hopscotch and Chinese jump rope at recess with the other girls, distracting myself, hoping that if I ignored whatever it was, it might consent to go away, but I did feel observed in a new way, as if the other kids were studying me differently. Even Mr. Samuels seemed to sense something about me, and whatever it was caused him to smile—or was it blush?

At home, the first thing I did was head to the bathroom, thinking to get to the bottom of the situation once and for all. When I finally did unfasten my pants and pull them down, the dark stain that had covered the entire inside of my pants and seeped through to the other side, like a new continent, shocked me. I was mortified. Everyone else must have thought I knew.

My mother took the pants and managed to get them clean. "You'll need to remember this in the future," she told me. "You can get bloodstains out of your clothing with cold water and salt. Don't use hot; that will set the stain and it will never come out."

"How does it feel?" my friend Terry asked me the next day at school. The way she asked confirmed my suspicion that the arrival of my period had become a scrap of gossip.

"Gross," I told her. And then, deciding I might as well try to convince her that it had caught me unawares, "I had no idea what was happening until I got home."

Fifth grade was the year when the first promised changes began to arrive, like relatives from an old country. They brought secrets. The worry they carried was the worst kind, based as it was on evidence, history. Alone in my body, I found myself at the center of a bewildering crowd. There was the self I felt like, which was different from the self others saw. And, thanks to changes my body had wrought, there was the self I had been made to expect, which was different, still, another transitory state that would last only as long as it lasted. There was the self my mother had urged me to embrace, in a spotless white dress for the world to see. And the potential self to which that virginal bride stood in contrast: the self I'd be when, according to Conrad, my body began to desire what it didn't yet know how to desire; the self that might choose to act upon what it wanted, then try to hide it. Is the self that is hidden different from the self that hides? What about the one sequestered in the imagination, no less real for lacking form? How many was I? How many were here for good, and how many were merely passing through?

My head started to feel like a Volkswagen Beetle into which had been crammed a hundred clowns. That must have been part of it, too: staring life down until it teaches you to laugh.

I could feel myself sliding over to the far side of a line, standing beside my mother and sisters, where before I'd only been facing them from a distance. My mother had taught Jean and Wanda to help her in the kitchen, something she believed a woman ought to know how to do, and sometimes when they did, they'd talk to one another not like mother and daughters but like peers. More and more, I was allowed to hear and know these things, too.

There was the story of an older Japanese man living in Fairfield with his daughter and her husband. My mother saw him almost every day on her daily morning walk. They greeted one another with smiles or waved from across the street. But one evening, with a troubled face, Mom told Jean and me that just that morning the old man had reached out and squeezed one of her breasts as they passed one another. Mom was upset. She already carried the walking stick my father had made for her, to scare away the neighbor-hood dogs that would sometimes appear from out of nowhere, defending what they viewed as their territory. Was she now sup-posed to raise it against an old man? Should she change her walk-ing route? The man lived in our neighborhood. How could she realistically avoid him? Hearing her dilemma, I knew I was no lon-ger a child. I understood the physical things a person must attend to, guard against, and protect from others when that person is a woman.

Mom did see the old man again on other of her walks—walks where he had waved and smiled broadly, even stepped in close and reached out as if to grab at her again, though she knew by then to cross her arms over her chest and hurry past. One day, weeks later and quite reluctantly, she knocked on the old man's door and, without being asked in, told his daughter what had been going on.

The daughter grew distressed. "Wait here," she'd told my mother. Then she disappeared from the doorway and returned with the old man, speaking to him in Japanese. He had shaken his head, looking surprised, staring at my mother as though she were crazy, as though he'd never seen her before.

"Tell him I'd rather not have to go to the police," Mom had said.

At word of the police the woman grew pleading. "*Papa-san* does not even know what 'breast' means! Please, *please* don't call the police!"

"Tell him," my mother had repeated.

The woman turned to her father and said something else in Japanese, and the old man nodded and dropped his gaze to the floor. Then, quickly, he had looked up at my mother with an expression she interpreted to mean, *Okay, you win.*

"He won't bother you," the daughter had said right before closing the door.

After that, when Mom saw *Papa-san* on walks, he stared straight ahead, though more than once she caught him shooting her an angry sidelong expression that told her he was upset at having been ratted out.

Hearing the resolution to my mother's story, I was reminded once again that I was no longer a child; again, I understood the choices a person must weigh in her mind and live with when that person is a woman.

Outside, everything seemed full. The hills were still that barren straw brown, but so much else was heavy with blossoms, birds, and butterflies—an abundance so exuberant and, I understood for the first time, so female, converged upon by a thousand demands. Some evenings, when the sky was still shimmering with that nearly invincible spring light, we'd sit up in the kitchen and joke together, the women in the family, about things only women understand.

III

UNINVISIBLE

AT CHARLES L. SULLIVAN JUNIOR HIGH SCHOOL, THE GIFTED kids and the regular kids converged like two prison populations let loose in the yard. It was fitting, then, that the school should sit at the top of a hill like a blocky fortress or a squat penitentiary. I had walked those same halls once or twice when I was just a toddler, following my mother to Michael's classroom so we could deliver his forgotten lunch or pick him up for a doctor's appointment. Those times, he'd knelt down with his arms spread wide and flashed his huge front teeth at me in a smile. No matter that he was just a gangly seventh grader; to me, he was a giant who'd scoop me up in his arms and spin me around or kneel down and let me climb up onto his back. Walking those same halls for the first few times as a seventh grader myself, I'd felt confident that I was indeed fulfilling some small but necessary bit of my destiny, taking my first steps along the path that my older siblings had mapped for me: junior high, then high school, and then, finally, the enchanted kingdom of college, where I'd find myself in a society of people just like the ones my brothers and sisters had brought home on weekends—the ones who were cultured yet kind; intellectual yet full of good humor. People who spoke with such knowledge and authority about the world that not only did it already seem to belong to them, but they also seemed to possess the ability to break off a piece and offer it to me.

Of course, the panorama of seventh- and eighth-grade boys and girls in my immediate vicinity was a far cry from all the young sophisticates my siblings had introduced me to. Mostly, we were the same piddling lot from last year, with the addition, in some cases, of a smattering of acne. Certain of the regular kids, under the onslaught of adolescent hormones, had become volatile; one or another was always willing, at the tiniest perceived insult, to step in close to the offender and whisper, "I call you out," the junior high equivalent of throwing down a gauntlet. The park adjacent to campus was the theater for such showdowns. We called it the Bowl, since it looked like someone had spooned out the middle with an enormous ice-cream scoop. Some days, as soon as the dismissal bell rang, a wave of boys and girls could be seen running down the hill toward the action. The first time I set foot in the Bowl was during the archery unit in PE class. The brute strength it took to string up a bow and the primal savagery of shooting an arrow at a distant target (we'd learned from a series of gruesome photographs how much damage a single arrow could inflict) only amplified my sense of the Bowl as a place rife with danger.

From the middle of the playground—well, it wasn't a playground, just a covered blacktop where we could congregate during lunchtime as an alternative to the cafeteria—it was impossible not to get drawn into people watching. Scanning the crowd, I'd try to gather a sense of what everyone was becoming and where the children we'd so recently been had gone. A lot of the girls had begun to style themselves as Like a Virgin–era Madonna wannabes, in tank dresses, fingerless lace gloves, and armfuls of black rubber bracelets. Some white boys had let their hair go long like fledgling rockers. The equivalent for the black and Asian Pacific Islander kids was to start dressing like B-boys in parachute pants and beanies and practice breaking and popping dance moves with names like *windmill, moonwalk,* and *centipede* upon big sheets of linoleum after school. All of these kids who had chosen to adopt a recognizable look or a style had also somehow taken on a different kind of know-how. I wouldn't call it knowledge, precisely, since most of it was likely just for show, but they'd caught a glimpse of what they'd wanted to be—on TV or in magazines, or maybe they'd been someplace different and scoped it for themselves—and used that as a pattern for who to become and how to do it. At thirteen, I was still just a taller version of my elementary school self. And though I wasn't alone, I wondered what it would feel like to be aligned with a movement, a group, a real sector of the wider world. It scared me, too, to think a kid could fashion herself into something she'd seen on TV, and be treated accordingly, and then, over time, start following that path toward wherever it led. My mother called things like that fads and told me they were fleeting. What would it mean to choose a path that was fleeting?

Oftentimes, I'd find myself eating my lunch with friends and talking and laughing about whatever it was that we were used to talking and laughing about, but also watching and concentrating upon one girl in particular. Her name was Emmy. She was beautiful and delicate, like one of the dolls my father had brought back from Thailand when I was just a baby, with dark hair that flowed past her waist. She spent her time with one or two other girls, and though I could see for myself that they talked and gestured with one another just like my friends and I did, Emmy gave off the impression of silence. Silence and grace. When school first started, people whispered about her, but the whispering ceased once her body, so far along in pregnancy, began to corroborate all of their rumors. I never once spoke to her, but I remember watching her with a mix of awe and fear—the same feeling I got, on one of the first days of school, seeing my friend Eilene's sister Leilani kissing a boy out on the edge of campus. It wasn't just one kiss but many, or else it was a kiss in many stages, a long, hungry dance they were doing with their mouths and their bodies. Everything around them seemed to disappear into silence, swallowed up in that same commotion-obliterating air that followed Emmy around, though perhaps this time it was really just a matter of perspective: I was in my mother's Volaré, watching through the rear window as the car filled up with knowledge.

SEX WAS REAL. IT HAD GONE FROM BEING SOMETHING WE learned about and recoiled from in disgust and horror to something people found ways of doing and talking about and flaunting. None of my friends was doing it, that I knew of, but I got the feeling that some of the kids who rushed to the Bowl after school weren't just fighting. There were rumors that you could find empty packets of rubbers in the bushes there. Once, after school, I saw Junior Jackson, one of the Breakers, and LeKneitah Nixon, an eighth-grade girl with enormous breasts and hips that she stuffed into stretchy tops and stirrup pants, goofing around under an overhang outside the gym. They were with a few other kids I didn't recognize. It was raining, so at first I didn't think anything of them all huddled together trying not to get wet, but when LeKneitah pushed Junior off her in a way that suggested she was defending herself, I slowed down. I'd have to pass under the same overhang to get to where my mom was waiting in her car. When I got a few steps closer, Junior and LeKneitah were all over one another, laughing like whatever it was had just been a game. Then I watched him work his hand to the inside of her shirt. "Smell it," she told him, laughing, throwing his hand back at him with her own, which had followed his under her top. My heart sped up. I didn't know what exactly they were up to, but I could sense that whatever it was, I didn't want to get myself mixed up in it. I worried about passing so close to them, but I was also aware of this: we were all of us black, and if I had chosen to shy away or show them I was afraid, wouldn't that somehow be worse than whatever it was they might have thought to do?

When I was close enough for them to notice me, I put a smile on my face and decided just to walk past as casually as I could. If I smiled, they'd think I understood what they were playing at, that I got it and thought it funny or cute, but that I wasn't going to get involved or let them deter me. "Hey." I nodded, or at least intended to. But instead of nodding back, they zeroed in on me. The way lions will ignore all the other gazelles save for the one likely to be taken down with the least effort. Junior grabbed me by the shirt, still laughing. LeKneitah and the others were laughing, too. I didn't discern malice in their laughter; it was just a pitch, a pulse, a rhythm that held them in step with their frenzy. They were so caught up I barely felt it was me they had their hands on. I could have been anything, a dog, a basketball, an empty coat. I was just an object that had come into their range of motion. I tried to pull away, tried to get out from Junior's grasp, but it was happening so quickly. A hand—I couldn't tell whom it belonged to—grabbed my breast and then, very quickly, let it go. Suddenly, I was pushed—by them or by my own will?—out of the axis of their commotion. I crossed my arms over my chest and tried to hurry away, not looking at any of them. What would my eyes have said, anyway, had they locked gazes with any of theirs? With their voices distinctly behind me, I heard one of the boys say, "Damn. Why do all the pretty girls have small chests?" I felt angry and violated, and foolish for what I'd managed to let happen. Why hadn't I just walked around them altogether? Failing that, why hadn't I stood up to them, manifested my own might? Why hadn't I even tried to push Junior off, the way LeKneitah had done? Is this how my mother had been made to feel by *Papa-san,* the old man who'd handled her once in exactly the same way? Perhaps the most vexing of the many thoughts rampant inside my head was my confusion over which group the boy with the question had been lumping me into.

Sex was everywhere. When we were watching TV and the topic of sex came up, my mom would complain that the world was "obsessed" with it. There were after-school specials and TV miniseries about it, and more and more, it turned up in the news. Sex could kill you, everyone was saying, and if it didn't kill you, it could ruin your life. Look at all the girls out there like Emmy. "Babies having babies," they called them, teenage girls pushing strollers or waddling pregnant through the mall. There was even new language for describing where they came from, these girls and boys getting into trouble or causing it: Urban Youth, though from what I could discern, the phrase seemed mostly intended as a euphemism for black kids and the occasional brown ones. We had Urban Youth in Fairfield, and we were a whole hour from the city. LeKneitah and Junior fit the profile, and so did plenty of the kids fighting in the park. To someone not paying very close attention, didn't I fit the profile of an Urban Youth?

Mom picked me up nearly every day after school. When I walked in the door, I dropped my things under the stairs and fell into the rhythm of home. My only real sense of the outside world was what came filtered to me through Phil Donahue or the breaking news. Within a few hours, Jean would arrive home from work.

If it was Friday, Dad wouldn't be long behind her, and the four of us would sit down to eat and to rehash the details of our week.

Whenever I talked about school, I felt like I was describing a place in which I saw myself as an interloper, a not-quite-neutral observer whose ongoing commentary was honed and rehearsed for maximum effect. I thought that watching and reporting was safer than getting too close to the center of some things. Telling my family about what the other kids were doing, particularly the kids least like me, was a way of keeping a little crawl space between myself and the chaos that reached out its hands waiting to snatch up anyone who got close. I'd brushed up against it that time with Junior and LeKneitah, and I spotted evidence of it all around me—in glances passed back and forth, in the boys and girls whose bodies glued themselves to one another any chance they got, not caring who watched—but I wasn't ready to let it have me.

The kids I only peripherally knew made for the best stories, anyway. And being able to tell a good story over dinner, a story that brought everyone to the point of laughter, was currency in my family. Like the one about Career Day, when Harold, an over-grown eighth grader with a baritone voice and full beard, had cross-examined a local lawyer who'd come to tell us about the ins and outs of his job.

"How much do you make?" Harold had asked, when he was finally called upon.

"Excuse me?" stuttered the lawyer.

"How much do you *make*?"

"Well, that varies somewhat, depending on   " the lawyer had stammered back, looking to our teacher for help.

"How much do you *clear*?" Harold wouldn't let up. He had a question and he wanted to know the answer.

It took a moment for our teacher to catch on to what was happening, during which time Harold continued to press the lawyer. He'd have been happy with just a ballpark figure, but after a couple of rounds of their back-and-forth, the lawyer, who was probably someone's father, finally admitted that he didn't feel comfortable sharing his salary with the class. After the bell, Harold had stomped down the hall toward his locker, angry at what he must have perceived as agents of the "real world" trying to keep him in the dark.

I'd felt pity for the lawyer. Wasn't he just trying to do a nice thing by coming and talking to a bunch of thirteen-year-olds? Maybe he'd also needed the bolstering that should have come from standing in front of our desks telling us what success in his career looked and felt like (once he began to buckle, I noticed that his suit had a sheen to it, a detail I knew would amuse my mother). But Harold was the real protagonist of my story. Big Harold, who looked and sounded like he'd probably been held back a grade or two at some point. Harold, who'd sit sullen and quiet all period long and then, incongruously, announce to everyone and no one in particular, "I'm handlin' my business!" Harold, whose curiosity on Career Day must at least in part have been rooted in the fact that he wanted to imagine himself as a lawyer, that he'd wanted to weigh that option against whatever else he'd been told was possible. Was it right to laugh? Maybe, but was I laughing at Harold's crassness or his ambition, or at the lawyer who didn't know what to do with this big Urban Youth grilling him about his finances?

I wasn't friends with Harold. I said "hi" to him in the hall, just like I said "hey" to Junior and LeKneitah, even after that upsetting encounter in the rain. The same way I looked back at any black face even if neither of us was going to stop and talk. The way my parents greeted every other black person they saw in the grocery store and the bank. Just a simple acknowledgment that said, *You are there. I see you. And I am here, and you see me. We are not invisible, are we?* Hadn't my story about Harold also been a way of saying that not only did I see him, but one way or another I even saw him as my own distant kin, the kind that might make you cringe but that you know you'd better go ahead and claim?

ONE DAY, FOR NO REASON OTHER THAN THAT THEY WERE IDLE or maybe curious, LeKneitah and two of her sisters walked over to our house to pay me a visit after school. I didn't know LeKneitah had even one sister; she'd always just seemed to exist alone. But she came from a big family, like mine. She and her siblings were close in age, not like me, the straggler, practically an only child by the time everyone else had grown up. At first, I wasn't sure if they were making fun of me. Probably everyone in junior high has to grapple with such a fear, whenever anyone reaches out in what appears to be friendly interest. But the girls came in and met my mom and Jean. They were nice. Did we eat slices of my mother's pound cake? Did I take them upstairs to my room? All I remember is the initial shock of their arrival, and then a feeling of bemused gratitude that they'd bothered to come, and surprise at how innocent the three of them seemed, away from school and all the horsing around. For whatever reason, talking back and forth excitedly all together, the girls seemed to have a faintly rural accent, and so my mother had called them "those little country girls" after they'd left, which she'd meant fondly, nostalgically. After all, she and her sisters had once been little country girls, too.

Once or twice afterward, when I complained of having nothing to do, my mother suggested I go visit LeKneitah and her sisters, but I never did. I felt more comfortable keeping their visit as just the briefest of brief stories in my head: "Remember the day LeKneitah and her sisters came to visit? It was like that year when it snowed out of the blue on Christmas morning. They only ever stopped by that one time, and they vanished before we could really make sense of them."

One place where I felt truly at ease—certain of why I was there, comfortable in the community that contained me, and impervious to the snares and pitfalls I had begun to recognize as part and parcel of adolescence—was in band. I'd kept up playing the clarinet since third grade, carrying the instrument back and forth with me to school and practicing in my room most days. Plenty of the kids I counted as my friends were doing the same thing with instruments of their own. We'd convene every day during sixth period in a double-sized trailer outfitted with risers. So many of my friends from GATE were there that it seemed our insular world hadn't been fully dispersed. But there was also the pleasure of being reunited with some of the kids from my first school, kids I'd lost track of after first and second grades: Benji and Bryan were in the horn section, and Kerry and Donna were fellow woodwinds.

It felt like a coming together in other ways, too. Playing, we blurred out of the categories that held fast to us at other times. We were white, black, and Asian kids—oddballs and nerds, as far as the kids who weren't in band were concerned—but when we touched our instruments and gave ourselves over to what vibrated out of them, we were in control, beholden to a power each of us housed. Music indulged our need to excel, but it taught us how to go about losing ourselves, too. Not to the kinds of risks or dangers that other kids had chosen to court but to sound and collective feeling. And we were good. In our black tuxedo jackets or green-and-white polyester marching uniforms, we swept most of our competitions. There was a high shelf of trophies lining the perimeter of the band room, and when he got worked up or angry, our teacher Mr. Taylor would jab in their direction with his baton. *"That's* why you're here," he'd remind us. "Now, straighten up!"

I wondered if Mr. Taylor was right. He certainly loved competition, and it was clear that he liked to win, but sometimes I suspected that our victories were compromises we made with him: let us hide here in this space between childhood and whatever sits just beyond it, and we will bring you a roomful of trophies. I certainly didn't relish afternoon practice, which had us marching through the surrounding neighborhood, serenading the residents with "The Stars and Stripes Forever." I don't even think I much enjoyed the band meets themselves, those competitions in hot truck-stop towns like Ukiah or Marysville, where we suited up in our green-and-white uniforms and our hats like ornamental buckets, where I took every step with a measure of anxiety, hoping the judges would see me as worthy or not see me at all. One of the drummers—one of the best drummers in the region but not someone who seemed to take it all very seriously—started calling us Taylor's Army, a moniker that never failed to coax a mutinous laughter. But it was true. Every day during sixth period and during plenty of weekends when other kids were doing whatever it was they did outside of school, we fell into step and obeyed Mr. Taylor's commands, nine deep, eight wide, minds erased of all but the music and our teacher's pride. And so we marched, obedient as troops, into the sun or with it searing into our backs, outsmarting our own fatigue, bolstered by the belonging that came with such a compromise. We marched, rank and file, heel-toe, heel-toe, backs straight, sweat dripping into our eyes.

THE NIGHT STALKER

THERE WERE OCCASIONAL WEEKENDS WHEN WE'D RETURN to the shape and sense of our old self again, my family. All seven of us home, staving off the outside world, which seemed to be inching closer all the time or else pulling us farther from the perfect seven we'd always been. Dad was still gone four nights out of seven, his absence punctuated by a smudge of oil in the driveway from where his Chevrolet leaked. Wanda had moved back to the Bay Area and taken a marketing job at a company that printed calendars and business cards. She lived in a sunny apartment on Guerrero Street in San Francisco and was saving money for a season in Europe all by herself, a foray into the world she had already begun to crave more than the world we all together made. Even Jean, who had reclaimed her room at home on the second floor and who served as my one barrier against the abject loneliness I imagined was the plight of an only child, sometimes chose to go out and do things with other adults, leaving me home clocking the time till she'd return to indulge me with her presence and attention. Conrad was in San Francisco, too, about to start medical school, which had been his dream since he broke his funny bone at age eight and fell under the spell of the white-coated doctors, with their air of kind-hearted superiority (that's probably not how he described it to himself, but that's how they've always struck me, and what I've always envied). Michael was firmly installed in his life at Stanford, an updated version of the self he had become immediately upon his arrival to campus. He now parked a red motorcycle in the vestibule of his dorm, and everyone had taken to calling him Spike, a hybrid of his high school nickname, Spider, and Mike. I wondered whether becoming Spike had required my brother to let go of a big part of the person he'd always been. Or, as I'd later discover for myself, perhaps it was simply a matter of having encountered bits and pieces of himself he'd never before taken stock of and deciding to give them a little extra space. Whatever it was, he was also mostly off on his own as an undergrad ninety minutes away, closing in on that future I'd never thought to account for when I imagined growing up: the future that situated us each in our own distinct lives, separated from the rest of the family by a world of distance, difference.

Sometimes, though, everyone came home. Maybe it was my mother who called them back, promising food, rest, and whatever else they needed. Or maybe home still held something for them that beckoned on its own and drew them of their own volition. Whatever it was, their being back brightened the otherwise long stretches of eventless summer with weekends of footsteps in the hallways and up and down the stairs. Those times, my father, whose car sat dripping oil onto the driveway as if marking its territory, would wake up early and set a pork shoulder or a turkey up to smoke, sometimes both. I'd lie in bed taking in all the happy clatter of my parents preparing the feast (out of necessity, it was always a feast when the seven of us were together: meats, breads, cakes, and holiday side dishes), eager for my brothers' and sisters' voices to fill out the array.

Sometimes my parents would get excited and turn our reunions into bigger parties, inviting the neighbors and some of the families from church and setting up the front and back patios like a restaurant, all covered in the blue tablecloths and napkins that my mom had sewn the very first time she'd thought to entertain on such a scale. Those times, we'd eat past our fill and then push back the tables and dance. I liked watching my father take my mother in his arms and lean down so that their cheeks touched. They'd both close their eyes and smile, and though there were plenty of better conclusions to draw about what that gesture might represent, the first thing that always came to mind for me at those times was Mr. and Mrs. Huxtable from *The Cosby Show*, which, by then, had given me something upon which to project, or in which to decipher, the things I understood about happy black families. It even came up sometimes at school, when one friend who knew my family would describe us to another who didn't. The default would often be "They're just like the Huxtables," and that seemed to set everyone straight. I supposed I was grateful that there finally existed such a convenient marker of what my home life looked like, relieved that some outside source was finally corroborating the balance and comforts of the life I knew. Maybe the Huxtables affirmed for them that there was such a thing as a happy black family—an alternative to, say, the black orphans or black project tenants or junkyard occupants of the other shows and movies my friends and I grew up on. Certainly, the wholesome Huxtable kids provided a perfectly timed alternative to Urban Youth, a possibility the larger culture seemed to incrementally consider and accept.

I clung to these gatherings, to the fact of them, to the voices and the racket and the lights on inside the house and out. I felt protected in the midst of so much cheerful activity, with so many adults to buffer me from the aspects of the night that, hours later, promised to poke and jab jeeringly at my sense of calm. For when the dishes were done and everyone else was asleep, I'd lie awake in the throes of a new panic: that whatever might have been deterred by the buoyant commotion we'd made earlier in the evening would be emboldened by the dead silence of two or three o'clock in the morning. Sometimes, I'd creep downstairs in the night to double-check that the front door and then the outside screen were properly locked. Oh, and wasn't there a ladder out by the side of the house? Though I wanted to sleep, tried desperately to trick myself into surrendering to exhaustion, my ears were too busy tracking every creak and scrape and passing car. It was a fear that only ever came when we were all home together, and it surged worst, I think, during the long, slow summer months, when we'd sleep with the windows open to let in the cool night air.

It was, after all, the summer of the Night Stalker, the serial killer who was taking California by rampage, breaking into houses at night and killing, raping, and mutilating the people inside. He used a tire iron on occasion or a machete. Once, after shooting a woman three times, he cut her apart with a carving knife. He carried home her eyeballs in a jewelry box, like souvenirs. Did I really think he would come for us? It didn't matter if it was him or simply someone like him, a copycat or even just a cat burglar, the thought made me crazy with anxiety, worried sick not so much for myself as for everyone I loved, defenseless and asleep in the deep center of night. What would life be like, and how could it be worth anything, without my parents and my beautiful brothers and sisters? What would be the point of living on without them?

Once, one of the girls Wanda used to bring home with her from college told us a story about having been robbed while she was home in bed. She'd just lain there, feigning sleep, while the thieves took everything and left her untouched. This story became a kind of gospel for me. At night, I'd lie awake trying to slow down my breathing and heart rate so that a thief, had he been checking, might mistake me for asleep. But the more I tried, the more the blankets across my chest seemed to heave up and down, raging as if racked by wind.

It wasn't until the sun began to tinge the sky with the first red strokes of arriving hope that I could let myself really drop off to sleep. When morning came and sounds from inside the house roused me, I'd spring up, grateful to be alive and eager to spin my night terror into a gag from which we might all derive a little fun. Lines from Poe that had fueled my dread just hours before (lines so enchantingly incantatory that I'd long ago committed them to memory) now seemed merely funny, a lighthearted description of my insomnia: "Above all was the sense of hearing acute. I heard all things in the heaven and in the earth. I heard many things in hell." I'd march downstairs reciting them like a ham actor, hoping the laughter they'd elicit might amount to reassurance, which I could stockpile for the nights ahead.

This fear of intruders even topped the fear I had lived with just a couple of years earlier, when children my age began to contemplate the possible repercussions of nuclear weapons. There'd been a whole unit in school devoted to the topic, and we kids had sat down in the library with our teachers and talked about our fears and what we'd do if we were the adults in charge. That had been right around the time that commotion was beginning to build about an upcoming TV movie called *The Day After*, about the effects of a nuclear war between the United States and the USSR, a movie that sprang to mind (though I hadn't actually been allowed to stay up and watch it) whenever my radio dial landed on Sting's voice singing, "I hope the Russians love their children, too." Back then, I tried to carry the fear inside me silently at first, not wanting to give it the weight talking it through would confer. But silence only made it larger. I'd lie down at night and feel it pooling in my arms, my legs, running into the tips of my fingers and bubbling up into the very top of my head. At school, I'd sit quietly in the library, not sure what to say, while visions of my own desolated neighborhood filled my mind's eye. Where would we go? What would we eat or drink? I could envision my own mother, pushing on for her children's sake, and my father, diminished by hunger, by radiation sickness, struggling at the helm of our household, though of course it was no longer a house. Why would we do such a thing? Why would we annihilate ourselves? When I finally asked my mother these questions, she offered me her lock, stock, and barrel faith in God as an answer: "I don't believe God will let man destroy himself." That single sentence, and the stolid authority of her belief, helped to calm some of my unrest. Had I pondered her logic further, I'd have probably wound up feeling even worse, for what I now think she meant was more in line with what the book of Revelation had told me: God won't let us destroy mankind; that's a job He has reserved for Himself alone.

Back in sixth grade, the other kids and I had gotten a bit of relief from our nuclear hysteria by inscribing postcards with messages of peace and then launching them into the air on helium balloons. That's how small the world was to us then. A few months later, a friend and I received word that our message had made it all the way to Hawaii, drifting on the same winds that, under different circumstances, could have been carrying toxic fallout. Never mind that the latex balloons had probably done no small amount of damage to the animals and the ecosystem; that concern wouldn't cross our minds for another several years. *Maybe,* the success of the endeavor had managed to suggest, *we will find a way to save mankind ourselves.*

I remember a still earlier fear that settled upon me in a similar way before I'd finally learned to speak it and break its spell. I was six and in the habit of playing across the street with a girl named Becky Billings. For a week or two one summer, one of Becky's cousins was visiting, a boy from a place like Fresno or Merced, where they had horses and rodeos. He told me, once when we were alone together, that he had a machine that could turn people into tiny dolls. "All I have to do is point it at you and you'll be a doll. Forever." This was his way of getting leverage, of bullying me to do as he said, and I was young enough to believe him. Luckily, he had no real agenda; he only wanted my fear, the promise of my obedience. Yet the threat of being made miniature and of being drained of my life transfixed, ensorcelled me. Would I still have a mind, I wondered, to think with? I could already feel the effects of the magic or the science silencing me, setting me in an inexpress-ible daze, as if I were already less human. I slept with the fear and woke up to it, yet still I went to the Billingses' to play. I hoped the boy would tell me it was all just a joke. He never did, but after he left, I approached Becky's father. "Is there really a machine that can turn a person into a little tiny doll?" I'd asked, relieved that it hadn't happened to me that time but fearful it one day might.

In fear, isn't there often an undetected tinge of fantasy? I cer-tainly didn't wish to be made into a toy, or zapped by a nuclear blast, or forced to watch my family slain. But the mind concocts such threats, I now suspect, as a way of testing itself, of closing off every possible door and seeing what other routes and outlets and modes of meaning it might find. When I feared those things, my mind raced with an ugly seriousness, a morbid determination—

but it raced nonetheless. We do these things to ourselves, I suspect, as a way of digging in deep to even just a hypothetical urgency. We do it during our waking hours, and then, while we sleep, our minds continue to toy with our fears by spinning strange dreams—dreams like the one about God and the Rapture that were still haunting me now and again. I suspect on some unconscious level, the anxieties we dwell upon provide us with a primitive, roundabout way of affirming the addictive delight of being alive. Like testing to see if a 9-volt battery still has juice by touching it to your tongue.

At the end of the summer, the Night Stalker was arrested. His name was Richard Ramirez. He was tall with vacant, spooky eyes. And he was handsome in a way that made him seem, in retrospect, even more dangerous. He was caught after fleeing an East LA convenience store where his picture glared out from the front pages of all the newspapers. Some neighborhood residents ended up taking him down by hitting him over the head with a metal pipe. Night was suddenly less menacing than it had seemed for months and months, but I was already sleeping well by then. When my siblings went back again to their own homes, safe in the adventures I imagined were their lives, I somehow always slept like the dead.

HOT AND FAST

I'D WALKED OR RIDDEN PAST THE LOCAL HIGH SCHOOL EVERY single day of my life since I was three, and it hadn't changed much. Just two blocks from our house, it sprawled on its lot with four wings fanning out from a large central quad and flanks of portable classrooms at its outer edges. There was a big weedy yard, fenced in for construction (or to minimize trespassing?) out past C and D wings, and I fantasized for a long time about scattering it with wildflower seeds, even talked to some teachers about it, though ultimately the weeds prevailed. Mom would rouse me for school using an intercom that connected my bedroom to the kitchen. "Tracy, time to wake up!" she'd call up, then ask what I'd like for breakfast. I found that getting up in the mornings was easier when the promise of food was involved and would send down my order—*two eggs over easy* or *French toast, please!*—as if she were the waitress in a truck-stop diner. Then I'd shower, dress (usually changing clothes two or three times before settling on an outfit for the day), line my eyes with the royal-blue kohl pencil I'd bought for ninety-nine cents in the makeup aisle of the grocery store, and put on a frosty lip gloss that had come for free with another department store cosmetics purchase.

Mom didn't sit down with me for breakfast, but we'd talk through the window between the kitchen and the counter with the three barstools, where I usually ate. Small talk about the day ahead. If there was a test or some other challenge involved, we'd pray about it together, briefly, as a way of setting my mind at ease. I'd eat my meal, ignoring the newspaper set up beside me on the counter. She'd move back and forth on the other side, tidying the kitchen or lining up the ingredients for whatever marvelous thing might be waiting to be eaten later that afternoon. It strikes me now as strange how little I recall of what we said on all those mornings. Did we talk? Perhaps I ate quickly, knowing there was not much time before the first bell would sound. Perhaps she was preparing my lunch, which I still brought with me at that stage of the game: a sandwich, a piece of fruit, and a slab of pound cake.

The first few months of my freshman year, I'd walk around the corner to the Johnsons' to pick up Qiana, who was a year ahead of me. It was a detour that made my walk a bit longer, but it was nice arriving on campus with a friend, especially an older friend, whose presence bolstered my own sense of belonging and who allowed me to focus upon things other than my clothes or my hair or the omnipresent self-conscious doubt that ran rampant among kids our age like a contagion.

The Johnsons were a black family that had moved into the neighborhood just before I'd stopped counting black families. At first, there had been only the Meekses and us. Then, later, the Beasleys had come, then the Johnsons, and before long, there were enough black families that I found myself no longer noticing when a house had suddenly begun belonging to blacks or whether they were people I was interested to meet.

It was through Qiana that I learned bits of the gossip about the older kids at school, especially the black kids. She had a huge crush on a beautiful boy named Jeffrey Steptoe, with a golden-brown complexion, honey-colored hair, and glittering green eyes.

He ran track and he usually had a girlfriend, but he was nevertheless the target of a great deal of hopeful feeling on Qiana's part. A lot of girls felt that way, but I didn't. Jeffrey was too pretty for my taste. I found my heart speeding up when I saw boys like James Holloway, a senior, tall and brown, with a sharp, clean profile that reminded me somewhat of my dad. Or Nigel, a black British boy who had somehow landed in Fairfield. He seemed older, manly in a way that was equal parts alluring and alarming. He carried himself like a person who knew things—not facts, or even ideas, but things rooted in experience—and that knowledge intrigued me in a way that caught me off guard. I thought long and hard about what it would be like to kiss him, until finally I gave up on thinking about it and directed my imaginary energy toward a handsome Vietnamese boy named Ton, who rewarded my interest with scant attention. When I felt particularly defeated by one or another boy's blatant lack of regard, Qiana was good for a story about somebody else's rollicking romantic life, which took my mind off my own troubles and even made me feel lucky for having nothing too hefty to regret.

Much of what I learned from Qiana's stories was disturbing. Boys pressuring girls to have sex and then turning against them once they'd gotten what they wanted. Or girls whose histories were so checkered, even at age fifteen or sixteen, that they sounded barely believable, except for the fact that Qiana knew them or knew of them from a close friend, or the rumor was so widespread it had to have at least some kernel of truth to it.

My mom had no idea what kind of information Qiana was feeding me. She'd let me ride to football games or movies with Qiana and her friends because it made her happy to see my circle of friends growing—or, more to the point, *darkening*—to include more black girls. I liked it, too, though I often felt I was playing catch-up with Qiana, trying to become older, more in the know, less of a kid in comparison.

When I'd arrive at Qiana's in the morning, she'd be upstairs getting dressed or working on her hair. I'd be told to go on up, where I'd stand half outside the bathroom while she primped in the mirror, just like I did on the nights Jean got herself ready to go out. Qiana's dillydallying usually made us late, but that came second to how much I liked the feeling of watching a transformation occur before my eyes. Most of the time, with both Qiana and my sister, what I found most compelling was the internal shift that occurred once the hair and makeup were complete, the way something eager and alive seemed to click on all at once in the mind and light up the face. That didn't happen when I stood before my own mirror lining my eyes and frosting my lips, and I wondered if it had to do with the fact that I never truly believed anything would change in my life: no boy would see me and fall in love or say "hi" in a way that gave me access to his heart, no matter how pretty I tried to make myself look. Perhaps some part of me was guarding against such a possibility, without my fully realizing it. But watching the shift happen in someone else told me that one day, when I was ready, it might also be possible for me.

There came a certain point when my first-period teacher began to balk at my tardiness. I began to excuse myself from the Johnsons' bathroom threshold and make my way alone to school, and then I eventually started walking straight to school, skipping the Johnson house altogether. Our friendship got more fleeting, relegated to the odd evening after school or the random idle weekend. When I did see Qiana after a lapse of any length, I would admire her new hairstyle or her new sweater, while feeling a vague sensation of culpability, like when I hadn't spoken to my relatives or gone to Sunday school in a while.

Sometime that winter, I got invited to something called High Life. I'd known about it since fourth grade, when Michael started attending some of its functions. "Is that where kids drive around in their cars and go to lots of parties?" a classmate had asked with hungry interest when I'd mentioned it way back when, bragging about all the things my big brother did with his time. "No," I'd explained. And then I'd watched the interest drain from his eyes as I told him that High Life was a Christian youth group that hosted Bible studies and found ways of making God seem fun for high school kids.

Surprisingly, Mom had been skeptical when Michael first wanted to join the group. I thought she would've been happy for anything that proclaimed God as its focus, but she'd insisted on inviting the leader, a man in his thirties named Rich, to our home for dinner; she'd wanted to get a sense of who he was and what he was preaching. Sitting across from him in the dining room, I took in his Prince Valiant bangs, cut straight across his forehead, which gave him a youthful air but also made him seem vaguely strange, like an adult who was trying too hard not to seem like an adult. He struck me then in a way I couldn't yet put words to. It's the way so many men of apparent faith have struck me in the years since: as odd, a trifle cagey, people whose inner lives are or once were a wreck and who have managed to hobble together just enough wherewithal to throw their burden at God's feet, where their relief could be seen to impart a feeling of redemption. I'm surprised Mom hadn't come to a similar conclusion about Rich. I guess he'd said enough of the right words—*Jesus, prayer, born again, saved*— to convince her their views of Christianity overlapped. Or else she'd merely trusted that Michael's head was screwed on straight enough that he'd know what to swallow whole and what to let roll past.

Rich still surrounded himself with popular boys from the two high schools in town, jocks mostly, who came faithfully to the gatherings he hosted. Sometimes, I'd see him around town with a small group of these boys, getting hamburgers or jogging through the neighborhood streets, and I found myself perplexed that a grown man (someone who had been grown since I was in grade school, if not longer) made a point of devoting all his time to a bunch of kids. Other times, it struck me that he was probably just lonely and doing the same thing most of us high school kids were doing: trying to find a way to fit in, to feel popular, to belong.

I was also motivated by the aura of popularity that seemed to cling to certain of the High Lifers. I thought it might rub off on me if I were to join their ranks, and so I started catching a ride once a week to a Bible study called Hot and Fast, held at Rich's house every Tuesday at 7:17 a.m.

"I don't like that name. 'Hot and Fast.' It's lurid," Mom said. "Why does everything have to be so provocative these days?"

I puzzled over the name somewhat, too, especially because one of the things High Life preached was that sex was to be avoided until marriage.

Hot and Fast *was* fast: it was over before 8 a.m. so everyone could make it to school in plenty of time for first period. But what was the *hot* part about? The word of God didn't strike me that way. There was a breakfast served, but it consisted of doughnuts straight from the box. There wasn't even a drop of hot coffee to be had (it would be another few years before anyone I knew ever drank the stuff). I found myself left with little choice but to con-

clude that the name was a salacious attention grabber, a stunt—
and that it had worked on me.

Nevertheless, I went. I ate the bear claws and laughed at the
jokes and bowed my head in prayer. I even, in the very beginning,
spent time thinking about the Scripture readings and filling in the
Bible-study worksheets. I tried and tried to convince myself of an
early lesson, based on John 3:30: *He must increase, but I must decrease.*
I wanted to believe those words for myself, but it was difficult.
How could I, at age fourteen, really and truly feel the need to let
God inch me out of my own not-yet-salient life? Where would I
go? I wasn't living a wrong kind of life. I wasn't doing any of the
things God had explicitly forbidden. In retrospect, John 3:30 seems
like the kind of prayer a much older person might seek to internalize, someone who felt the tug toward some kind of looming
destruction or who, in light of his past mistakes, had given up trying to control things on his own. *He must increase, but I must decrease*
might have been Rich's prayer a dozen years earlier, back before
God had begun to fill up the empty spaces in his life. My empty
spaces, on the other hand, were empty because they were brand
new; I couldn't yet feel the kind of desperation-born drive to give
them over straightaway to God. Still, I repeated the verse to myself
for the whole first week, wondering what it might be capable of
changing in me.

Did I ever even tell Rich about how I'd met him years before
when I was a little girl? I probably knew it didn't matter, that I
wasn't one of the kids he was interested in. I was quiet, lacking the
dynamism of the older jocks or their tall, long-haired girlfriends.
Those kids were the ones who showed up early and left late, who
sat on one another's laps or joked around in the kitchen or huddled
on the floor while we prayed. Perhaps I thought that, a year or two

down the line, I'd come to fit in with the kids Rich really seemed drawn to. Sometimes, my mind drifted off to imagine a future in which I was one of the chosen, called to stand before the group and tell a story or explain a game. I longed for the courage and the knowledge that could have proved I belonged there with those kids who hadn't yet found reason to notice me.

There was one girl people noticed, Becca. She came to matter quite a lot to a man named Dennis, the other adult who worked with Rich in the High Life ministry. It was rumored that Dennis was successful at whatever he did—banking or law, something that brought in a lot of money—and he was soft-spoken and serious in a way that contrasted effectively against Rich's Peter Pan demeanor. Becca was pretty in a mild, pleasant way—a tall messy-haired blonde, natural and unadorned. She seemed to return Dennis's interest, though he was in his thirties and she was just starting her senior year in high school. Some mornings, if my ride and I arrived early enough, we'd see the two of them cuddled together, practically spooning on the couch. It was blissful, if the tortured longing of two people driven wild by their commitment to chastity can be seen as a kind of bliss. It stirred in me feelings of pity coupled with deep envy.

Were they dating? Dennis seemed like the kind of man who would have approached Becca's parents with his intentions—intentions that would likely have been serious. I wonder what my parents would have said if I were in her place. Would they have been irate at him or me for letting our feelings for one another turn to love (Dennis and Becca were rumored to use the word *love* with one another), or would they agree that God had led us to one another? I wasn't sure I could imagine letting myself be persuaded, the way Becca had been, that loving a man so much older than me, and marrying him, would be more important than going off on my own to discover what life in college tasted like. I wonder if Becca was afraid that loving someone brought to her by God would cut her off from the many things she might find on her own. Sometimes, I'd pass the entire thirty-eight minutes of Hot and Fast thinking such thoughts and wondering what it would feel like to let Dennis hold me in his arms like that in front of everyone, even God.

Did Becca and Dennis have secrets, stories like the ones Qiana liked telling, about what boys and girls did when they were pretending to be men and women? Did they and the other kids who called themselves Christians believe in God enough to obey Him, or was God a pretext for some other thing we were all of us seeking without our knowing it? Was Hot and Fast calling, all along, to our appetite for that which whispered enticingly, the things we'd been warned to look beyond, to stay away from, to talk ourselves out of wanting?

I wanted to be liked—to be wanted—the way Becca was. Who at that age wouldn't covet that kind of belonging? And so it was not quite an accident that I came to be friends with Becca's younger sister, a sulky, mannish sophomore named Diane, who stood a whole six feet tall. Diane made blunt, crude jokes that caught me off guard, and she didn't care much about being pretty. She wore men's rugby shirts and traipsed around campus like a big, irreverent Muppet. She wasn't pretty or even popular, but she struck me as cool. It also felt like an accomplishment, or the next best thing to an accomplishment, to be friends with Becca's sister. Perhaps that meant I was inching toward my goal of blending with the crowd that claimed Becca or at least being recognized by it.

My friendship with Diane wasn't much. We sat together sometimes at Hot and Fast. Sometimes, Diane and I and another girl would eat in the quad together at lunch. Sometimes, we'd find ourselves crossing campus in the same direction at the same time, and we'd match our steps to one another's and find some nonsense to laugh about before our paths diverged. Diane made deliberately gross faces or contorted her lanky body into impossible postures, like an animal put together upside down and backward, just for fun. She burped loudly and on purpose, like a boy. She made a celebration of being awkward, and despite my desire to be none of those things—to be, instead, pretty and poised and to attract the attention of Nigel or James or Ton or someone like them—I embraced the strange spectacle of her company.

There was one thing I didn't like about Diane. She never called me Tracy. In keeping with her penchant for blunt irreverence, she insisted upon calling me Black Girl. "Hey, Black Girl!" she'd call out from behind, and I'd cower on the inside before turning around to greet her. "What's up, Black Girl?" she'd ask when I bumped into her in the quad, and I'd miss a beat trying to find something equally sharp-edged to throw back in her direction. I never found anything equally sharp-edged. I couldn't even find anything adequately witty to say about her height, and through trying, I learned that it's generally not productive to mock someone taller than you are; no matter what you say, they are always up there looking down at little you.

"Oh, come on," I said more than once. "Stop calling me Black Girl, White Girl." But Diane didn't mind being called White Girl. I guess she took it as a given that there was nothing inherently wrong with calling a white girl White Girl. Like calling a tall person tall, it didn't sting.

In May, when everyone was passing out school photos, two-by-three-inch pictures of themselves that would be printed in the year-book come June, Diane surprised me by asking if I wanted to swap photos with her. It was a gesture loaded with meaning. The more pictures you exchanged, the more popular you were. I bent down to retrieve one of mine out of my backpack and thought about how I should fill up the space on the back. It seemed like an earnest moment, though I also knew that it, like everything in high school, was an opportunity to show how cool—or betray how clueless—you really were. *Hey Diane,* I wrote on the back, and tried to walk the line between kind and funny. This, after all, was something that would outlast our high school friendship, something meant to say that no matter how glib or word-shy we'd been on a daily basis, the feeling between us was one of warmth and friendship. Maybe even belief that the future for the recipient would be filled with success. I jotted down a message that seemed befitting of the occasion, signed my name, and handed Diane the photo, making a mental note of how many pictures I had left to distribute and to whom they should or shouldn't be offered.

"Thanks," Diane said. "Here's mine."

I didn't read what she'd written right away. I held on to the photo, wanting to will it great meaning. My collection was already growing, and I liked the heft of the stack of photos in my hands, a stack I could shuffle, like a deck of cards. When I got to class, I flipped the picture over and read the back—but first, I held my breath and made a tiny wish: "Let this be nice." I knew the odds of that were grim, but I thought a genuine inscription would prove that I mattered to Diane, which would mean that I might one day come to matter to the others, the ones on the inside of all the fun I watched each week from afar.

Thanks for being my friend, the inscription read, though the only thing I saw, the thing that spoke loudest or truest, was the salutation at the very top: *Hi Black Girl!* I carried the photo in my backpack with the others for the rest of the day, but when I sat showing the pictures I'd collected to Jean and Mom, I edited Diane's out. Later that night, I dropped it in the trash compactor, a place I was certain no one would see it and from which it wouldn't manage to escape.

Maybe Diane was a bully. Probably she was that catchall word that applied to most of us: *insecure.* She might also have sensed that, deep down, her friendship represented a social opportunity to me, that I hoped it might grant me permission to jump several social lanes to merge with Becca and her friends. Had Diane grown adept at sussing out that kind of opportunism? I told myself mine was hidden, but it turned somersaults in my stomach whenever Becca or someone like her acknowledged me. It's funny. Where did I think all my discomfort—the social anxiety that left me, for the most part, without a single word in my mouth or head—would disappear to on the day Diane finally delivered me to the popular kids? At that point, would I just wave to her over my shoulder or look at her with such transparent intent that she'd understand that my use for her had vanished? Did she sense what I really wanted from her and choose to ignore it? Or did she know it was so impossible it didn't matter, that I'd never get past her, I'd never make it to her sister's world.

Black Girl. Every time Diane said those two simple and accurate words, I fed my own voice to the familiar silence that came around whenever it smelled pain. I fed the silence every time this strange tall girl called me out of my name, just as I fed the silence every time I failed to ask my mother and father what names Jim Crow had tossed their way when they were my age. Perhaps the shame that ensued and that I mulled over sometimes at night, wondering what Qiana or Nigel would say if they ever heard Diane refer to me that way, was enough of a distraction to keep me from acknowledging my actual dislike for that big, ugly, rude, brazen, cunning girl I so desperately wanted to claim as a friend, as an intermediary between myself and the kids whose easy, happy, carefree belonging I craved.

SHAME

M Y MIND WAS IN TOO MANY PLACES. I'D BE APPLYING FOR college in a year, and everything I did, whether it was my intention or not, became an item for my college calling card: student leadership; French club; dance company. I wrote for the school paper, trying to come up with gritty features that had to do with the world outside our campus bubble. I conducted two or three interviews for a long piece about a new homeless shelter in town and felt a flush of professional gratification when our faculty adviser allowed me to keep the word *damn* in one of the quotes. With a teacher who had chaperoned a trip to Washington, DC, the year before, I started a relatively inactive branch of the Junior State of America club. I stuck a "Dukakis for President" bumper sticker to my locker and rode some nights with a friend's parents to meetings of the local Democrats Club, or whatever it was called. Behind all of this activity was the notion that if I could just get out of Fairfield—get to a real *somewhere*—I'd be able to do something genuine with all my theoretical interest in the world. I'd converge with the people I'd been waiting all my life for, and together we'd find our true place. It was a different time from the one kids live in now, an era when someone in my position could have the luxury of not knowing and not worrying, when the specifics were still far enough in the future that I could trust them to work themselves out. All the details had to do, in the meantime, was wait for me and exert whatever magnetism they could in my direction.

My teachers recognized something in my ambition. One afternoon, Mr. Catania, who'd agreed to let me take economics as an independent study, told me, "You're going to get lots of opportunities because of who you are."

I liked the sound of that. Didn't it mean I was special, deserving of opportunities?

We were standing near his desk in the classroom, with the door open to after-school comings and goings. I was on my way home, just dropping by to deliver a paper on the topic of opportunity cost.

"You're an African American woman," he continued. "You should take advantage of the opportunities that will bring you." My heart sank. Where he'd said "opportunities," my mind revised the statement to hear "handouts"—a word that instantly conjured the look and taste of those ancient bricks of government cheese Nella had once brought around, the ones we'd eventually ended up throwing away. I'd been brought up to do the kind of work that would put me above such offerings, to shine so brightly I'd have to be rewarded for my merits and nothing less.

Mr. Catania could surely read the distrust in my face, which he tried to quell by suggesting it was a new time in the world. It was the Oprah era, and suddenly people were not only willing but *eager,* falling over one another to listen to someone who looked and even sounded a lot like me. Exceptional Oprah, who'd changed the world—hadn't she?—with her cocktail of intelligence, empathy, and affability. Of course I wanted a life and a voice—a public voice—just like hers. But the advice stung nevertheless, because it also told me that it might be hard to be seen for who I was beyond or beneath the category to which I most visibly belonged. I told myself that Mr. Catania was wrong, though I didn't erase his advice from my mind. At home every afternoon, the mail brought brochures from colleges across the country. Mr. Catania's voice whispered in the back of my mind whenever the word *diversity* was printed among the catalog copy.

I was one of a group of prospective students flown out to Connecticut for a weekend visit to Trinity College. It was my first solo flight, but I'd been seated in the row beside an Asian girl named Audrey, who would be one of my roommates for the weekend. We hit it off in the air and bonded on the very first night in Hartford over the fact that neither of us was interested in the Jell-O wrestling event our hosts planned for us to attend. Looking out at the audience (a fairly homogenous sea of white faces, who on the whole seemed rather engaged by the sticky affair), I realized we must have been asked to campus in an effort to recruit students of color.

Audrey wanted to go to Yale just like her father had, and so did our other roommate, a black girl named Carol, who was a junior at a fancy Connecticut boarding school. Later that night, shivering in the dorm where we were camped in our sleeping bags, I decided that my dream was to go to Harvard. Conrad was living in Boston; he'd graduated from medical school and earned a prestigious fellowship in internal medicine at Massachusetts General, and so I'd told Audrey and Carol, "My brother lives in Boston," as a way of cementing my own blood link to such an ambition.

When I got home and asked my mom if she thought I could get into Harvard, she'd looked at me with those large eyes of hers and smiled, saying, "You can go to Harvard or anyplace else you put your mind to."

SETTLING BACK IN TO THINGS IN OUR HOUSEHOLD, I NOTICED TENsion. There was something upsetting our mother, and she whispered about it with Jean. Well, they weren't whispering really, but they spoke about it in fragments and quiet tones, as if it were something they no longer needed to reference by name. This vague *it* seemed to bother my mother more, but her disappointment—or was it anger?—rubbed off on Jean. They'd gossip about it, then pray about it. Their tension seemed to hover in the room, lingering but never rising very high, like the smoke off dry ice.

I guess I trusted that whatever it was, it didn't apply to me. If it did, I'd surely at least have had some guilty inkling about what I'd done, a feeling of shame just waiting to be summoned. I was so in the dark about the *it* in question, I knew I had to be in the clear.

But the murmurs continued. When Easter rolled around, I observed how Mom seemed to be preparing for the family gathering (Conrad wouldn't make it home from Boston; he'd be on call, but the rest of us would be there) with an unusual preoccupation. She still baked the cakes and the rolls, still stuffed the bird and glazed the ham, but the girlish eagerness that usually characterized her preparations for such occasions wasn't present. There was something dogging her mind. I helped in the kitchen, trying to amuse her with stories from school like I'd always done. She laughed when she was supposed to, but at night the prayers resumed, and so did the whispers.

On Easter, the revelation came. Michael arrived with his girlfriend, a slight, pretty, timid-seeming girl who didn't say much and followed him everywhere he went, as if she were afraid of being left alone with the rest of us. She was white, but that couldn't have been what upset my mother. My siblings had already brought the occasional white boyfriends and girlfriends home for visits without alarm. No, something else was at stake.

I could read the tension—and judgment?—in Jean's movements

and my mom's. They were perfectly cordial, but the warmth, the ease, the play with which we always welcomed guests, especially special guests, were absent. Then, while we were all waiting for dinner, Michael and his girlfriend (her name was Kathleen, like my middle name and like Mom's name used to be before she'd changed it to Kathryn) lay down together on the couch for a nap, their arms around each other and limbs entwined. The way their bodies fit together so easily and relaxed like that into such a familiar, unselfconscious sleep made perfectly clear what had been causing our mother such unrest.

"Did you see that 'nap'?" Jean had asked me that night after Michael and Kathleen had left. Of course I had; it had taken place right in the middle of the family room. We'd all seen it. I'd practically sat and watched it, for a moment at least, before busying myself someplace else out of a feeling of intrusion or impropriety.

They were living together. Was this Michael's way of showing that he was an adult, of embracing or even validating his decision to live as he wished? I was too young then to think about how natural it was for a man his age (he was twenty-five, after all) to fall in love and have sex and make a life with someone, even without waiting for the certainty or the ceremony of marriage. I was too young and living too much in my own head to have feelings like that of my own. Or else I still believed that I should be ignoring those feelings, apologizing for them, talking myself into putting them off for a later time.

Michael's freedom, and the way he'd chosen to announce it, unsettled me. It meant that life was not the obedient animal I'd been taught to believe it would be. If it wasn't, then what else that I'd been plotting, planning, waiting to receive, might turn out to be disconcertingly different from what I'd expected? And it meant that we as a family weren't quite what I'd thought we were, weren't the five perfect, dutiful children for whom every good thing had been reserved. Mostly, I suspect it unsettled me because deep down I understood that I, too, would soon deviate from our mother's wishes, and that when I did, it would tear her up inside and threaten to build a wall of disappointment between us.

I thought about Michael and Kathleen living together, wondered what it looked like, what they did. Did they feel proudly defiant or diminished by the rift their choice was causing? And did it mean that Conrad was out there sleeping with girls, too? Conrad, who had never done a wrong thing in my eyes and who never could, I was sure. Conrad, whom even our mother seemed to look up to (he looked a little like her father—I think that was part of it—but it was also just him, the way he seemed to carry something brilliant inside himself), what if he was defying our mother's wishes, too? Wouldn't it mean that, no matter how I tried or what I told myself, I would fail her, too?

I couldn't manage to unravel that logic-knot, and so I backed up to the thread I could decipher, the one I had more clearly before me: Michael and Kathleen on the couch, sleeping the deep sleep of lovers, something my parents—that all adults—had the propriety to do behind closed doors. Michael, causing all the whispers and the sighs and the accelerated prayers. How could he? And, perhaps more quietly, silently in the very back of my mind, was this: why should it be him and not one day me? Why should he be able to do it and flaunt it and get away with what I knew I'd feel forced to hide or deny no matter how old I was?

For weeks, I stewed, upset by the upheaval in my view of the world—our world—that the revelation had caused. The next time Michael came home, I barely spoke to him, was deliberately cold.

It hurt me to treat him that way. I was acting upon borrowed feelings and hurting myself in the process. And worst of all, perhaps I was hurting my brother, my sweet, humble brother, the one who deferred so often to Conrad's authority as the older son or his status as the doctor. Being cold to Michael left me cold inside, but I kept it up until I couldn't bear it any longer.

"Talk to him," Mom had urged me. I don't know if she wanted me to let go of my resentment or if she wanted my words, whatever they might be, to have some kind of a chastening effect on my brother. Once, when I was very young, she'd dictated a letter for me to write to one of Conrad's college roommates who hadn't been paying his part of the phone bill. She'd thought that anyone would feel guilty about being reminded to do the right thing by a child. I'd sent the letter, not thinking of how it would make Conrad look, and the roommate had paid up, but the conversation I was being urged to have with Michael was altogether different, one for which I had no script and little wherewithal.

It was just before dinner. I remember sitting on the couch in the upstairs sitting room. Michael came up because he knew I wanted to speak with him. It was a heavy moment—we both knew it—and I still didn't know what to say. I'm sure he was anxious about what it would be. Did he feel guilty for shocking our mother? For being the one to show me that the world, the real world, could be messy and painful and that such choices—the choices that would hurt or upset the people we love—were absolutely necessary?

"I'm sorry I've been mean to you," I said. I can't remember what he said, or if he said anything, but it was clear that there was more that I must say in order to come clean and break the spell of tension and distance my behavior had cast. It wasn't a word like *sex* or *sin* or, for that matter, *God*, that needed to be spoken.

Those words were implicit, part and parcel of our mother's worry. I'm sure she'd used them at one point herself—that is, if she had indeed sat down and had her own heart-to-heart talk with Michael.

All five of us were good kids. I don't think any of us wanted to do wrong. But we censored ourselves growing up in order to prevent the need for conversations like the one Michael and I were having. I wonder how much our being good in the eyes of God and our parents came out of the fear of being confronted as having failed in one way or another.

Once, in the eighth grade, I'd put off doing the final bit of work on a social studies report until the Sunday before it was due. It just happened that on that same day, instead of going home after the church service, we went to the house of some of my parents' friends. It was an impromptu invitation, the carryover of a conversation that had started on the steps outside the sanctuary. We stayed for one of those long Sunday lunches that fall under the rubric of "supper," and as the sun began to set, I felt a rising agitation. Finally, I interrupted my father to tell him that I needed to get home and finish my assignment. We made an accelerated good-bye, but when we got into the car, my dad turned to face me and said, "I'm disappointed in you." It was the first time he'd ever told me such a thing, and it split me open. I cried all the way home and felt miserable as I sat poring over my index cards to piece together the finished paper.

Michael probably felt like that—like he'd done nothing wrong but had failed nonetheless because someone he loved, someone with extraordinarily high expectations, had been let down by his actions—when I blurted out, "I'm just—I'm just so disappointed."

The words drew tears. Mine were tears of shame and regret at having, in just that very moment and with that particular phrase, broken Michael's heart. Perhaps the part of me that had been angry for weeks had chosen those very words for precisely such a purpose, but immediately, I felt small. Why hadn't I just focused my attention in the direction of things that genuinely concerned me? And, more to the point, what was preventing me from apologizing for the error of my disappointment and the haste of my judgment? What has kept me, even after all these years, from offering my brother the kind of apology he deserves, one that would yank me out from behind the safety of having been young and impressionable; one that would expose me for what I was, someone lying carefully in wait, biding her time, determined—I knew it even then—to do the very same thing as the person she blamed: to grow up and leave home and live her own life honestly, unapologetically, doing exactly as she pleased?

MOTHER

"MOTHER IS GOING TO COME STAY WITH US FOR A LITTLE while."

The smells and the heat and the idle restlessness from that ancient visit to Leroy came racing instantly back when my mom broke the news about my grandmother's imminent visit. For a moment, I was back in Mother's house, trapped and restless, and separated from my mom by an invisible gulf.

"Mother has started forgetting things," Mom explained to my sisters and me. "I'd like for her to come out here and let us take care of her for a little while." The phrase *out here* carried with it a silent nod to our father's belief in California as the antidote to life in the hot and gritty South or in fast-paced, dangerous New York. In opening our home to Mother, we were hoping to help ease her mind, to give her the chance to regroup and come back into her real self, to realize that she was only tired—exhausted and nothing more.

The way I saw it, Mother in California might have meant a bit of sunshine and fresh air for her, but it meant the opposite for us; our lives would feel more like her life, and our home would feel more like that house with the strange smells and the long, flat hours stretching on and on into the distance. It might also mean that my mother would disappear again into the self she had become in Alabama, the one I couldn't hold to tightly enough.

Compounding my dread was the fact that I was now a senior in high school and had begun to feel intense pressure from a part of my mind wholly dedicated to the task of tabulating the Embarrassment Quotient of every situation. The idea of Mother as an indefinite houseguest sent that embarrassment meter shooting into the red.

As Mom related it, Mother had started behaving strangely about four months ago. My aunts, who had her with them in New York, said she would insist upon going out to run errands and then wander off, mistaking the streets of Pelham and Mount Vernon for those of Leroy. At any given moment and with minimal instigation, she would become dead set on giving anyone, everyone, a good old-fashioned whipping. Someone might offer her a cup of coffee, and she'd reply, "Go on out in the back and git me a switch, 'cause I'm fixin' to whup ya," forearms tensed like snakes homing in on their prey. Aunt Gladys claimed to have narrowly missed a good beating by perching herself on one leg and raising her arms like a kung fu master, making B-movie martial arts noises until Mother called her a fool and stalked away.

"I don't know how long she'll need to stay with us," Mom continued, "but it should do her good to get away. I know my sisters need a break."

I'd seen Mother only a smattering of times in the span of ten or eleven years since I was last in Leroy. She'd visited us now and again, and there had been a Christmas sometime not too terribly long before when the extended family had congregated in California. Those visits were brief and blurry to me, though her presence, and the conundrum it posed, loomed large to me always.

When she finally arrived that spring, she was so much slighter than I remembered. Of course, I was bigger myself, but there was something different about the scale of her. She was wiry, and her breasts and stomach had shrunk away to almost nothing. She'd also given up her thick glasses. Her eyes, once cloudy with cataracts, were open and clear, and I tried to take her in as if through them rather than my own, thinking that if I could see her afresh, perhaps I'd be able to hear and understand and love her the way I should have the first time around.

Mother stood on the landing just inside our door, inching forward as we each hugged her, welcoming her into our home. What if we should succeed? What if being sweet with her, just as we had been asked, could lead her back into our lives and back into the world the way it was supposed to be? When it was my turn to hug her, she felt strong beneath her coat. And underneath the perfume one of my aunts must have dabbed her with in preparation for her departure, she smelled just like the tobacco and the woodsmoke and the cane syrup of Alabama.

She was quiet, wary. Evenings, she'd sit with Jean, my parents, and me, and Wanda sometimes, too, in silence. Sometimes, under her breath, I thought I heard her muttering curses. In the afternoons while I was at school, she tried to elude my mother's watchful eye and venture out into the streets she thought would lead her back to her own house, her own life. At first, I thought she must just be eager to return to her own familiar belongings, the places she knew and liked, but one evening, when everyone was home, she touched Conrad's thigh and called him by my grandfather's name: Herbert. "No, Mother," he told her, gently returning her hand to her own lap. How far into a past only she could recognize would any of our voices have to travel before reaching her? Perhaps all the way back to the place my mother used to reminisce so much about, the one I thought would still be waiting for us in 1978—where Christmas morning meant ripe, sweet oranges and wrist-thick peppermint sticks; where the cotton, melons, and chickens, the whole cured hogs and the catfish swimming in the pond belonged to them; where the brick house on its vast acres made a world all its own, set back, perhaps sometimes only moments at a time, from the world beyond, with its rigid facts and despicable truths.

Truths like the story about one of my distant relations, a great- or a great-great-uncle—someone Mother would have known when she was a young woman in Leroy—who stopped into a bar one night after having sold hundreds of acres of his own timber, his pockets bulging with the cash, or just having the poor sense to boast of it. He'd peeled a few dollars from a fat roll in sight of the wrong pair of eyes. Or else he'd forgotten how quickly news traveled in that town, and his need to slap a few backs and stand a few drinks had given word of his good fortune time to overtake him on the road. It's possible I have the story wrong. He could have gone straight home. It could have happened on his front porch or in his own house. It doesn't matter. One way or another, the bullet would still have found him—that bullet or some other—affording one or another white man the ease with which to walk away with all that money, confident he had nothing to fear, accurate in his hunch that, though he'd just killed another man, the law was on his side.

Occasionally, Mother managed to escape her daughter's gaze, wandering the streets of our neighborhood like a vagabond or a prophet, but we were always able to find her. In a neighbor's yard. Walking slowly up or down North Texas Street. Arguing with the cashier at the doughnut shop. Once or twice, when the police were enlisted to help, Mother was convinced we had called in some corrupt sheriff from way back when, and she glared at us with incredulous contempt.

No matter who found her, Mother always came back angry—for being kept prisoner, barred from conducting her affairs. Our response was to humor her. "Sorry, Mother," we'd submit. Only my mom dared correct her. "No, Mother," she'd say. "You're in California now." But no one told her *when* she was—that her husband was gone, and Mama Lela, too—that even if she were to "come to" here or anyplace else, she'd still likely find herself unmoored, an alien adrift.

Despite the discouraging fact that having Mother with us was improving nothing, my mom continued to try, giving her things to do with her hands, asking her to cook or explain or reminisce, anything to slow her descent into the disease we'd all by then started to call by its proper name.

I remember the sorrow in my mom's eyes when she told me Daddy Herbert had died. I was only four or five years old, but I recognized a heartbreak so undisguised it collapsed me in tears. *My mother's father has died*, I told myself. *My mother's world has been touched by death*. But really, what I was crying for was myself and the fact that my mother, having come from a man who was susceptible to death, might one day die herself. I wept and wept, my body buckling under a weight I was too small to have ever considered before, a weight that pushed in from all sides. My mother had been touched by death; it was no stranger to her. There was no way to undo that, no way to make death forget her name.

But this time, it was something else she stood facing. What did she see in Mother's face, the brow knotted in doubt, the mouth crimped shut in anger or fear? What did she hear in the silence Mother mostly gave back? I never asked. Caught up in my own adolescent crushes and fantasies, worries and preoccupations, I barely stopped to think what kind of trauma this must have amounted to for my mom. I could see that she was more than tired, that she was mentally exhausted from the stress of wanting to stop time and fix whatever was broken inside Mother—but I said nothing.

I began finding reasons to linger after school, not wanting to rush back to the disquiet I'd come to feel with Mother at home. Sometimes, I stopped into a favorite teacher's classroom as he was erasing the boards, and we'd talk for a few minutes about poems or novels. Other kids were racing home or changing into gym clothes for sports practice. The band, which I'd quit after eighth grade, was off in the distance; the brass notes and percussion traveled through the air and reached us almost languidly. I was motivated by something I couldn't articulate. I was sniffing out what else the things I was reading might offer me, some way of seeing or being in the world that might help lead me . . . where, exactly? I only knew the very real wish, like an itch under the skin, to get there. When my teacher and I talked about a poem or a story, I felt its words rolling toward me in great waves that crashed, receded, then gathered force and returned. The language and how it hit me assured me I was withstanding something, that language was marking me. But sitting there day after day talking with that man as if what we said to one another had never before been said—as if the sound our voices made together really did matter—that was marking me, too.

My teacher was young, just a few years older than Wanda, who by then was already thirty-one. Perhaps I'd fallen so easily into our unfolding conversations because I was used to confiding in people his age. Because of his age, and the fact that he was relatively new to the school—unlike other of his colleagues, he had never taught my siblings or met my parents—he represented a different kind of authority. He wasn't handsome. He was exaggeratedly tall and angular. But he was earnest; he talked about works of literature and art as if they were the keys to a deeper, more genuine way of living. I don't know that he lived that way outside of the classroom, but from the way he talked, I knew he wanted to. Sometimes, the two of us would walk across the quad to the school library, and he'd pick a book off the shelf for me to take home. It was on one of those afternoons, while my teacher was disappeared in the meager stacks, that I noticed a portrait of Conrad hanging midway through a lineup of former Students of the Year. "That's my brother," I told him when he reemerged, as if Conrad up there on the wall might help to assure him that he was justified in devoting so much time to a girl half his age.

Soon I began stopping by his classroom every day after school. My teacher would turn one desk around to face mine, and without feeling it happen, we'd talk for an hour, sometimes more. Then I'd collect my things and walk home, with an optimism that helped brace me against whatever unease Mother might have been stirring up at home.

One afternoon while I was at school, Mother cornered my mom in our front yard, brandishing an actual "switch," a young branch she'd yanked from the shrubs and stripped of its leaves so that, were it to strike someone, it would cut quickly through the air and hurt like the devil. There was an attempt to reason, then a standoff, and then a struggle. My mom, racked with her own grief, was no match for Mother's desire to be done with the bewildering time and place in which she found herself, and to be done with all of us. How could my mother strike back against an old woman whose anger was not anger but fear swirling in every direction? How could she lash back at her own mother, even if doing so was the only way to save her?

Seeing her mother like that must have tipped Mom into a state I didn't associate with her, a state of panic, and that thought activated my concern. Did she run for cover? If she had, Mother might have taken advantage of the opportunity to get away. Did she lurch for the arms that whirled the switch in the air like a knife? Surely the promise of one of Mother's beatings (a promise Mother, incidentally, made good on) would have been secondary to the threat Mother's escape would have posed. Mom must have called out for help, because eventually a neighbor, glimpsing the tussle through his front window, emerged to help corral Mother back indoors.

By the time I got home, everyone in the house was slumped under a mix of enervation and fright. Jean had taken me aside and told me all the details in a voice barely above a whisper, not wanting Mom to have to relive the day's events by hearing the story narrated again. I remember that I felt guilty, but also, I am ashamed to admit, lucky, to have been away when the struggle took place. My mom made some calls. By evening, she'd found a way back into herself as we knew her, into her voice and her mind-set as our mother. She had even mustered a thin, brittle laugh at the skill with which Mother still knew how to hand out a whipping.

When Aunt Gladys arrived to take Mother back to New York, she dispelled a small part of our anxiety. She was younger than my mom but older in a kind of visceral experience—strong, tough even, but still feminine. Aunt Gladys had the family eyes—large, expressive, and deep—and my mother's strong, wide nose that married an unexpected vigor to her beauty. She had a physicality that Mother submitted to more easily. Aunt Gladys was a switchboard operator at a hospital in the Bronx. "Op-er-a-tor!" she sang into the receiver, when she was on the job, like a lady in a movie. She laughed easily, and her laughter was either big and explosive or silent but perceptible, seeping out practically from her pores.

It didn't seem that a woman like Aunt Gladys could ever be tired or that she might secretly be dreading the family work that lay ahead in New York. "Okay, Mother, here we go," Aunt Gladys said when the day finally came for their departure. When she and Mom said their goodbyes, the physical mirroring I always recognized in the two of them inverted. Aunt Gladys was, for a moment, the original, and it was my mother who resembled her—not the other way around. My mother's eyes, her nose, even the dimples in her cheeks, were, for a moment, not working together to conjure an image of herself but rather one of her sister. Something under the surface united them, too. A knowing and a sorrow I had not seen in my mother for a very long time.

EPISTOLARY

THE HILLS WERE ALREADY PALE, THE STRAW COLOR THAT Californians call "golden," which meant the winter rains were a distant memory. There was the sense of things flowering, stretching open. In our after-hours meetings, my teacher had been acting distractedly. His eyes fidgeted when we spoke, avoiding my own. "I'm worried about you. You don't seem like yourself," I finally said, fearful that he might be tiring of our visits. By this time in our ongoing conversation, it didn't feel strange to me to say a thing like that. We were friends. We had entered into a shared language. We wanted to be the characters in books, even the ones like Prufrock or Jude the Obscure, who circled around and around in their lives like bubbles in a drain. I never stopped to ask myself why, in the face of every other possible scenario, either of us should want a thing like that.

On the last afternoon before spring break, he handed me a letter. It sat in a folder behind an essay I'd written, and he asked me not to read it until I got home. The rest of the school day was heavy with suspense. I zipped the folder into my backpack to protect it from my own agonizing curiosity. Did I already suspect what it would say? A year earlier, an older girl had told me how, when she was in his class, he'd once been so pleased with another girl's work he'd blurted out: "If I weren't already married, I'd propose to you right now!" What had I done with that information? Is it what led me to his classroom every day after school? Did it hover around us those afternoons while we passed a book back and forth taking turns reading passages aloud to one another, our knees almost touching beneath the desks? *If I weren't . . . I'd . . .* Where did those ellipses propel my mind? I retrieved the letter from my backpack once I'd put some distance between myself and the campus. I wanted time to take it in before I reached home.

> *I've begun to realize that my feelings for you*
> *are different now than they were just a few short*
> *weeks ago . . .*

I suspected he had already said more than what he'd once said to that other girl. I walked the blocks home avoiding the cracks in the pavement while my heart galloped. He loved me. It was a dangerous revelation, entirely inappropriate. He'd certainly understand if I chose not to meet with him anymore, to revert to being an ordinary student who handed in her work and raced past his classroom on her way home at the end of the day. He understood that even the fact of the letter would weigh heavily on me, as a secret I would probably feel obliged to guard regardless of what my response would be, and he apologized for that presumption. The letter was written in the same wiry script that cluttered the margins of all the essays I'd written for his class. I folded it into a square that could fit in the back pocket of my jeans. When I got home, I placed it on my dresser, in a wooden jewelry box that played *Für Elise.*

Twenty-five years later, and with children of my own, I ask myself what it was that assured him he'd be safe in handing me such a chronicle of forbidden feeling, safe even in acknowledging the facts to himself. When a teacher says such things to a young girl, it usually leads to a heap of trouble. Even then, I knew as much. When I was in ninth grade, people had whispered about a tenth-grade girl they claimed was having an affair with one of her teachers. Her story disturbed and perplexed me. Whenever I'd pass that teacher in the halls, his blank stare seemed to both hide and advertise a lurid appetite. I thought of the two of them doing things to one another in his classroom, of her driving to visit him at home, which is how the rumors described it. Did she like it? Whose idea had it been? Could it have possibly been hers? And what exactly was the *it* that bound them? The thought was like a film reel that would flicker in my mind for just a few frames before disintegrating. I told myself that a girl who'd get involved in a situation like that must have been lonely, crying out in a visible way for attention. But whenever I saw her, she had on an exuberant smile; she was tearing through the halls, yelling over her shoulder. The next fall, that teacher was gone. Fired, people said. But the girl was still the same.

My adult self still can't figure out what made my teacher sit down to write such a letter to me. What had made him decide to come out and say it? What did he think saying so would do? I was not unloved, not a girl for whom such an admission might produce the kind of gratitude that would result in unrestricted access. Taking my home life into consideration, I might have been guilty of having had too much love. We used that word at home a lot: "I love you." "I love you, too." And we meant it. We hugged and kissed one another. We talked and laughed together. We spent weekends and holidays, our whole lives, really, talking and laughing and feasting on this thing we never had the need to call by any other name.

When I was still just a very little girl, my father would appear in the doorway at the end of the day and I'd race up and hug him around the leg, not letting go until he bent down to scoop me up in his arms. Or I'd lean into his chest while he held me in his lap, his gentle, sturdy voice creating a cushion around us that blotted out everything else. By the spring when I received the letter, I was too big for these rituals. And my father was still gone most of the week; he'd moved on to a different job, but the commute was the same, and I saw him mostly on the weekends. An awkwardness had crept into the times when my father and I were alone together. He was still the same man, but there were moments, more and more of them, when I'd anger him with some small thing—sassing my mother or stomping off in disgust at some request he hadn't seen fit to grant—and he'd grow terrible before my eyes, glowing from some inextinguishable inner source. Still, even when I was angry with him for standing between me and what I wanted, there was also a part of me that drew comfort from the fact that he hadn't diminished, was just as mighty as he had always been.

Things with my mother were different, too. Growing up, I was always at her side, her silent satellite at her doctor's appointments and ladies' lunches. Or she'd pack a picnic for just the two of us—sandwiches sliced into triangles, along with squares of her buttery pound cake—and we'd sit by a pond watching the ducks bicker over our crumbs. On days when we did nothing but stay at home, she was always nearby, sewing or baking, humming to herself as she filled the space around us with her calm warmth. Those were my favorite times, the two of us alone together passing long, happy stretches in companionable silence—a wordless quiet inside of which I could feel myself simply be. But more and more at age seventeen, I found myself resisting such closeness, feeling intruded upon when we were together. I needed space. As if the fact of her and the claim she'd always had upon me, her youngest, had grown

into a threat to the scope of my imagination and to my vocabulary
for what I was deciding to want. Had I been a different person, one
of my friends at school, say, perhaps it would have been as simple
as choosing to hide from her the fact that I was having sex or drinking alcohol or smoking pot. But I wasn't doing any of those things;
it was nothing as tangible as that. What I needed was the privacy
to find out if I even had desires of my own and, if I did, to figure
out what exactly they were.

My teacher's letter changed things. It made it suddenly and
forcefully clear to me that I could—already *did*—have desires.
With the letter in my possession, I passed the spring break with an
unfamiliar feeling of agitation. I wasn't hungry or tired; I couldn't
keep my attention in one place long enough to read or have much
of a conversation or even watch a TV show through to the end.
But I also felt chosen, like a character from a novel, as though I had
only just then begun to feel my life. Alone in my room, I tried to
hold my hands perfectly still before me, and when I couldn't, I realized with some elation that I had finally found occasion to tremble.
Or my teacher's name would appear in my mind, and suddenly
my breath would get out of step with itself or a wave of longing
would cause my whole body to quiver, and I'd think, *So this is what
it feels like to swoon.* I'd envision versions of my life in which he
and I let ourselves love one another, though I was never myself in
those scenarios. I didn't know how to let myself think those things
about the self I knew. Didn't every available source on the topic
agree that it was wrong to love a man, as I told myself I did, who
was married to someone else; wrong to do the things I sometimes
tried to imagine we would do if only we'd let ourselves? I felt like
a mermaid carved into the prow of a ship, straining ever forward,
though the distance was shrouded in fog. *Yes,* I told myself, *I love*

him, too. And in the days and nights before classes resumed, I found some way of telling him so in my own handwriting, the spaces between words like the distance a thought or an impulse must cross before it becomes an act.

On the first day back to school after spring break, I asked permission to leave my first-period Shakespeare class to run across the hall and deliver an assignment to my teacher. I couldn't wait even until the end of class to get the letter out of my possession. I interrupted him teaching to hand him my response, tucked in the same manila folder he'd used for his letter to me. The other kids wouldn't think to notice anything strange about this; they never did, even though the exchange tripped off a back-and-forth that would continue throughout the spring and even into the summer after school was out. We fell shy of saying the kinds of things that actual lovers would have said to one another (the truth was, we barely touched one another, never even kissed), but somehow we never managed to run out of things to say: *This is what I'm thinking . . .* Or: *This is what I am reading . . .* Or: *This is what I am learning and what I am thinking about what learning a thing like this means . . .* I was taking an evening art history class at the local community college that semester, and I found myself transcribing passages from my lecture notes (which seemed suddenly to ripple with previously undetected nuance and meaning) into his nightly letter: *The first sign that the Roman Empire was about to collapse was the fact that the figures on the coins became larger and less distinct.* Or I rushed home from dance rehearsal and wrote to him about how strange and powerful I'd been made to feel rehearsing a dance we were performing to Stravinsky's *Rite of Spring.*

Those were the kinds of subjects we bandied back and forth, subjects I believed would help me to become an adult in the way I imagined I wanted to be—a model based less and less on my parents and more and more upon a character like Goethe's Young Werther: sensitive, artistic, impassioned, worldly, discerning. I couldn't yet see that such a character was also woefully naive and doggedly self-destructive, and neither was my teacher's stake in our correspondence based terribly much on what was practical or patently true. He wrote in blue ink, and his cursive gestured out like his thin arms or like his eyes, which darted off and up when he was closest to saying what he meant to say, giving the impression that he was intercepting each idea as it flew past. Every day after school, somewhere in his house, a house I never quite knew how to imagine, away from a wife I would not allow myself to think about, he sat and wrote page after page to me. And every night, I hunched over my own desk, a black oak desk my father had built, writing back to my teacher.

I called him by his first name. A simple name. A solid name. One his father and grandfather had carried. The name with which he signed his letters and by which he insisted I call him. I wrote his name and said it to myself, and the plain, flat sound of it caused me to smile. I smiled whenever I heard his name, even if it was attached to someone else, which was often, practically every day.

Every now and again, I'd lift my eyes from the inky imprint of my own voice to scan the low hills on the horizon. At seventeen, I hadn't seen anything. I only knew how much distance I wanted to cross but nothing of what it would look or feel like or what it would leave me with. How did I write about that? But every night I did, just as he did—as if during those few hours before sleep, sequestered by some excuse about schoolwork or a book too good to put down, we each disappeared into the same place, the same blank plane where nothing but the weightless platonic shapes of things sat.

Through all of this—all of the letters in which we professed our love even while also, possibly for conscience's sake, going to great lengths to posit that love as spiritual, as higher than ordinary love—did it once occur to me that my teacher was not an ordinary thirty-four-year-old man? If it did, it was only to reconfigure him in my imagination as an exception, a rare being, my soul's companion, my *Paraclete,* which was the word he taught me to use in thinking of him, a word he'd culled from the Bible. If my mind or conscience ever attempted to configure him another way—if I found myself watching from the outside and seeing what the sight of us must have suggested to a careful observer—I shooed the thought away, retreating to that other sphere, that blank plane, the space where things were not just themselves but their higher selves, their perfect platonic selves.

That spring and summer, I kept friends my own age at the same arm's length as I did my parents. I preferred to spend much of the day alone, reading poetry aloud to myself and letting the lyric *you* summon a version of my teacher. I read poets like Christina Rossetti, trying to hear her words as if my teacher were speaking them to me and to claim them along with the wish that I myself might one day be capable of fashioning such words into an address of my own:

> I dream of you, to wake: would that I might
> Dream of you and not wake but slumber on;
> Nor find with dreams the dear companion gone,
> As, Summer ended, Summer birds take flight.
> In happy dreams I hold you full in night.
> I blush again who waking look so wan;
> Brighter than sunniest day that ever shone,
> In happy dreams your smile makes day of night.

I took to my room, my bed, reading, writing, daydreaming, extrapolating from the tiny sliver of passion that I had been privileged to house. I felt so alive; I didn't want or need other voices cluttering my days.

EARLIER THAT SPRING, THE FIRST COLLEGE I HEARD BACK FROM was the University of California, Berkeley. I had been admitted. When I shared the news with my teacher, he gave me a hug. When I shared it with friends, a boy named John, whose first choice was Berkeley and who was still waiting for his own letter of acceptance, sneered. "Of course *you'd* get in," he said, suggesting that the news was only owing to affirmative action. The comment stung more than a little—I've remembered it all these years later—but it didn't undo the relief I felt and the delight I took in the ensuing days imagining what it might feel like to be a student at Cal.

Weeks later, the other letters arrived, all at once. It was a school day, and I was home for lunch period. The mailman himself was curious about the four thick envelopes from colleges, and he rang the bell. "I thought you might want to see these right away," he said.

I had been praying for a yes from Harvard ever since the conversation with my mother, more than a year before, when she told me I had it in me to get in. I'd spent what little time was not wrapped up in being smitten with my teacher imagining life on the East Coast. Mom and I stood on the landing opening the envelopes, each of which contained a letter of acceptance. I couldn't wait to tell my friend John, to watch him try to chalk everything up to affirmative action, though I wondered to what extent he might have been right. I wondered whether this was the kind of opportunity Mr. Catania had been speaking about when he told me to take advantage of the things that would be handed to me and whether, by his line of reasoning, I should feel proud or ashamed.

It didn't matter. There was no denying that my life was about to begin. I yelped and leapt up into the air. Mom squealed with pride and squeezed me tight. Had she been that happy, that relieved, and that excruciatingly proud when her own acceptance letter from Alabama State had arrived in the mail? And had Mother wrapped her up in a hug that felt at once like a warm embrace and a push into the oncoming rush of experience?

When I shared the news with my teacher, he made an announcement to the entire class. In his next letter, he told me that he felt a complicated mix of emotions: pride and an indescribable reluctance.

Graduation came. There was a picture of me hanging in the library by then, in the same lineup where Conrad's photo hung. Marching in the ceremony with my class, I knew I should have felt more, should not simply have been waiting for the speeches and the celebrating to be over, but leaving high school didn't strike me as meaning all that much. Only that a whole four years of waiting and vying for college were finally done and I could get started, get on with things—though September felt so far away, another occasion that would take its good time in coming.

A group of girls I'd known forever were moving into a house together with some boys that they seemed to be passing around among them. It was a freedom that made me envious. They knew what they wanted and were brazen in taking it; they'd grabbed on to an agency that was still far-off for me. I figured that once I had crossed the country for college and set myself up in life on my own I'd be able to give myself that kind of permission. Until then, thinking and writing about what my heart felt (the heart, yes, but not the body, whose vocabulary still eluded me) was plenty.

What did my parents think when, come summer, there was an envelope addressed to me in my teacher's handwriting every afternoon in the mailbox? They must have suspected some kind of an infatuation but trusted that I wouldn't make any serious mistakes. Sometimes, I thought back to Dennis and Becca, the couple from Hot and Fast who had fallen in love despite a similar difference in age. Dennis had been forthright about his intentions. He wanted to marry Becca, and it was in his power to do so. Not like my teacher, who was already married, who said things to me in letters that he hoped would never be sniffed out and dragged into the light by my parents or his wife. Whenever my teacher's wife came to mind, I hurried to tell myself that she didn't notice, that our life was a separate life from their life, and that it happened without hampering anything outside of itself, that we passed it back and forth between us invisibly. I told myself this, but I knew it was a lie. Why else did I sometimes feel so heavy inside, so anxious and despondent? Why else did I worry that she would one day grow curious about what my letters said, curious enough to break open the seal and read one for herself?

I spent my days during the summer working at the computer company where Michael was now a systems analyst; it was a job he'd helped arrange so that I might save money for the coming year at Harvard. I shared an office with a woman named Claire who had recently gotten married. Our desks faced opposite corners of the room, hers by the window, mine just to the left of the door. I can't say with much certainty, now, what I actually did there, but I had my own telephone extension and a voice mailbox that held messages only I could retrieve and to which I would listen first thing each morning. Sometimes, there were messages detailing tasks requiring my attention in the office. Mostly, though, I knew my teacher had called during the night and left me a message. His words, the sound of his voice: these are what I remember of those days at my first job; these would tide me over until the afternoon when I could rush home to the mail.

But one morning, the message I found told me that I shouldn't write to him anymore or try to call.

"I've told my wife about us, and the situation is delicate."

I listened to the message again and again. It was a fist in my chest, a punch someone had landed there, refusing to retract his arm. The weight of it pushed into me and stayed. I was angry, didn't know where to direct my thoughts or how to slow them down, how to go back to being the person I was before, the one who felt, suddenly, like a faraway stranger.

I lived like that for many days. I couldn't explain much to anyone about what had happened or how I was feeling. I mentioned to Claire that my mentor—did I use that word or just describe someone to whom my relationship was that of a protégée?—had asked me not to contact him because I made his wife uncomfortable. *Uncomfortable.* Surely I knew his wife was livid, as I'd have been, too, had I been the wife, though I didn't want to dwell on her stake in the situation. Claire didn't say much, but at the end of the summer, as a going-away gift, she gave me a copy of *Anna Karenina.*

The affair—that's what I had begun to call it in my mind, hoping that word might wean me of the desire to have it back—had left me heartbroken. I tried to tell myself that, in the grand scheme, I hadn't lost so much, hadn't even disrupted things to the extent I could have. I knew my life would go on more or less as it had been preparing to. I'd leave home, and time and distance would begin immediately to do their work. I tried to tell myself that my teacher had been lucky, too. Nobody had fired him; there was no transgression that would have warranted it. I told myself our restraint had saved him, for there was nothing terrible or irreversible, nothing as bad, I thought, as physical betrayal to recover from. In the absence of palpable fallout, I was afforded the luxury of being swept up in a kind of manic, narcissistic grief, willing my own feelings of bereavement to blur into the losses and disappointments borne by the characters populating the novels I worked my way through before the summer's end. I told myself I was becoming one of them, someone who had suffered, who had weathered something true and beautiful and therefore doomed to be short-lived. I told myself I was finally awake to what we'd sought together, my teacher and I.

When we did eventually speak, he suggested that we meet to say goodbye. On a sunny mid-summer afternoon—one too pretty and mute, too simple, it struck me then, for the occasion—we sat down for brunch at a restaurant more than an hour away, a place frequented by utter strangers, people in groups of two or four or six, smiling over baskets of pastries or stacks of French toast. We talked for only part of the time and spent the rest of the meal moving the food around on our plates and looking mournfully into each other's faces. I don't want to denigrate it now by trying to imagine how we must have looked to the other diners. I just want to say that we sat there filled with happiness at the sight of one another and with a very weighty kind of sorrow at the fact that we'd likely never see each other again. After the meal, we spent the next several hours walking the many passageways and colonnades of the Stanford campus. My brothers had long since graduated. It seemed imperative that we surrender to our separate futures in a place where no one would recognize us, a place running over with so much deliberate beauty.

When he dropped me off at home, it was dusk. Before he left, he walked around to the trunk of his car and handed me a lawyer's accordion file heavy with all the letters I had poured my young self into. It was a weight that dropped me to my knees as soon as I was safely alone behind closed doors.

POSITIVE

ONE WEEKDAY AFTERNOON TOWARD THE END OF THE SUM-mer, my mother stood in the kitchen facing my father, Jean, and me. We all knew she had been to the hospital recently for tests, though I was perhaps the only one who didn't know with abso-lute certainty what exactly the doctors had been testing for. It was like her to keep such things quiet, not wanting to burden us with worry. She had probably gone alone not only for the tests but also for the results and kept them to herself until a moment when we were all together. Nevertheless, it shames me to think that I could have been so caught up in my own selfish dramas and excitement about school that I hadn't even noticed her fasting before lab pro-cedures, hadn't read the deliberate tranquillity or the visible trepi-dation with which she moved during the days or weeks when the results she awaited were still unknown.

She had been hospitalized once when I was in first grade, after an episode of what had been described to me simply as "hemor-rhaging." When I'd asked what the word meant, I was told, "Mom's bleeding, and they don't know why." I didn't know to worry. But I was lonely for her when it was just my father and siblings and me on our own for a string of days, cooking our meals or eating food prepared by various neighbors. One particular devil's food cake, which I dug into every day after school like a hungry orphan, stands out in my mind as an emblem of that time. And then, a few days later, she was at home, our life was back to normal, and I never really thought about it again.

On that late-summer day, my mother told the three of us that her biopsy results had come back positive. Instantly, Jean's face contorted in fear. She ran to my mother and bent over her, in tears. My father looked down and held his head in his hands. It took a moment for my mind to process it all. *Positive,* I reminded myself, *is bad.* I knew this much. The word *cancer* had circulated within my earshot for years. The tagline KNOWN TO THE STATE OF CALIFORNIA TO CAUSE CANCER had popped up so often that I'd started to view cancer as the destination to which nearly every route, one way or another, would likely lead. "Next thing you know, peanut butter will be known to the state of California to cause cancer," Jean had scoffed once after a news segment identifying another compound found in Krazy Glue or diet soda or anything else in the average pantry as the newest in our state's running list of carcinogens. But on that particular August day, in our kitchen, the word entered our home as if calmly, through the front door, looking us in the eyes and calling one of us by name.

When I was very young, I would sometimes awaken from nightmares furious with my mother for putting herself in harm's way: going outside in her nightgown to shoo away a bear or letting strange men into our home when no one else was there to protect us. Underneath the anger, though, was always relief that the bear or the dangerous men weren't real; already they were on their way to wherever dreams go when they disappear. Yet, on that particular late-summer afternoon, the danger in question was real. An assailant called Cancer had installed itself in her colon and was already launching its attack from within.

She wanted to be strong. She wanted to stand on faith there

in the kitchen with the windows open and cool air blowing the curtains up and back, but I could tell she was afraid by the way she steadied herself with both hands against the countertop and smiled an almost apologetic smile.

"I know that God can heal me," she said. I was old enough by then to notice how thin her voice was and also to hear its timbre as distinctly female. Not weak but welcoming, cordial. As though she had just asked if we would like milk with our tea. She was not going to kick and scream or cause a scene. Certainly not before God, whom she had just allowed a loophole by employing the word *can* where I would have wanted her to say *will*. She was going to wake one morning soon, dress in a skirt, blouse, and pearls, pin her hair in place, and blot the excess makeup from her face. She was going to apply two dabs of perfume and enter the hospital with a smile for each of the doctors and nurses and technicians who'd be thinking whatever it is that people who see cancer every day must be in the habit of thinking. And then she was going to close her eyes and pray silently as the anesthesia dispersed into her lungs, saying to herself, *Fear thou not; for I am with thee: be not dismayed; for I am thy God: I will strengthen thee; yea, I will help thee; yea, I will uphold thee with the right hand of my righteousness.*

It was too big an upheaval to fit my mind around, and so I only attempted to parse it in part, by doubling back to the recent memory of a girl who'd graduated with me. Her mother had been diagnosed with cancer during the first part of our senior year—or had my friend just been quiet about it until then? By then, she was coming only intermittently to classes, and it confused me that she should be behaving like the kids who broke rules and racked up Cs and Ds as a matter of course. It confused me that she should be taking what seemed like such a lax view of her own future.

Wouldn't her mother have been happier knowing her daughter was set to follow a sounder path?

On that particular late-summer afternoon, while my mother did her best to relay to us the information provided by her doctor, thoughts of that friend seeped into every crevice of my mind. How I used to ride to school in her mother's old burgundy Saab every morning of seventh grade. And how, nearly every afternoon, my mother would pick the two of us up and take us by the Thrifty drugstore for a ten-cent cone of rocky road ice cream. How during junior year that girl had taken a job at one of the department stores in the mall, and how I'd dropped in sometimes to say hello when I was there squandering time on weekends. How she'd written a poem, just months ago, that our teacher (before he had become *my* teacher, belonging to me alone, as I saw it) had thought enough of to liken to Sylvia Plath. During her mother's illness, my friend took on an air of mysterious glamour in my mind. She came to seem more grown-up than the rest of us, staying home to attend to serious matters, driving herself around town behind the wheel of her mother's old car. And, though she never revealed anything about her emotional state—not even in that poem, which, like Plath, had found a way to speak through some sort of a fierce or mythic mask—I'd spent part of our senior year envying what I guessed was her great complexity, my friend's profound depth.

For a sliver of time on that late-summer afternoon, I allowed myself to blur into her in my mind. Again, it was like watching the reels of a film, only this time it was I who moved for a few frames through my friend's life rather than my own, feeling older, just as my friend had seemed to become to me, a half-dozen months before. I was looking for the thing that made her life seem so much more real than mine and wondering if that thing would find me, too, as a result of my own mother's illness. My thoughts drifted for what felt a while, though it could only have been an instant, a quick flash of images that took up a fraction of a heartbeat. And how wrong, how awful, but also how true that a trickle of eagerness, a readiness to rise to the occasion, crept in before I put my thoughts back in perspective and put my mother back into the center of the scenario. Looking up, I caught my sister's gaze, so like my father's, with his high cheekbones and sharp, straight, perfectly sculpted nose. Her eyes held on to me, boring into me without blinking, as if she could see the gears racing in my mind and was willing me to remember that this was not an occasion for anything but sorrow or anger—or pigheaded faith.

My mother's surgery was scheduled for early September. I realized with a start that I wouldn't be there for it; I'd already be across the country for school. She decided to forgo chemotherapy, hoping it would suffice to have the cluster of small tumors—polyps, she called them—surgically removed. Knowing next to nothing about what happened to people with cancer, it didn't occur to me that such an approach might not be aggressive enough. I didn't ask Jean or our father or even Conrad, who would have known something about cancer, if they thought the surgery alone would be sufficient or the course of treatment correct. This was still a time when I fundamentally trusted the soundness of my parents' judgment. It's a funny thing to try to articulate now, because I can very clearly see the contradictions, the ways that I had even then already begun to discount my parents' view of things—by picking apart the weaknesses in my father's ideas about the world or by backing away from some of the features of my mother's religious beliefs. One way or another, my decision to carry on the way I had with my teacher must also have necessitated a discounting of my parents' judgment. Yet, despite all of this, when it came to my mother's cancer, I remained under the impression that my parents, merely because they were my parents, possessed inherent knowledge of what was right.

It wasn't until years later, after we were both parents ourselves, that Conrad and I finally discussed the plan of action that our mother had taken in responding to her cancer. It turns out that he hadn't been given the opportunity to weigh in when the tumors were first detected because he hadn't been told. Our mother wanted to keep this a secret from as many people as she could, her family included. She came from a generation—a time and a place—that viewed sickness as a private matter, not a topic up for discussion. Disease, especially cancer, responded best to stoicism, charting its course according to fate, which my mother referred to as God's will. It was for private reasons, then, that my mother didn't seek recourse to additional opinions. Her doctor in the brand-new military hospital that my father's service had entitled her to receive care in, free of cost, said the surgery alone would be enough, and my mother believed him. That became the narrative we aligned ourselves with. Besides, other opinions might have opened up room for answers that I, and perhaps they, wouldn't have known what to do with. Answers that told us, with an unfailing certainty, how things would one day end. So we moved about during those next weeks, shopping, cooking, working in the yard, packing up my belongings for school, all the while repeating what we knew and what we hoped would bear out as truth: "The tests showed a few small malignant spots, which the doctor will remove in a couple of weeks."

I'm not sure any of us kids could know what our mother's view of the situation truly was, what she said to herself at night after the last words between her and our father had been spoken, what she was praying for when she closed her eyes over a plate of food, what passed through her mind while she stirred a pot or trimmed the ends off a bouquet of roses. I suspect that, as she went about her days and nights, she was reminding herself to believe that God would deliver her—not only from the illness but from the fear of whatever it was He had decided to deliver her to.

IV

KATHLEEN

IN THE FIRST STRANGE AND STRANGELY FREE MONTHS OF LIFE on campus, I didn't make much mention of my mother's cancer. Either I had convinced myself that it really was gone, because the polyps that contained it had been cut out by the doctor, or I was afraid that introducing her to my friends by way of such a story would make that the only story about my family—and me. On the occasions that I did speak of the cancer, I was careful to lean toward the past tense, emphasizing the fact that she was fine, that the surgery was a success and there was now nothing to fear. This was partly because that's what my mother, in her weekly phone call, was eager to have me believe—she used the word *eradicated*, which seemed to ride on the wind of a massive exhalation, the kind preceding a statement like "That was a close call"—and partly because I was afraid of considering the situation from any other vantage point. But I think it also had to do with wanting to pre-empt the look on anyone's face—a mix of condolence and abject pity, as if they'd just learned that I grew up a foundling—that arose whenever I said, "My mother was diagnosed with cancer."

Whenever someone managed to look me in the eye and say "I'm sorry" in the way people did once they learned that malignant tissues had been removed from my mother's body, it frightened me more than the idea of cancer itself, which by the winter was moving around freely in my mind like old shrapnel, lying dormant for whole long stretches before jostling up against something that registered an alarm. At those times, my mother became a specimen, someone beholden to the whims of a near stranger's polite curiosity. If the person was familiar with illnesses of that sort, then I'd have to field a set of follow-up questions that made me feel like a kid in a spelling bee: *What kind of cancer is it? What stage is she? How is she responding to the chemo? Has she been given a prognosis?* And if it was someone who didn't know what to do with such a pronouncement, his expression—a mix of fear or discomfort bordering on distaste, as if I had just sneezed in his face—seemed to flatten my mother out and pull her away from me, like the heroine at a drive-in movie.

Naming what was happening had a way of making it irrevocably real and making my mother into someone I was suddenly aware I had only barely known.

What could I tell anyone about her? Not just about how she'd taken care of me or what I felt like in her company but about where she came from and who she'd been long before me. Throughout my growing up, she'd entertained me with stories of farm life. One afternoon when she taught me how to cook a chicken, she'd reminisced that, at my age, she would have been told to go wring the bird's neck and pluck its feathers before dressing it for roasting. When I helped her roll out biscuit dough and cut it into circles using the mouth of a coffee cup, she'd sometimes remind me that she had learned to do the same task when she had been a mere five or six years old, standing on a chair by the kitchen stove. There were always bits of her childhood popping into our day-to-day life together, but her past remained an assortment of disjointed parts. I'd backed away from so much out of fear of what it might force me to accept, namely that along with these quaint or colorful facts of country life came a darker portrait, of struggle and injustice.

Dread of such narratives—stories like the one about the great-uncle way back when, the one who'd been killed for the money in his pockets—caused me to stifle the very questions that could have afforded a more continuous view of my mother's story and the story of her—of our—people. My mind, in its eagerness not to know too much, had managed to focus on all the wrong details: how disgusting it must have been to lift the bird up by the head and swing its body around in the air or how surprising that a five-year-old could learn to measure ingredients to the correct proportions. What my squeamishness had cost me was beginning to feel a bit like my birthright.

I knew that my mother had also been a "gifted child," graduating from high school and leaving home for college at age sixteen. When I was honest about my own motivation for excelling in high school—leaving home and situating myself in a world of my own choosing—I couldn't help but imagine her feeling the same way as a girl, looking out the kitchen window in Alabama and thinking of what it would be like to cast herself in a different kind of life. Growing up, hadn't she leapt at the chance to spend her summers with her grandmother in the city of Mobile? And didn't the story go that she had long ago changed her name from Kathleen to Kathryn mainly out of annoyance at the way southern mouths seemed to add an extra lazy syllable every time they addressed her? Maybe she thought of that *Kath-a-leen* as the kind of girl she wanted to leave behind—someone without enough taste, enough poise, someone forever stuck on those red-dirt country roads, not going anywhere quickly enough for Kathryn's liking. How changed my mother managed to become, how possessed of a quiet refinement, pointing herself toward a future not even she could have named. And how selfless and heroic her own mother seemed to me then, as I thought about her in this other light—Mother, with all her wits and young fire still about her; Mother, with her stock-steady wide-legged stance and her gaggle of younger children at her heels; Mother who had given my mom a dozen siblings out of the fierce desire to save her from the lonely plight of an only child—letting her daughter come to her own conclusions about the world, conclusions that ultimately led her farther and farther from home.

I imagined Mom arriving at college with the big green steamer trunk that sat for so many years in the garage of our family house in California. It probably contained five dresses and three pearl-button cardigans, a single quilt, two sets of towels, and photos of her sisters perched on stools and smiling kittenishly into the camera. In addition to a Bible, which Mother had probably inscribed with my mother's name, there must also have been other books, which she'd eventually found space for in the room she rented near Alabama State College for Negroes.

The few stories I knew about my mother's time as an undergraduate were like the bits of advice I'd been handed before leaving home; they rattled around from time to time making themselves heard, but mostly they just sat there gathering dust. There was the one about the young man in the library who had been so enamored of her legs that he'd asked her to marry him each and every time he caught sight of her. And the female professor she'd once accompanied to a conference whose sense of simple elegance had forever impressed her: "She brought just one skirt, a jacket, two blouses, and a sweater, and she never wore the same outfit twice," Mom recollected whenever she helped me pack for any kind of trip.

Freshman year, I tried to hold on to the image of my mother as a young woman hugging a stack of books to her chest, smiling over her shoulder at that boy from the library. It must have felt good, being noticed, having a whole four years ahead of her like a blank script. I tried to imagine what she vowed, in those first days or months on her own, to become. I thought of it as I stood before my own dorm-room mirror, sizing myself up, and as I walked across Mass Ave. in traffic, feeling for the first time that I was part of a real place, a place with history. But it was hard to hold on to the thought of my mother before she was my mother. I'd get a glimpse of it, just briefly, and then the knowledge of her as my mother would barge in and refuse to leave. Did Mother— who would only have been in her thirties at the time—struggle with a version of the same thing? When I could see past the tired, angry old woman Mother had become, I sometimes pictured her trying to envision her daughter in that new life. Did Mother smile or frown at the idea of Kathleen refashioning herself into Kathryn, someone other than a country girl from Leroy? Was this fuzziness, this coming in and out of view, anything like what my mom felt in 1990 trying to envision me?

In the fall of 1952, when my mother was entering with her class, the Reverend Fred Shuttlesworth, the civil rights activist and a cofounder of the Southern Christian Leadership Conference, would have been finishing his master's degree on that same campus. "Were you a part of the Civil Rights Movement?" I remember asking her when I was in Ms. Dyer's third-grade class.

Her eyes smiled a little when she answered, as if her mind had gone back to the exhilaration of that time. I could recognize the pride—and something else, something more private—enveloping her. "I went to Dr. King's trials," she said. "And after Rosa Parks's arrest, I went to her trial. I was a part of the Montgomery bus boycott. We all were. We carpooled and walked for a whole year instead of riding on the segregated buses."

And I tried to hold on to the image of her walking along the wide, sun-blasted sidewalks of Montgomery, a place I could only envision in black and white, like an old newsreel. I always saw her with a Sunday hat and a handbag dangling from the crook of her arm, walking with her back straight and her head held high as bus after empty bus rolled past. Even if she was only part of a crowd, a throng of students whose names or actions would never rise to the surface of that written history, how intensely alive must she have felt, and how like a pioneer, to be among those making a claim for a different kind of existence. And how unprepared, how timid and afraid. How could it have been any other way for a country girl of sixteen in a world where so much was at stake?

I arrived in Cambridge eager for small freedoms. I wanted to go out at night. I wanted to be able to wander the streets of a city, to disappear into bookstores and movie theaters. I wanted to be able to drink alcohol and kiss boys. My young mother must have wanted some of those things, too, but her drive must also have been for something larger and less private. She must have left home at least in part so that she could stand alongside the other members of her generation and take action in the ways her parents had probably warned her against. Arriving, for her, must have felt not only like one of the first inklings of her own personal independence but also, and perhaps more emphatically, like the first euphoric indicators of a new era in public history.

Did she feel as free—and at times as alone—as I sometimes did during that first autumn on my own, striving to carve out my space in a world where it seemed that so little of what I'd spent my short life learning and believing actually mattered? And was there a sense of conflict for her, as there was for me, in breaking free from the place and people who had raised her? A sense of guilt in choosing the new life as preferable to the old? Because my mother had done it—had laid down the old life like a too-small garment and stepped eagerly into each layer of the new—I told myself I wasn't completely defying her when, one by one, I let my own wishes and desires replace the values she sought to instill in me. But if I really felt that way, why didn't I ever tell her so?

Sometimes it did feel like she must have heard me as I thought, must have been there with me even if only in minuscule tokens: the lace she'd tatted onto the edges of my towels, or the whiff of Jean Patou's "Joy" (the bottle belonged to her; she'd said yes when I asked, completely ignorant of its extravagance, if I could pack it among my things) that I sometimes wore to class on the insides of my wrists, never smelling completely like myself when I did. I wasn't quite my mother then, either; maybe I was the idea of her younger self, the one I sometimes tried to reach with my thoughts, the one who would surely have wanted to live in that delicate exhalation of jasmine and new grass and, deeper under the surface, a living kind of heat. Like a young woman's wish, if such a thing could be weighted to the skin.

SOMETHING BETTER

I WAS MAKING STABS AT WHAT WAS BEGINNING TO RESEMBLE A lifestyle. In it, I found myself jogging along the river in the evenings or taking the T into Boston to meet Conrad, who was still a fellow at Mass General, for dinner. Some nights, my best friend and I ignored our course work and sat instead in the open-air patio of Au Bon Pain, drinking coffee and discussing our friendship, which we had come to call our "relationship," proud of the gravitas such a word seemed to impart. I'd also found the thing that would constitute my first real breach of my mother's trust, and sure enough, it was a boy.

I hadn't been looking for him. After the end of the affair with my teacher (which, because it was chaste, probably didn't count as a full breach), I'd thought it might make sense to take some time off from even thinking about love, let alone falling into it. It wasn't hard. There was so much else to command my attention: the difficulty of my classes (German social theory during the fin-de-siècle; a seminar on the bildungsroman; an expository writing class on the writers from the American South; French) or the distance that seemed to exist between me and so many of the other students there, students who, from what I could discern, were exponentially better at the things I always thought I'd been so good at. But then the boy was there, announcing his interest—a thing that had only happened once and only then with a man I could never really have, never even let myself really try to have—and once that happened, it was as though a part of my brain (a part located equally in the head and in the body) wouldn't relent. I thought about the boy liking me, and I thought about all the reasons why I liked the boy liking me, and why I liked him regardless of his liking me, though it was his liking that had certainly set the whole series of events into motion. I also thought about how infinitely better it would be to love a boy my own age, a boy without a wife, without the need for strange meetings and secret letters. I thought about it for a while, with my head and with the part of the brain that did not reside in my head, and I liked the way such thinking made me feel.

It happened slowly. At first, we just had meals together in the Freshman Union; then there were weekend outings, usually in groups; and then eventually we ran out of ways of skirting around what we wanted from one another. Like most things of such a nature, it started with a kiss, which led to other kisses, and then, over time, those same two parts of my mind began to come up with more interesting feats to attempt. Because everything was equally new to both of us, the boy—my first *boyfriend*—and me, it all seemed harmless. More than harmless, it felt natural and there-fore innocent. Or natural and therefore inevitable. I wasn't quite sure how to consider it, but I was eager to find out.

Back when the school year first started, I'd signed on to take part in a Bible study run by other first-year students on campus. I suppose I'd wanted to know if there was a way to make good on my parents' concern for my spiritual well-being by seeking out my own version of the faith I'd grown up in. I didn't know what I wanted to discover, but I hoped it wouldn't sound like the sermons I'd gotten used to hearing back home at First Baptist, the ones with their tendency to wheel back toward a predictable enough moral before I'd really gotten the chance to consider anything. It struck me as odd that while so much of the Bible was the story of radical disruption—tragedy, miracles, near-impossible leaps of faith—in church, there was always such a rush to get to the moral, the message, the Good News. We never lingered long enough upon what such extremes of despair or grace or believing would have felt like from the inside. We never tried to understand why those people would have struggled, never drew them close enough to ourselves and our own desires and flaws to love the parts of them that were likely to be most like us. How could the God they submitted to feel sufficiently real if we didn't first allow the Bible's human characters to come to life, if we didn't come to recognize and understand all that was wrong with them before God showed them His grace? Those questions struck me as important because I thought I had begun to live as an adult, an adult with regret and disappointment behind her—and more than that, there was the stark reality of a parent's illness to consider. I thought my life had gone from being a child's life to a woman's life, and so I wanted to know what the women and men I'd only ever thought of as symbols might have thought and done and weighed in their hearts or minds against the promises of God. What would salvation have cost them? What, if I were to take it on the terms upon which it seemed to be offered, would it cost me?

For one of the first study sessions, I volunteered my dorm room, a two-bedroom arrangement I shared with two other girls, Noelle and Vivian. We had a flimsy foam couch in the common room that unfolded into a guest mattress. Our three desks faced three different walls upon which hung impressionist reproductions we were only allowed to affix in place with poster gum (on cold days, the posters would start to come unstuck and curl up at the edges). Noelle's desk was littered with empty Diet Snapple bottles. Vivian's was ordered and tidy, and her belongings in neat stacks gave off the impression of being costly, probably because she'd told me about the $10,000 allowance wired into her bank account every few months. On the day of the Bible study, I made a space on my own desk for a plate of Oreo cookies and a two-liter bottle of soda. It was the best show of hospitality I could afford with barely a three-figure balance in the bank.

At around seven o'clock, after dinner was over, my roommates cleared out and three other first-year students arrived: a midwestern black kid named Glenn with glasses and a toothy, smiling mouth; an Asian girl I recognized from one of the other floors of my dorm; and a plump, dark-haired white guy I'd met at one of the social gatherings held during prefrosh week. If they had met ahead of time to discuss a plan for how things ought to proceed, I wasn't aware. But soon enough, the white guy was leading us in prayer the way it had been done by so many others in the past, asking for guidance, soliciting God's mercy on behalf of our fellow students who were as yet "unsaved." It reminded me of High Life, the Christian youth group I'd longed to be a more central part of back in high school, and I felt similarly skeptical that such young people could be so settled in the terms of their faith. The sight of us going through the familiar motions as if by rote put me in mind of what I least liked about church. An anxious, irrepressible agitation rose up and wrapped itself around me.

"May I say something?" I interrupted.

After a brief pause, which I took to mean yes, I launched into a rapid-fire declaration of what was sitting on my chest. "I really want to get to a place where we can stop asking all the same old familiar questions about the Bible, questions we've been taught to answer in the same way every time. I want to figure out if there are other ways of seeing what it means to be a Christian. Questions like, what kinds of conflicts did the disciples feel when Jesus told them to spread the word, and what about all the different views of who Christ was? Maybe there's something in all of this that nobody's named before, something . . . ," and there I faltered, not knowing exactly where all of my blather was leading. "Something better."

Silence.

"Don't you think that together we might be able to figure out a better way of hearing all of these familiar Bible verses? Don't you want to find a new language for interpreting God's will and all His rules?" I was carried away on the gust of urgency I imagined the original disciples must have had way back when.

The voices out in the hallway sounded happy. A group of kids was taking a study break. Inside, an icy divide had opened up between my guests and me, and I saw how foolish I looked in their eyes. I thought I had meant what I'd said, but it was hard to tell through the embarrassment. Was I so naive as to believe in my desire to have the cake (security as to my spiritual well-being) and eat it, too (sleep with boys, acquaint myself with the many enticements of the secular world)? Hadn't I grown up hearing that God's charge to His servants was to be in the world without being of it?

The echo of my words and the disapproval of the three young Christians that lingered in its wake seemed to be telling me I wanted two things that weren't compatible. I had been operating under the assumption that college was a place for unraveling conundrums, but none of the others seemed willing to offer me a hand. They'd eaten a few of the cookies and drunk some of the Coke, but we weren't communing. So I made a hasty decision. Before they were even out my door, I washed my hands of the

Bible-study kids. If God is and was and always will be, I assured myself, then it wouldn't be a terrible idea to save Him for later.

After that first humiliation, I bumped into Glenn, the black kid in the group, just a couple of times. On both occasions, it was early morning and I was on my way back to my dorm room after a night spent with my boyfriend across the Yard, what my friends and I laughed about together as the Walk of Shame. The air always felt wet and dim in those early morning hours before the sun was high enough in the sky and before most of my classmates had dragged themselves from bed. That early in the day, not yet fed or caffeinated and still a bit groggy from the night before, I felt as though I were merely a game piece being moved across a board. In such a state, Glenn's very presence was like a reprimand, not just from God but from my parents. A reprimand for quitting the Bible study, for abandoning the habit of going to church, for taking advantage of this luxurious and expensive education (the fifth my parents had saved and budgeted and paid for) to forget where I came from and run stark wild. I didn't see Glenn much more after that, but I thought of him and what he represented one morning when, awakened by the campus church bells, I noticed that a packet of condoms had been tossed onto the eaves outside my window.

ONE WINTER SUNDAY IN MY SECOND SEMESTER, ON A WHIM, I decided to try again to see if there might be a place in my new life, even just a few hours every few weeks, for God. Perhaps I thought that if I did a better job of it than I had before, I might find a version of Him that was better suited to my dilemma. I was certainly tired of telling my mother no each time she asked if I was going to church. My mother, thinking only of my well-being, refusing to dwell overmuch on, or talk at length about, her own still not-fully-out-of-the-woods bill of health. I thought of her and the Jesuses she loved. The one tender and lamblike who loves the little children, as well as the fierce protector, the vanquisher of fear and sin, the one who stands at our sides like a bodyguard. I thought of how much it meant to her that I not only continue to believe in Him (I did, actually; it would have been an act of deliberate and concerted will to scour that deep-seated belief from my mind and my heart) but that I honor Him with my words and my actions. *They profess that they know God; but in works they deny Him.*

It's funny. I never once worried that God would abandon me. I trusted that God understood what it meant to be eighteen years old and awake to the miracle of independence. I trusted that God could see my heart, and I took Him at His word: *I will never leave thee nor forsake thee.* My recurring spiritual worry had little to do with God or Jesus, two interchangeable versions of the same largeness. It had everything to do with my mother and wanting her not to fret as she'd fretted, all the way up until they were finally married, over Michael and Kathleen. Was my mother's worry rooted exclusively in what God thought, or might there have been some room within it for her own pride? For needing her friends to see that she had succeeded in instilling in us the proper values and the proper degree of devotion, for the urge to be the one among her peers who had gotten everything right. *Raise up a child in the way he should go, and when he is old he will not depart from it.* And how much did her worry have to do with compliance? With wanting to ensure that she had done right by us and in so doing done right by the God who had promised to love and keep us, but also—as we full well knew—to judge each and every one of us according to our works?

The second time around, I decided that reaching out to God should be simpler, a matter of going to Sunday service at the campus church and just seeing what happened. I woke before the

Sunday bells, and daylight flooded my room like an affirmation. It was a sunny, crisp winter morning, the sky an exquisite blue, dappled with clouds that could have been cut from a child's drawing. There was a woodsmoke smell on the air and a bite to the way it came up against my bare face. It was the kind of winter morning that a Californian like me could revel in, something beautiful and bracing, proof that the seasons were real, designed not just to be enjoyed but endured. I walked across the Yard thinking how funny it was to be doing by choice what I'd just months ago given myself permission to view as the distant past, my life B.C., Before College. Campus and community members filed into the stately brick church—stately but quiet; not proud of itself, but certain beneath its gleaming white steeple that stood taller than the tallest trees. My heart accelerated to a canter in anticipation of the perspective that might help me to resolve this bundle of jangled ideas I guess I'd have to call my spiritual dilemma.

I entered through the wide-open doors, saying hello to all the faces, shaking hands, feeling the ebullience of participation. I walked down the aisle toward a middle pew on the right. Along the way, I was handed an Order of Worship booklet emblazoned with the university's crimson seal. Compared with what I was used to back home, everything felt so elegant, so tasteful and discreet. Even the paper—dense card stock—was several steps up from what was used at First Baptist.

I sat nervously until the congregation was signaled to stand; then I stood. A few minutes later, we all took our seats again. It happened more than once while a chamber music ensemble played, and then we joined together to sing "Holy, Holy, Holy." I felt like a guest at an expensive restaurant, excited and suddenly, for no good reason, self-conscious. I'd done this a thousand times over through eighteen years of Sundays. I'd risen and sat, sung and listened, bowed my head and whispered affirmation on cue my entire life, never once concerned about getting anything wrong. (Well—I'd visited a Catholic church once or twice with friends, and felt nervous then, but that was different. The Catholics, according to my parents, were too caught up in ritual; they didn't know how to come to God without the assistance of a priest. There was nothing too important to worry over where the Mass was concerned because, at least according to my parents' logic, in comparison with a Catholic, I was the more spiritually evolved.)

I looked up at the fine architecture, the high-paned windows and the Corinthian columns. The pews were pristine white with mahogany trim and looked as though they had been carved, one by one, by some master artisan. At First Baptist, the pews were rustic oak upholstered with orange burlap, as if we were all congregated in somebody's 1970s recreation room. Sitting in Harvard's Memorial Church, I felt what I felt in so many of Harvard's various places: like a person of privilege, of "good breeding"—or rather, like someone pretending to be. Once I was settled in enough to forget all of these thoughts, what I heard more than anything else was what wasn't there: the absent voices of the two elderly sisters ever present at First Baptist, the ones whose singing always scraped to the tippy-top of their register and screeched through to the end of every hymn like roller skates with metal wheels.

At First Baptist, everything was familiar, a simple dance that had worn grooves into the floorboards, but this new series of movements was almost Byzantine. I followed the other churchgoers as best I could, keeping quiet during the responses and at the tail end of the Lord's Prayer, since I wasn't sure which closing was preferred. There was something in Latin, the language that always reached me like a reprimand of my public school education, a reminder that I had not been born into the kind of advantage that so many of my peers had, a reminder that no matter how smart I was or how apt I had become at utilizing the opportunities I'd been given (yes, Mr. Catania, I would by then have been willing to concede that a great many opportunities were given as much as earned), it was luck above all else that had landed me there.

When the sermon finally began, I was hopeful that some part of the message would signal our proximity to what I'd been craving, something other than run-of-the-mill religion with its white-bearded (and, unless I was trying very hard to see him as otherwise, white) God and His threats of punishment. Something that didn't seem designed to lure me in with promises of simplifying my existence when what I favored, I told myself, was complexity. Something I wouldn't feel compelled to apologize for or outright hide. Something that might bridge the divide between the God people always described and the one I thought I knew or wanted to know.

The reverend was black, like Pastor Gainey at First Baptist. His wasn't the earthy hardscrabble blackness of Alabama or even Chicago. It was aristocratic. Like that of the free blacks living in antebellum America, certain of whom also happened to be slave owners. He was daintily refined. His voice was slow and melodic. There was an elegant cadence by which his words arrived—a few at a time and then a pause, a few more and again a pause—as if he were leading us along a trail dotted with petits fours. He made a point about how God was much more interesting than the Bible makes Him out to be. *Yes,* I thought, *yes, this is why I've come.* And about how the Gospel was an admonition to a fearless kind of submission, an invitation to a new kind of freedom. At that glimmer of paradox, a bolt of excitement flashed through my mind. What if, sitting there just then, I found myself truly caught up in belief? How would it feel inside a future like that?

In my last months attending First Baptist, I'd used most Sunday sermons as a time to settle into thoughts I never had sufficient privacy to mull over at home. Those times, too, I'd find my imagination racing toward a future, building a model of what my life might look like in five, ten, twenty years. I'd imagine the city where I'd have settled and the home I'd come back to at night. (I'd pieced its various rooms together from my mother's Spiegel catalogs and the advertising inserts in the Sunday paper. Sheets and towels, rugs and candles, dishes and plush couches and ottomans that added up to something sumptuous and mature.) I'd imagine walking through each of my rooms, feeling the beautiful objects collected and arranged for my own comfort. Always there was a faceless man just a room away, reading on the couch or taking a shower, cooking us pasta, filling glasses of wine, and like the couples in all the catalogs and magazines, the ones whose happiness and chemistry seem to be held in place by all the carefully chosen furnishings, that man and I would end up sitting cross-legged on the floor, laughing, leaning against one another with the effortless ease one takes as shorthand for true intimacy.

At first, I forgot to notice how tenuous my grasp upon the minister's voice had become. Already, without sensing it happening, I'd taken two, five, fifty steps into my ready-made future, that momentous day's sermon now nothing more than a cadence, traffic outside a city window. How warm, the room I'd built in my mind. So habitable and real it caused my breathing to quicken. Using my own recent sexual experiences as a template, I made my way toward the part in my fantasy where the man and I led one another to the big paisley bed heaped with pillows.

The minister and all the other churchgoers were by then tiny specks out on the horizon, sailing happily on the current of his homily, and I was left behind wandering circles in my mind.

From as far back as I could remember, I'd taken it as a matter of course that the death of my body would mark the beginning of something else. Sometimes, I tried to work it out in my head like a riddle: *I am not a soul, but I possess one. When I die, I will become what I possess . . .* But then the noise of this world always rushed back in to convince me of the here and now that required my attention, my eager participation. And just like that, the soul would vanish. That portentous Sunday was no exception, though when you believe in the soul, the idea of it never stays gone for very long.

When I was three and riding back from a doctor's appointment, I looked up at my mother, with the sun on her face and the calm certainty she seemed to move and live within, and said, "Mommy, I want Jesus to come into my heart." It was the received language of the Sunday school classes I had grown used to attending week after week, but what I took it to mean was this: *I feel filled with love. I'm not afraid. I want a name for what this means. I need something to call it.* I didn't think to wonder if I was speaking in metaphors. My mother pulled over and let me say a prayer, and whatever it was felt real, as if she and I really were in the presence of a third being who had agreed never to lose track of us. Maybe we made it ourselves, but when I was by myself, it was still there. It was like being assured I was part of a story that, no matter what else, would never cease to keep me in its sights.

It would have been nice not to have had to care about anything other than the private certainty that God belonged to me. It would have been nice not to have had to worry about whether my believing was visible to others. But there were lots of things it would have been nice to have that I didn't. I was reminded of that fact many times each day.

Left behind by the homily and miles away from the other

churchgoers, whose minds, at least from where I sat, appeared to be actively trailing the minister's words, hearing them and chuckling or murmuring, or merely nodding to themselves as the meaning sunk in, I realized I had no idea what the story was that I was a part of. I didn't yet know what was important to me or what would remain important years down the line, after the thrill of experiencing these first freedoms, and the weight of living with what they brought, had passed. But I wanted to believe I was right when I told myself that the God I'd learned to believe in so long ago was still there, bigger and more real than I had imagined, and that He was long-suffering, abiding, that whatever He was would blaze bright and undeniably near when the thing that led me to Him was not obligation or fear. I had no idea what that thing would be. Illness? It had intensified my mother's relationship with God but only slightly. Abject circumstances? It was hard for me to envision a scenario in which I would allow myself to hit bottom. I felt too cautious, too conscientious for that; such a descent would seem to require an act of concerted effort. Besides, no one in my family had ever hit bottom, and they'd probably see to it that I didn't, either. Maybe, if a powerful relationship to God were to happen for me at all, it would happen the way so many of the things in the Bible happen: by means of some unforeseeable mystery, upon a *day and hour no one knows, not even the angels of Heaven, nor the Son, but the Father alone.*

Stepping back out into the late-morning daylight, I was, if decidedly untransformed, nevertheless bathed in an earthly peace. The Yard brimmed with human traffic. The clouds maintained their distance, silent and luminous with their faraway, patient knowledge.

THE WOMAN AT THE WELL

I SPENT MY FIRST SUMMER HOME FROM COLLEGE JOBLESS; THE application I filed at the public library never panned out, and even the bookstores in town—the two at the local shopping mall specializing in mass-market paperbacks—lacked the need for my part-time help. So I read. I watched television. I wrote letters. I ran around town with my mother, the running around we'd always done: shopping for groceries, "junking" through thrift shops, trying on clothes at department stores. The fact that we did the same old things together made it seem like she was her same old self: healthy, taking care of everyone else, never requiring more than a tiny favor, a quick hand at something or other. And, with the exception of a new sense of relief—more than relief, of joy—at having survived the surgery and lived the many months with no new dark spots spreading like moss on her insides, she may as well have been identical to how she was before any of us learned she was sick. No, after the worry that gripped our home when I'd left that fall—worry I'd only partly been able to internalize, being so selfishly and single-mindedly fixated upon reaching the promised land of college—I returned home that summer with the distinct impression that it was *I* who had undergone the most drastic of changes.

Preposterous as it now seems, the impression had something subtle and unexamined to do with my mother's wish that I move within a cloud of hope or, more accurately, of ignorance to the stakes she was gambling on. Certainly, I knew then that cancer kills, but she told me over and over again that her cancer was gone, that God had healed her. And because those were the things I wanted to believe, I believed them.

Soaring over the country in the cabin of a 747 only to touch down in the strip-mall suburbs, I felt like Icarus on the descent. I'd felt it after flying home at Christmas, too, when I'd first seen my hometown through changed eyes. There had been so much I wanted to apologize for, so much I wanted to tidy up or correct, if only to protect my own sense of where I had come from. The plain, cookie-cutter houses. The acres and acres of parking lot. And oh, the people. How many of them now seemed dim and fat, trudging along behind shopping carts piled with products that seemed to confirm an utter lack of imagination and taste?

In the back of my mind that summer was a constant awareness that in three months' time I would be describing these very days and nights to my new friends back at school—characterizing them as quaint or pathetic, editing the details just enough so as to carve out a strategic distance between me and what was beginning to feel like my old life. Without my deciding it, an air of supercilious contempt crept into much of what I saw about the place I came from. Mostly, I was lamenting the absence of freedom. The freedom to come and go as I pleased, with whom I chose and for reasons I did not need to explain. I missed the thrill of having places to be and the ease of passage that felt a universe away from life in Fairfield, where nothing and no one was knocking down my door and where I'd have been hard-pressed—carless and unemployed as I was—to get anywhere even if they had been.

One afternoon, my mother walked into the family room, where I sat propped against the base of the couch watching reruns.

"I'd like you to do something for me." From her tone of voice, I could tell it was something I would not look forward to doing.

"Okay," I muttered, "what is it?" The question didn't have anything to do with my having the option of saying no. I simply needed to know to what extent I ought to embrace the approaching sense of dread. Was she going to suggest I spend the afternoon with one of her elderly friends or that I run a dust cloth over the furniture in the living room? Or could she have been preparing to ask me to walk the five blocks to Kmart and parade home with a mortifying and unwieldy thirty-six-pack of quilted toilet paper?

It is safe to say I was even more of an adolescent than I'd been when I left home. After nine months away, I had become silent, shirking, always inching toward whatever corner seemed to afford even a momentary scrap of privacy. And judgmental. How small my parents had become, suddenly, in my estimation. My once-elegant father, whom I'd always likened to Cary Grant because of what sounded to me like a mid-Atlantic accent (in truth it was probably just the remains of a southern twang after thirty or more years of disuse), had become coarsely ordinary, fraternizing with our simple neighbors, sympathizing with the wrong politicians, eating with such gusto that I regretted having learned to love the very same foods. To top things off, he had discovered a penchant for country singers like Merle Haggard and Willie Nelson, music that would have been decidedly laughable back then in the dorms. Nowadays, Willie Nelson's voice puts me in immediate mind of my father and causes my eyes to well up with tears, but that summer, finding LPs of Garth Brooks and Clint Black propped near the stereo, I grew anemic with humiliation.

I'd been pulling away from my mother subtly ever since the season of the affair with my teacher, which had taught me to hide the feelings and wishes that love set into play. I knew how to put my errant thoughts and wishes on mute when Mom and I were together and how to be vague about certain specifics of my coed life. But the best proof that I was still an adolescent is the fact that I came home feeling like an adult. It was that knowledge—the knowledge that I'd snuck and grown up—that brought with it a self-consciousness I had never before noticed during my times alone with my mother. Stranded, idle, and suddenly cut off from everyone and everything that shaped my new sense of self and purpose, the need to put some distance between my mother and myself suddenly felt urgent, desperate. I had jumped ship on the life she'd been guiding me toward for nineteen years, and I could tell she knew. She looked at me from a different kind of distance, as though I'd gone feral and she was afraid I'd threaten her with my teeth if she got too close. Of course, most of the time, we still laughed and talked like we used to. And I was still capable of eliciting her great broad smile or coaxing her to laughter, usually when there was a group of us around the table after dinner, but the silences between us when we were alone together seemed different. I sensed that she was aware of everything I wasn't saying, and the fact of it produced a very articulate variety of wordlessness on both our parts.

Sometimes now, I wonder if she might have been waiting for me to approach her and ask what she felt and thought, what it felt like to be her at that unthinkably harrowing juncture in her life. Sometimes, too, I wonder if she ever hoped I might sit down on the side of her bed and tell her what my life felt like and what it was composed of. Not just what I knew she wanted to hear but the truth, my truth.

But no matter how much of an adult I fancied myself to be, I couldn't do that, couldn't open the door onto my world and invite her in.

Did I really think she'd have been surprised? I'd felt that way about Conrad, too, and had tried to hide from him the fact that I was sleeping with my boyfriend. One Sunday morning, he drove to Cambridge for coffee and called me from one of the campus phones in the Yard. I'd had to hurry to get my boyfriend out of the room and make it look like I was just waking up, but I'd done a sloppy job and had had to come clean. I was expecting Conrad to look at me with disappointment, to reprimand me in some way, but all he said was "Relax, Trace. I was in college once, too, you know." That may not be how my mother would have responded to the situation, not with her youngest daughter, the baby of the family. But if I had been more courageous, like Michael had been after he met Kathleen, we could have moved past the shock and into a relationship where plain, unabashed truths might be asked for and offered.

At the time, though, it didn't seem fair to me that what in many other families would have been considered natural or even healthy development for a girl my age should open up such feelings of guilt and shame in mine or that my mother should view my inevitable ascent into adulthood first and foremost as a threat. Even so, I told myself it was nothing compared to what some families went through, nothing in comparison to what Mom's friend Nella from the adult school had had to confront when, right around the time I was entering junior high, her daughter, Lisa, began showing the unmistakable signs of addiction.

The whispers back then were about crack cocaine, whispers that seemed to be corroborated by Lisa's newly strange behavior. She'd disappear for days or weeks at a time and then turn up looking ravaged, desperate, and wordless, or else brimming with an infuriating laughter when asked to explain. I'd spared my mother the turmoil that had aged Nella and drained her spirit of its vigor.

The big, mirthful woman who had been such a fixture of my childhood withdrew. Her face was drawn and serious, and the songlike laugh was gone. I rarely saw her after things became serious with Lisa. I heard that Anthony became a football star at his high school, but once Nella stopped coming around, Anthony, too, dwindled to just a memory, an echo of a hushed rumor.

I hadn't done a thing like that to my mother, but it was no great feat; no one had expected me to. What they had expected, I reckoned, was that I would walk the line my mother had sketched for me with her own exemplary words and deeds.

Standing before me on that summer afternoon, about to reveal the details of the favor I'd have no choice but to agree to, my mother was impeccable in her pastel skirt and blouse, with her hair sculpted into a neat chignon. She looked pretty and kind and solid, like a matriarch, which is what, over the years, she had become. In the old photos, she is girlish and sexy, a young woman testing her power in front of the camera. But standing there above me that day, the only word that came to mind was *proper*, characterized by virtue and propriety. There was nothing in her life that she could not have stood before a great crowd and testified to, and though that had become her strength—what everyone praised her for, what even we had begun to attribute her apparent recovery to—there was a part of me that had come, just a little and all at once, to resent it.

"First Baptist is hosting Vacation Bible School next week, and I'd like you to volunteer to help with one of the classes."

I'd grown up at First Baptist. I'd hardly missed a Sunday in all the years of living in Fairfield with my family. Through grade school, I had learned the Bible lessons taught with paper cutouts on a felt board. I'd saved my coins for the collection plate and happily risen to sing the hymns. I'd run around on the steps outside the main sanctuary with the other children while my parents greeted their friends and caught up on the week's events before heading home for supper. I'd even begged, at age six or seven, to be baptized and stood stiff as a plank while I was tipped back into the symbolic water (for the occasion, my mother had sewn me two new dresses: one to wear under the white baptismal robe and another to change into after the first one got wet), but suddenly the thought of spending more than the requisite two hours once per week at the church felt like a sentence. Perhaps because I was already in the habit of seeing my experiences at home through the eyes of my friends back at school, I quaked at the prospect of having to make sense of Vacation Bible School. *Oh, no,* I thought. *Not that place. Not that battalion of billowy, perfumed ladies with their faces creased into joyless smiles. Not their sons and daughters, serious and old beyond their years, faces fixed in—spare me!—godly resignation.*

Not terribly long before, on a Sunday when we'd invited a young deacon and his family home with us after church, I'd been the target of a very matter-of-fact dismissal when the man—an otherwise pleasant-enough father in his forties—noticed my copy of *Of Human Bondage* on a side table. From the look he'd shot me, he must have decided then and there that Maugham's novel was little more than a handbook on S and M. If only I had had the wherewithal to set him straight. Instead, I sat stock-still in my seat, feeling as if I'd done something wrong. Maybe I'd felt chastened because the book, no matter what it was about, signaled to him that my appetites were for the world and not for God, an insinuation I'd have been hard-pressed to refute. I remember the sneer he'd shot me later, when flipping through some albums propped by the stereo, he'd seen something else not to his liking. At the time, I was still in high school, still technically blameless as far as his moral compass was concerned, and so I couldn't help sensing that what he was seeing in me was a projection of some dark facet of his own inner life.

Though there were surely exceptions, it seemed that the church people with whom we tended to socialize were often just different enough from us to make me self-conscious or squirmy and uncomfortable. It was more rare than not to happen upon a family who seemed to resemble us: grounded, functional, cheerful, and made up of real people, but my parents persisted in trying, perhaps out of a sincere wish to add to their circle of friends or perhaps merely out of the obligation to be welcoming to our brothers and sisters in Christ. Maybe it was also designed to show my siblings and me—with the emphasis, now that my siblings were all grown up, on me—that it was possible to reserve a space for God in an otherwise "normal" life.

But I did not want to go to Vacation Bible School. Not even for one week if it meant I'd have to spend part of every day with the other volunteers who all said they wanted to be missionaries when they grew up. And what if that deacon hadn't been off base in pegging me as a bad Christian? On how many occasions in the previous nine months had I underplayed my upbringing in the church? Hadn't I avoided taking a popular Harvard course on the Bible after hearing how, on the very first day of class, the professor had the habit of asking every student to raise a hand if he or she believed that the text was the true word of God? And I still didn't know where the line stood in my mind between a life of the mind and one of the spirit—not to mention the body, which was also becoming a topic of increasing consequence to me.

"All right, if it's important to you," I told my mother, and though my voice said a lot about my true feelings on the matter, both of us knew I had no choice.

Several days later, I reported to a Sunday school classroom in the annex behind the main sanctuary building. After a few minutes, a group of third and fourth graders found seats and waited, fidgeting, for the class leader to address them. His name was Theo, a young man, about twenty-one or twenty-two, who studied accounting at a local college (as a precursor to theology, which he planned to take up in graduate school). Theo led the lessons each day, but he didn't actually design them; that had been done by the group of ladies (his mother was one) who decided that the emphasis in the classroom this season should be "Ministry." To that end, they'd picked a set of parables from the New Testament about Christ and the disciples. Theo spent part of each class narrating the stories that many of the children had already heard, about the loaves and the fishes, about Jesus healing the blind man and the lame man and raising Lazarus from the dead, and about the woman who washed Jesus's feet with her hair. I was mostly there for reinforcement. I didn't say much, but I helped with activities, walking around the room and whispering encouragement as students drew or glued together projects meant to illustrate the lesson. Every day, we concluded with a reminder of how, just as Christ and the disciples preached the Gospel, these children should spread the Good News to their friends and family.

It wasn't as painful as I'd expected. No matter how I thought I felt, the church was a familiar place to me, where much of my childhood had taken place. I remembered sitting in that classroom, or a room just like it, and eagerly demonstrating my knowledge of God's word. And I remembered later giggling with some of the other girls while scouring Song of Solomon for instances of words like *breast* and *loins*. Mostly, I was comfortable there because the stories were all so familiar to me. I didn't mind letting myself wander through them, filling in the details about who those people must really have been, trying to envision the disciples as human beings with smells and appetites and voices and teeth—as people like me who felt that God was real but who were also susceptible to a great many other things the world told them were real, too. While Theo was guiding the students through the text, pushing a little too hard to make them see what he had been told to make them see, I tried to imagine what all the Bible's men and women—whether they were real figures or simply metaphors in this book that was also, on top of everything else, a work of great literature—might have felt in the presence of the ambassador for the all-powerful God, the mind of the universe.

One afternoon, we came to the story about the woman at the well. In it, a Samaritan woman encounters Christ sitting by a well. "Everyone who drinks this water will thirst again," He tells her. "But whoever drinks the water I give will never thirst." They speak for a few minutes about salvation, and He convinces her that He is the Messiah by telling her about her own past: that she has been married five times and that the man with whom she is currently living is not her husband.

Theo glossed over the implications of the five husbands by describing the woman as "unclean," a term he didn't quite manage to define for the children. Instead, he looked my way and allowed a flicker of accusation to travel from him to me, waking me from my daydream about the ordinary human passion the woman must have begun to feel for that young man who preached so far and wide about love and compassion. And then it struck me. Just like the deacon who had been horror-struck by my summer reading, Theo must have thought of me as a fallen woman.

Was it something I happened, at that very moment, to be un-
wittingly projecting—that I had, indeed, defied the Bible's admonitions to remain chaste until marriage? It couldn't have been
my clothes; there was nothing suggestive or revealing about my
T-shirts or my jeans or the demure dresses I always wore on Sundays. Was I releasing some pheromone that only devout Christians could detect? There must have been an explanation for why
Theo—and, come to think of it, some of the other churchgoers
that summer—seemed suddenly to regard me with discernible disappointment or barely disguised contempt.

And then, slowly, like a photo taking form in a basin of devel-
oper, I began to understand the rumor that was circulating among
the congregants of First Baptist. I had been within earshot when
it was first set loose at a ladies' prayer luncheon in our own dining
room just days after I'd arrived back home: *And Dear Lord,* a white-
haired woman in fuchsia had said, with her arms raised Southern
Baptist style so that they seemed to hover in the air like rabbit ear
antennae, *we pray for Kathryn's daughter Tracy and her relationship*
(she'd paused just before that word, as if not sure she ought to use
it) *with her boyfriend.* The six or seven ladies sitting alongside, my
mother among them, had responded with some hushed variant
of *Yes, Lord* and *We lift her up to You.* I was tiptoeing past the dining
room table with a saucer of coffee cake to bring upstairs to my
room when the prayer went around, when I heard my name and
the unspoken assumption—that I was in danger of surrendering
my virginity or, worse, that it had already gone the way of my
milk teeth. Everyone's eyes were closed, but fearing that a reaction
of any kind on my part would merely serve to confirm what they
had all been instructed to suspect, I strode past with all the poise
I could summon, not breaking stride and with my chin up. I told
myself that once I crossed from the parquet dining room floor to

the carpet of the family room, I would be safe. Step by step across the hardwood floor, I willed my face to remain serenely blank. Every other day, it was the span of a few quick steps, but just then, the family room seemed infinitely far away. Step by step, I forced my features into a blank, placid expression and denied my eyes the opportunity to steal even a quick glance at the ladies at the table, lest any of them were watching. I walked past as though nothing were out of the ordinary, like a man who maintains unblinking eye contact when lying to your face.

Sitting that day in the air-conditioned Sunday school building with its three windows overlooking a concrete walkway and lawn dappled with trees, I felt an ire rise in my throat. Suddenly, I was livid at Theo and his mother and the chain of churchgoers who had passed that kernel of gossip back and forth under the guise of prayerful concern. For the first time, I allowed myself to savor a single dram of anger toward my mother—not for her wish that I remain the girl she had instructed me to be but for her need to discuss with others the girl she feared I was vying to become. I felt something else, too. Pushed as I was to consider the conflict that had been set into motion by my decision to go against what I'd been taught, my anger mingled with my nascent sexual knowledge, forming a very exhilarating third thing that seemed to fit quite nicely under the name *Independence*.

It was almost lunchtime. Some of the kids had grown restless from hunger. Some of them only came to Vacation Bible School in the first place for the meals or because their parents wanted them kept busy and out of the house for a few hours each day; it struck me as funny, thinking that my mom might have wanted the very same thing for me.

"He stands at the door of your heart and knocks," Theo was

saying in yet another attempt to persuade the kids to give their barely formed lives over to the Lord.

I walked over to an empty seat at one of the long classroom tables and, sitting down, took out a piece of paper and a pen.

God is not that small.

I wrote it over and over again, until Theo commanded us to bow our heads in prayer.

A STRANGE THING TO DO

THERE WAS ONE OTHER SOURCE OF ANXIETY THAT WOULD
have been felt not just by me but by my parents as well that
summer: just a few weeks before classes were set to resume, I was
planning a trip to Portugal with my boyfriend.

My parents had agreed to let me go because I was an adult and
possibly because I'd presented the trip to them as something other
than what it actually was. "His father and stepmother have a house
there, and they've invited me and about eight other kids to come
and stay there for a couple of weeks." That was mostly true. There
would be a whole group of us there, all together, boys and girls.
But in order to justify my going and to dissuade my parents from
envisioning me as party to the kinds of carnal behavior that leaving
the country with one's boyfriend surely conjured in their minds, I'd
had to assure them that my boyfriend's parents would be there the
whole time as chaperones, which was not true. Every time the trip
was brought up, I was careful to mention that his parents would be
there, that they were behind the invitation. Sometimes, I'd mention them just randomly as the property owners, which, I hoped,
implied that they would be present the whole time, dutifully mind-
ing their property (and their son). I mentioned them so often that
I began to feel a kind of nervousness about meeting them, though
of course there was no threat of that because they wouldn't be
there. The fact that my parents never asked to be put in touch with

my boyfriend's father and stepmother stood out to me then as a sign that my story was credible; they must have believed it, I told myself, just as they must have trusted that my correspondence with my teacher was nothing to worry about. Of course, it may well have been precisely the reverse: my parents wanting to allow me my freedom and hoping, as they'd hoped with each of my siblings before me, that I'd use it wisely. Hence, my mother's prayers all summer: *We pray for Tracy and her relationship with her boyfriend.* Hence the need, for full effect, for me to be within earshot of such prayers whenever possible. She hoped it might not be too late for me to choose to do the right thing.

My father was less subtle. After dinner one night, he held my gaze steadily in his and said, "We don't condone what you're doing." He didn't say more, and he didn't need to. His words, and the look that accompanied them—not an angry or a judgmental one but one of frank honesty, like one adult addressing another—had hit home. I felt sorry that the choice I made—the choice I was desperate to follow through upon and the life I thought it might point me toward (a life of travel and of meaningful kinds of experiences and, finally, of the adult love I'd taken so long to really trust was available to me)—meant having to lie to my parents or live knowing I was the object of their regret. When I was really honest with myself, I knew it meant both lying and knowing, which put an uncomfortable damper on whatever else I'd set out to feel.

Because my parents didn't approve of the trip—they merely allowed it—I'd had to save up the money on my own. I had spent two grueling weeks working on the dorm crew at the end of the spring semester—cleaning dorms and helping to prepare the campus for commencement and reunions. Not only was it backbreaking work; it was the kind of work that made me feel as if I were undoing whole chapters of the history of American racial progress. There I was, black, on my hands and knees, scrubbing the bathtubs that had been dirtied all year long by the children of the privileged class. Never mind that my own dormitory bathtub was just then being scrubbed by someone else, what the job forced me to feel was a kind of abject need and a subservience that I was without recourse to refuse. I left work with a kind of shame at what I had inflicted upon myself. But if I hadn't, who would have paid for my plane ticket, and how much longer would I have had to wait to taste that bit of sought-after independence?

Back home, Wanda paid me a bit of money each week to clean her apartment (I did a lackluster job but not out of the same sense of embarrassment that had characterized my stint on dorm crew). I believe she took pity on me, having recalled how she, too, had gone against our parents' better judgment in taking her own solo trip to Europe the year she turned twenty-seven. Mom and Dad had worried that she might come to harm, that she'd be opening herself up to too much risk, that she was wasting time and money when she ought to have been finding a real job. But Wanda had gone anyway, needing to feed her sense of adventure, needing to test out her appetite for the world, wanting to know who she would become once she set foot outside the confines of her familiar world. I remember how galvanized she'd seemed upon her return home. She glowed with a joy at what and whom she'd encountered, and with a different sense of herself, too. She had new clothes—gladiator sandals bought in Greece and bohemian chic clothes from France and Italy. Sometimes, she'd let me borrow an oversized Fiorucci belt or squeeze my feet into a pair of her tiny shoes. After I'd worn her London Hard Rock Cafe T-shirt to school several times, an older boy muttered under his breath, but audibly,

"Never been to London." I was crestfallen but only partly so, for if my sister had been off to see the world, it meant that one day I'd get there, too.

Michael had spent half his junior year of college in Austria. We still teased him sometimes about the calls that would come through from heavily accented girls looking for him, girls he'd surely made some impression upon while he was living in their country. He didn't feel as strongly as Wanda or my parents that I ought or ought not to be making the trip. Once, when the subject of my plans came up, a friend of his from work, a woman, told me, "Spike said to me, 'I can't get over the fact that some guy is porking my sister.' And do you know what I told your brother? I told him, 'He is if she knows what's good for her.'" And while I didn't quite warm to the term "porking"—it turned my relationship into something sordid, a drunken punch line and nothing more—the comment reinforced the extent to which, no matter what I said, it was a given for everyone in the know that I was very likely to be having sex. Maybe that was Michael's way of processing the mix of surprise and understanding that accompanied his discovery that I, too, had crossed over from a state of innocence.

Sex. Put like that, it sounds merely as if I had been initiated into the animal kingdom, had been activated in my biological destiny to move fully through the evolutionary cycle of birth, reproduction, and death. Sex. The noun that had hung over so much of my adolescence like a threat, like a plague to be avoided, like a snare waiting to snap me up as if I were a rabbit or a careless bear. Sex. The noun that encapsulated so many different kinds of verbs, all different shades of more or less the same thing: sleeping together, fucking, fornicating, being up to something, playing with fire, making love, living in sin. But also being caught up in the wordless feelings of elation and suspense and surprise that, I now knew, made everything—all of the longing and the waiting and the little anxieties about being wanted or not—worth it. Being alive and unafraid in my own body and feeling in control of how, why, and to whom I let myself go. It was a step into a world where the terms were less easy to pin down, where feelings and facts and opinions sometimes did funny things in response to one another, sometimes refusing to lie still. It was a world where, for once, I knew that what I thought I'd known all along, what I'd been taught to know, while still true in many ways, was not the only truth. Where, finally, I was flawed and implicated and awake to experience in a way that felt like a gift. Sex. What a strange thing to do, to want to do, and yet, what a strange thing, too, to get so bent out of shape about. What a strange worry to carry, especially if it's not you you're worried about but someone else. Sex. The thing that made me *me* as distinct from my parents and that made me finally feel older, finally mature in a way that nothing could undo.

It would have been nice to have had someone to talk to about it. Instead, I spent a lot of time thinking about what it all meant. I started to write a play in which a woman sitting up naked in her bed was having a version of this conversation with herself, describing what it felt like to lie down under the weight of her lover and feel the rest of the world slide off the edge of the bed. Then I began to worry that my mother might find the play and read it and be horrified by what she saw, so I tore it up and put it into the big black garbage cans along the side of the house.

And one other thing happened that summer. Despite my determination to make the trip and the cost it exacted upon my relationship with my parents, there was scant encouragement from my boyfriend, Andreas, that I should follow through on my plans to meet him and the others in Portugal. He spent part of the summer at home in Massachusetts with his mom and part in Germany with his dad. He didn't call, seldom returned my calls; when he did, the line was gripped by a painful, static-fleeced silence. He sent me two letters in the course of three months, and while he did not tell me not to come, neither did he reveal any excitement at the prospect of seeing me again in August. For most of the summer, I was left to wonder if he was still my boyfriend at all. Yet I had so little experience with boyfriends and so little recourse to romantic advice that I convinced myself I ought to go anyway, that he must have been as excited to be reunited with me as I was to be reunited with him. At the very least, I had such an appetite to reassert my connection to the world beyond Fairfield and to the physical intimacies Andreas and I had only just begun to experience before the school year came to an end that I decided, helter-skelter, come what may, to go. And so I went.

In the San Francisco airport waiting for my outbound flight, I bought a pack of cigarettes and went into the smoking area to reacquaint myself with a social habit I would pick up and abandon a number of times before eventually dropping it for good. I'd had to temporarily quit while I was in Fairfield, but I was deep enough into the belly of SFO to feel home's hold on me suspended. In the dense haze of first- and second-hand smoke, I breathed in thick lungfuls of relief. I sat next to one of those large, communal ashtrays full of sand and hours' worth of spent cigarette butts. The large, ugly concrete object struck me as pathetic, stuck in place, just as I had been stuck at home, biding my time. It would have been nicer to be sitting and smoking on a couch in someone's living room or outside on a bench with the fresh air blowing the smoke off and away, but my being there among the smokers and the ashtrays was freedom. It was me doing what I felt the urge to do, going where I felt the urge to go. Whether the feelings of having been stifled by the smallness of home were real or exaggerated— whether they were innate, a genuine product of my own heart and will, or artificial, like the conventions that tell us we ought to laugh at certain things and cry at others, things that, in reality, have no bearing upon our actual feelings—I sat in that smoking area feeling as though a tremendous yoke had been unfastened from around my neck. I was permitted again to listen exclusively to my thoughts and whims and to act in accordance with whatever they said. My thoughts and whims told me to finish my cigarette, and I finished my cigarette. My thoughts and whims told me to go to Portugal, and I was going to Portugal, with both genuine excitement and nicotine jittering in my stomach.

On the flight, I drank red wine with my meal. I tried to sleep, but the excitement prevented me from dozing off. Eventually, I made my way back to one of the smoking rows and struck up a sporadic bilingual conversation with an old man on his way to Lisbon. We drank what the Portuguese flight attendants called "white coffee," and when his English broke down, I did a patch job with my passable French. I have no memory of what we discussed, only the feeling of jet-set sophistication and the white coffees and the smoke and the ever-shortening distance between Europe and me.

On the connecting flight between Lisbon and Faro, I noticed that there were some of Andreas's friends in the rows. I knew two of them from school; a third was one of his childhood friends from home whom I'd heard of but never met. The realness of them put me in mind of my repressed anxiety. Surely they had been in touch with Andreas over the summer, and surely they already knew some of what I was waiting to find out. Was that a nervous shifting of the eyes? Was it embarrassment, pity, anything at all? I felt at once shy and determined to demonstrate how perfectly at ease, how unflappably confident I was. Moreover, I felt the need to show how very wonderful I could be—how smart and wry, perceptive and fun. It was exhausting, and finally I felt as though I could have slept, only by then there wasn't time, and besides, sleeping didn't strike me as a terribly appropriate way of reinforcing what I sought to project just then about myself.

Faro was parched and sat under a cinematically blue sky. The sand and the sandy hills reminded me of how California was supposed to be: golden. The constant sun cast everything in a radiant luxury, even the remote, dusty town with its pebbly roads that wound up and down through the hills, even the bare-bones unmarked cafés, where couples or groups of elderly men sat very still sipping from tiny cups of coffee and smoking. It looked to me like a town in an old-fashioned Italian movie, the kind where you can hear footsteps raking over gravel or echoing against the stone buildings when the characters walk.

I knew as soon as I saw Andreas that his feelings had changed. I could see it in his eyes and in his bearing. He'd been in Portugal for two weeks already, so he was tanned, and he looked leaner than I remembered. He stood there smiling a new, knife-sharp kind of smile. He welcomed all of us, the three boys and me, in the same way, as if we were his guests and nothing more. Perhaps it was merely an unimpeachable hospitality to which I was unaccustomed, something regal and cool, in his blood on the German side. But it felt like more. It felt like the continuation of our summer-long silence, only now it was loud, because I was in its presence.

The house struck me as a small villa, as far as I could tell, though it was my first villa, and I couldn't be absolutely certain that's what it really was. It was remote, a drive from the center of town along a narrow, winding road. It had grounds, upon which grew, among other things, fig trees (my father grew figs at home, and I recognized those unusually shaped leaves). There was a swimming pool adjacent to the kitchen, which was separate from the house, in its own cabana. The room Andreas led me to, and which the two of us would share, was obviously the room where his parents slept, with a large bed canopied in mosquito nets. What a pang it caused me to see something so luxuriously romantic, knowing that the romance I'd tried so lovingly, so doggedly to nurse was on its last legs. Still, that night, after the dinner that the whole group of us had prepared and stayed up late in the garden eating, Andreas and I made use of the big bed, trying things we hadn't been bold enough to try upon one another months earlier in Cambridge. It was exhilarating and felt earned, affirmation of everything I'd hoped to claim upon my arrival. We talked, too, reinitiating ourselves into each other's voice and life. I don't remember, though, much of what we said. It was an evening that unfolded in a way that struck me as the exact opposite of the winter night when I'd lost my virginity, a night spent in my minuscule bedroom in the dorms, a room barely larger than the twin bed where we'd lain (for that reason, in part as a joke, I'd hung above my dresser a print of Van Gogh's painting of his bedroom in Arles, which looked spacious by comparison). On that first night, things had happened slowly, timidly. It wasn't rough or jokey or clandestine, the way sex had been made to seem, to me at least, by kids who had been doing it, or playing at doing it, back in high school and junior high. It had felt momentous and real. I'd enjoyed it. Though it had also weighed on me as something my parents and God would have frowned upon as wrong.

My first morning in Faro, as if in answer to my mother's prayers, when I turned to Andreas hoping to begin again what we'd left off with the night before, he sat up and put into words what, deep down, I had known enough to fear: whatever had once existed between us was now over. He didn't know why. And though I'd read countless novels in which love, courtship, and marriage constituted the central drama, I was so lacking in real-life knowledge about such things that I had no idea how to let him go with any modicum of grace. I had no idea how to grieve the thing that had felt so like a gift, like the beginning of my life as someone other than my mother's child. I cried. I battered him with questions. I sulked, and I suffered through the better part of two weeks sharing the same bed with someone who no longer wished to be my lover. It alerted me to yet another function of sex, which is to open up new depths within the self that can be filled just as easily with elation as with a merciless, leaden sorrow. I finally understood why, apart from God and the Bible, my parents might have wanted me to wait, to keep myself safe from such extremes of feeling for just a little while longer. But instinctively, I also understood how important it was to let such pain in, to embrace it as another function of being an adult, and human, of striking our bargain with the world.

Pain. Somehow, it was never too far around the bend. When I was a child, I'd viewed its promise as part and parcel of the reverie of deep feeling. *One day, I will house a tremendous heartache. One day, I will reel with a singular ecstasy.* It was a lesson I learned from the stories of the ballet, and later it was books and movies and soupçons of gossip that sustained such a belief. But there was also the pain I shrank from, the pain that stood watching me, wanting to speak to me, to tell me what it knew about my parents and grandparents and the race of men and women I'd descended from. The pain that knew my name and that had something to teach me, something it wanted me to learn and never forget. Every time I saw it there in the periphery, I froze; I shut my ears, averted my eyes, turning instead to what I thought at the time was pain's antidote: silence. I was wrong. I could see that finally. Silence feeds pain, allows it to fester and thrive. What starves pain, what forces it to release its grip, is speech, the voice upon which rides the story, *This is what happened; this is what I have refused to let claim me.* Suddenly, I understood, though no one had taught me. I understood, because what I wanted, what I needed more than anything, was someone to listen to my story, someone to help me starve even this pain—this small, private pain—so that I could stand up and figure out how to go on.

The first time I told the story, it was over the phone to Conrad, quickly, in sobs and fragments. It solidified the reality of what had befallen me, and if I knew what was happening, it was likely that I would make it out okay. Telling the story bolstered my sense of hurt and anger and, the longer I considered it, my sense of having been entitled to something better. Yet it also tamed the pain, giving it a shape, a beginning, a middle, and, eventually, an end. I told the story to myself sometimes at night, looking back for all the signs, all the salient motifs, rehearsing for the ways I'd tell it again when I returned to school in a week's time.

Here, the mother that I now am must stop and smile. My daughter, who is not yet in kindergarten, already knows some of the merits of telling one's story. "When we tell our stories," she and her classmates say to one another at their progressive Brooklyn preschool, "we make power." They came up with that statement together, writing a play to perform for us, their parents. They even put it into a song, which means, with luck, my daughter will remember and come to truly understand what such a thing means.

I had read novel after novel without realizing how often the narrator was doing just that: claiming the power to name and state and face the events, even the most awful events, making up a life. *This has happened to me, and because I can see it, can call it up and face it again for you, can stand my ground while I sift through it for nuance and meaning, I am stronger. Telling my story, standing here and telling it to you now, is both a prayer for power and the answer to that prayer.*

One afternoon that summer in Portugal, sipping vinho verde in a beachside restaurant, I met a young man and woman who were traveling together. They were in their twenties, just a stage or two ahead of me in life. They were from England, ambiguously ethnic—maybe Indian or Persian?—and the fact that they spoke English and that they were the first nonwhite people I'd met since my arrival provided me with an easy pathway to conversation. They were happy. When I laughed at their jokes, I realized it was the first time I'd laughed in days. I joined them at their table on a patio overlooking the sea, and I told them my story. The mood their company created urged me to tell it with less drama, less dejection, which, in turn, urged me to see and understand it that way. For their ears, the story became more matter-of-fact, less of an ongoing saga and more of a hard-and-fast occurrence, an event that had happened and been processed and had since ceased to reverberate.

They invited me to a disco. "Bring your friends, if you want," they offered. "Bring your ex and you can make him jealous," they'd joked.

It sounded like good medicine, and I was eager not only to see them again but not to disappoint them, especially after they'd managed to boost my spirits so effectively. I told Andreas and everyone else, and the eight of us agreed that we were up for a night out.

There wasn't enough room for all of us in the tiny Fiat somebody had rented, so I rode in the car with the Brits. Andreas's roommate and a girl the roommate had once dated but who had since gone back to being just a friend sat in the backseat with me. I remember the moment when the three of us, all at the same time, realized we didn't really know these people, that they might not be who they said they were, and that they could be taking us anywhere at all, no matter what they'd told us or how nice they'd seemed. It was a fear I read on the face of the girl when she turned to look at me and a fear I mirrored back to her. Then, realizing there was nothing to do but wait and see where we were going and what happened when we got there, I leaned back in the seat and looked out at the night—a night that was at first pitch-dark and that gradually lightened as we approached the center of town, with its restaurants and nightclubs—and I felt, rising up out of my fear, the thrill of that nameless going. It was neither the end of one chapter nor the beginning of another but rather a deep, vacant, weightless Now that would last as long as it lasted and lead to wherever it led.

I, TOO

"I DON'T KNOW WHAT THAT WHITE BOY DID TO YOU," MY COUSIN Nina said, "but whatever it was, it must've been bad."

That wasn't her way of asking me to tell her all the nitty-gritty details of my breakup with Andreas, which was now nearly a year behind me. She was commenting upon the recent change in me, one of many she'd witnessed over the span of our relationship. I was no longer the goody-goody girl she'd encountered on her first visit to California when we were both children—though as far as she, in all her savvy urbane know-how, was concerned, I probably had more than a little of that child left in me. For her part, she still had a portion of the sass that had hit me like a cold front long ago. But our child-selves were buried beneath other things, having been tempered by the growing up we'd managed to do in the dozen or more years since we first met.

The change Nina detected was knotted into the dreadlocks I was cultivating, and it was stippling my underarms and legs, left unshaven in defiance of I'm-still-not-quite-sure-what. It was evident in the newly acquired rhetoric—phrases like "the White Power Structure," "Women of Color," and "the Black Community"—that had begun to pepper my speech.

I'd gone militant.

If Nina was right, she'd succeeded at pinpointing a connection I hadn't myself been willing to acknowledge. As far as I was concerned, my awakening had started in the fall of sophomore year, with a course on African American literature. When we read Ralph Ellison's *Invisible Man,* I'd felt, possibly for the first time, like I was capable of looking at racial injustice without blinking and of really listening, letting things unfold before me, jab at my heart, and kick my mind into motion. Reading the novel, I'd understood something I hadn't ever considered: listening to a protagonist is easier than listening to a person speaking in the flesh, even if the two might be saying the exact same thing. The protagonist invites you into such an intimate proximity, asking only to be heard, and then proceeds to say a thing like, "I have been hurt to the point of abysmal pain, hurt to the point of invisibility." If someone said that to my face, my esophagus would tighten, my temples would flush, and my heartbeat would thump louder in my ears. I'd retreat, too ashamed and too guilty to stand there listening to what the world had insisted, again and again, upon doing to a person with skin hued like my own. And yet the voice on the page, saying these very things, entered me differently. My eyes raced across the lines, chasing down every sentence. It was more than simply loving to read, more than simply loving a good story. It was about realizing I was capable of opening my eyes and ears in such a way as to accept the truth of what I was reading and admit the pain.

Novels, essays, and poems about race in America did hurt, but they buoyed me, too. I'd never read so many books by black writers before. Ellison, Hughes, Hurston, Baldwin, Wright. I'd recognized a version of my own daydreaming, my own longing for the future and for true experience, in Janie, the protagonist of *Their Eyes Were Watching God.* Janie's "Looking, waiting, breathing short with impatience. Waiting for the world to be made" became my own tendency to lurch with all my imagination toward a moment when my life would magically begin. And once that bond was cemented, once I'd claimed a piece of the character's subjectivity as my own, it was almost as though following Janie through the rural black world of the novel, immersing myself in her experience and in the details of the place she belonged to, was a way of undoing the fear and squeamishness with which I'd once reacted to Mother and her corner of the South. Janie, or rather Zora Neale Hurston, returned a piece of what I had rejected when I was too young to know better.

I could feel these novels healing and enlarging me. Ishmael Reed's *Mumbo Jumbo* reminded me of the vibrant cacophony of voices making up my extended family—the playful and pointed way words could take on a life of their own, *signifying* (another new yet instinctively familiar concept for me) in many directions at once. I felt a heady joy that Jean Toomer's *Cane* might sweep from one register to another so quickly—that one writer might be able to claim dominion over so many different lexicons, saying, "You are the most sleepiest man I ever seed" in one breath, and "Night winds in Georgia are vagrant poets, whispering" in another—without seeming concerned with who was listening, trusting that the reader was listening in the exact right way. These texts allowed two different parts of my person to mingle, perhaps for the first time. The part that lived in and understood blackness as a thing apart, a thing unto itself; and the part that lived in and understood language as a vehicle for deep feeling and complex thought.

One night, the phone in my dorm room rang. It was a friend from high school, a tall gangly blond boy named Jacob, who had always been shy and clumsy but brilliant, a voracious reader. We'd talked on the phone in high school about Baudelaire and Oscar Wilde. Jacob was a year younger than me, and our friendship hadn't lasted long past my graduation, but it was a thrill to hear his voice again, and because we'd always shared what we were reading, I tried to tell him about the books I'd been devouring in my class.

"But," he countered, "is African American literature as good as our literature?"

The statement struck me as layered. For one, he'd presumed that he and I belonged to the same *our*. Having grown up together, I suppose that, one way or another, we did. But the *them* his *our* presumed was pointed both at me and away from me, for if I grew up to be a writer, as he knew I one day hoped to do, the books I'd write would not belong to the *our* he assumed, the *our* he recognized and privileged.

"Oh, but you're different," he said. "Race doesn't really count for you." He was doing the thing that whites sometimes do to the blacks they admire, which is to strip them of their blackness, as if doing so were a kind of favor.

I had talked about this at length in my seminars on race, but I didn't feel hopeful that Jacob would follow me through the nuances of such an argument, so my next tactic was simply to answer his question directly. "African American literature is part of the canon. It's American literature. *Invisible Man* is an American masterpiece."

But Jacob's hesitation, the pause before he assented, drowned out everything else we had to say to one another.

When I hung up the phone, I was fuming. "Who does he think he is?"

My roommates sat by, listening to my rant. Two of them were white, but they certainly knew what I meant. It was the early 1990s, after all, and everyone at Harvard was caught up in the conversation about Identity. At least everyone I knew. Identity was a badge, a discipline, a spectacle. It was something you could claim, something you could deconstruct, something you could interrogate, something you could even wield if need be. Identity surprised us during those years, spinning in countless ways upon axes of race, class, gender, sexuality, and whatever else we were willing to consider. It was exhilarating to be so astute, so dexterous, so chameleonic. It was also helpful, at a time of life when so many feelings remained out of reach, burrowed deep beneath the skin, to believe that identity was something that could be mastered.

The spring of sophomore year, galvanized by the thinking imparted by my first-semester foray into Afro-Am (that's what we called the discipline, back then), I'd enrolled in an eight-person seminar, which introduced us, in the first weeks, to the work of Booker T. Washington, Malcolm X, and W. E. B. DuBois. I also took an Afro-Am cinema class taught by Spike Lee, who flew in from New York once a week for the lecture. During discussions, Lee poked fun at a white girl in the class named Stokely and a black boy whose speech had been tricked out with urban slang in what may have been an effort to compensate for the fact that he'd graduated from Exeter. My studies convinced me I was beginning to live in a new language. I discovered cultural critics who taught me to interrogate notions of Otherness, who argued that loving blackness was a means of political resistance, and who gave me the terms within which to consider a thing called Black Consciousness.

Conversation in the seminar room, which sat across the street from the Yard and let in some of the commotion of Mass Ave., was lively. There were many of us who were exploring the discipline not merely for intellectual edification but as a means of recovering something we believed had been withheld by the mainly white schools many of us had attended and the culture, which, when we were children at least, had the habit of making us feel guilty or ashamed for the victimization of blacks by slavery and racism.

But it wasn't just about self-esteem. We discussed that in the first class, when we'd covered the texts that had once designated

Black Studies curricula for just that purpose, to repair black self-esteem. But that was decades ago. The language of such a time, and many of the theories and practices it had given birth to (theories of "Afro-Centric architecture," for example), was already dated, played out. Now it was much more fruitful to interrogate the subtleties informing the conversation about race and to "read" (my new favorite verb, at least when applied to things that weren't literal texts) the relevance of a whole number of offshoots from the topic. That semester, I wrote a paper exploring why so many black revolutionaries had become conservatives during the Reagan era. Privately, I wondered if the assignment might help me learn more about my father, who had never been a revolutionary, but whose service in the military had made him even more fiercely patriotic, and who had voted for Reagan, both times.

Afro-Am meant many things to me and galvanized me with new energy for my studies. But there were moments when I also doubted that it was enough to become an expert on Blackness. Maybe it was enough for the white students in the class, who had no literal skin in the game as I saw it, but for a person like me, how could Afro-Am ever fully be a bloodless pursuit? Wasn't there always going to be an unconscious ulterior motive behind the things I sought to clarify for myself and for others?

Sometimes, my classmates and I talked about the work of black writers as if it always involved some kind of tricksterism or sleight of hand: "Phillis Wheatley is speaking in code. Nobody will listen to her if she doesn't praise the Western God. Nobody would even believe she'd written those poems herself if she didn't have the white man's stamp of approval at the front of the book." But what if such a thesis were equal parts true and untrue? What if the language Wheatley had adopted had also gotten inside of her? What if she believed herself when she said, *'Twas mercy brought me from my Pagan land, / Taught my benighted soul to understand / That there's a God, that there's a Saviour too?* Would that make her less worthy of our attention?

"It would be a wise idea to concentrate in something in addition to Afro-Am," my friend Chris told me. He was a senior who had also been in that first Afro-Am lit class. His presentation on Ellison had impressed me. "Ellison wrote for the little man behind the stove," he'd said. He was proposing a reading of *Invisible Man* that had been inflected by Ellison's essay "The Little Man at Chehaw Station," in which the author recalled being cautioned never to forget about the unnoticed, unassuming little man sitting quietly in the corner—the one who knows more about what is at stake aesthetically and culturally than everyone else. Chris's comments illuminated for me the sense of Ellison's epic reach by tempering it with a sense of his humility. That afternoon, I'd felt my eyes trying to morph my friend into my image of Conrad. It was a way of acknowledging my respect for him and my wish to do what he was standing there doing, which looked to me like mastering the material, casting it in a new light, adding new layers to the conversation our professor had prompted. I wanted to be able to do that.

"If you're interested in the field," Chris had coached me, "you should think about doing a joint concentration in English and Afro-Am."

Having a foot in both realms seemed appropriate. For while there was a version of me who knew and revered the literature my old friend Jacob had called "ours," there was also a version of me who believed she was a nationalist.

As a "nationalist," I attended Black Students Association meetings and participated in the verbal sparring that often erupted around the topic of black women who weren't dating black men. I wasn't dating a black man—I wasn't dating anyone. Maybe the hurt my heart still felt from having been broken up with (by a white boy, yes; would it have hurt less if he had been black?) required me to claim a kind of strength, an authority. Granted, it was an authority that was merely theoretical—one that lived primarily in the words I strung together in my essays on topics having to do with the countless combinations of gender, race, class, and subjectivity—but as I saw it, a theoretical authority was better than no authority at all. And it gave me a language for thinking about the world, a language that deepened and complicated the ways I saw myself.

Some weekends, needing a brief respite from course work, dorms, dining halls, campus gossip, and roommates, I'd take the bus to New York City. After so many years of living thousands of miles away from my aunts, uncles, and cousins, and of imagining that there were many impassable worlds between us, I was finally getting to know that branch of the family for myself. Those visits had also, finally, wrested the city itself from my father's narrow view of it, erased for me his contempt for the sprawling, messy, raucous frenzy of the place. There on my own terms, letting my eyes climb past the trees to scale the high-rise buildings that never fully seemed to surrender to the sky, I'd felt filled with agency, as if the magnitude of what was human—the skyscrapers, clock towers, mammoth bridges, and the wide avenues electric with traffic—had enlarged me. I could see very clearly why a person would *choose* to live in a place like that, why a person might race to fall into step with the river of pedestrians, everyone moving with an aggrandized sense of his or her own going—walking, sprinting, climbing, closing in on something always just a little way off. There was a privacy to the place that intoxicated me. A quiet at the center of that racket into which a person could disappear, if she wanted to.

Sometimes the quiet of my thoughts, and my ideals—which I took to be thoughts I hadn't yet had the opportunity to act upon, like the one about being a nationalist—was intruded upon by one of my relatives. Like Nina asking what on earth had happened to me. Or my aunt Ursula wanting to know what kind of job I hoped to get with a head full of dreadlocks.

"I'm not interested in the kind of job that would discriminate against me for wearing my hair in its natural state."

I can now see how the steely rigidity with which I rattled off my new beliefs might have been disconcerting. My mother was unsettled by my new appearance; she thought I looked unkempt, though she grilled me less about what else my appearance signified. But my aunts were not my mother, and they gave themselves permission not just to worry but also to badger me.

"There's a little boy at my school," Aunt Ursula had told me, "whose mother put his hair into dreadlocks. I see him on the playground yanking it out, one lock at a time. He feels stuck. It's not fair."

"You can be black without going overboard about it," another voice had chimed in. "Why stir up trouble trying to make such a big statement?"

They were telling me that blackness wasn't a costume and it wasn't a battle but something most people lived inside of quite naturally, not wrestling with it or feeling obliged to wave it around. Like it or not, they also meant to remind me, blackness was also a factor that made some aspects of life harder. Of course I knew what they meant. Of course I knew they were right, but up until that point in my life, I'd mostly kept my understanding of blackness inside. Couldn't my aunts see how elated I felt, finally having the permission and the tools to voice my own thinking about race and to unpack such thinking for others (whether or not they wanted to hear it)?

As far as my New York family was concerned, I was late to the party. They'd lived a great portion of their lives in the South, after all. Even my cousins who were raised in New York had had the benefit of regular visits to Alabama, where they, unlike me, had felt at home. They'd been given the language I hadn't or hadn't been willing to receive, and it freed them from having to talk their way through what being black meant. Had they been told to always be *twice as good*? Maybe, but they'd also been told it was a flaw of the white world to require such a display.

I made a trip to New York one weekend in order to visit the Schomburg Center for Research in Black Culture, a branch of the New York Public Library devoted to the African diaspora. I'd read about it and was eager to be in the space, to soak up the feeling of all that black art, all that black thinking. My aunt Carla had driven me there, and on the way home, she'd given me a tour of the Harlem neighborhoods, weaving along the blocks of Striver's Row and, farther north, pointing out the abandoned buildings that had once been magnificent, too, but that now stood gutted like doll houses on burnt-out blocks. After dark, as we were heading back down Lenox Avenue, I'd pointed to the silhouettes warming themselves around garbage cans whose contents had been set aflame.

"Wow!" was all I could say, spinning around in my seat to take in the sight for as long as I could. There was something about it that delighted me, something real, something that reminded me, perhaps, of the invisibility Ellison's protagonist described.

"When I graduate, I want to come here. I want to live in Harlem, with all these beautiful black people," I announced. It felt like a homecoming. The little sliver of blackness I'd known growing up in California, a sliver that sat inside the walls of our family house, or inside the silence of my mind, leapt now in joy to know that there was an immense realm whose facets gave back occasional glimpses of itself.

"Those men are *homeless*," Aunt Carla said. I could hear the echo of my father in her voice.

"But there's something so . . . so *beautiful* about them." It was the only word I could access quickly enough to answer her. I didn't want to be just my old self, the one for whom race was a private meditation and nothing more. And while I surely didn't want to be one of the homeless warming myself by the heat of a trash can set afire, I didn't want to be a stranger to that reality forever.

"Your parents did everything they could to make sure you wouldn't have to suffer. Why would you want to go backward?" Aunt Carla was asking.

It was a question that on one level made sense to me. But on another, it didn't, and I wasn't able to answer it—not yet.

On the Greyhound back to Boston, signs everywhere told me how much farther there was to go. Bridgeport. New Haven. Providence. I treasured that feeling of drifting between places. It helped erase some of the anxiety about where, in the real scheme of things, I was supposed to be headed, and it helped take my mind off the loneliness I sometimes felt now that I was no longer in love, no longer anybody's urgent destination. Moving over ramps and bridges, and back and forth across lanes, I relaxed my grip around the confusion, the sorrow, the independence, the wanting, the shifting allegiances, the insatiable wondering that fueled so much of my life. High above the ground, watching the bus's shadow skimming north on Interstate 95, I felt vacant, expansive, subjective, far away. Like a cloud pushed along by the wind.

TESTIMONY

IN THE FALL OF MY SENIOR YEAR OF COLLEGE, I WAS LIVING IN
Somerville, in an off-campus apartment with a roommate who
was, from what I gathered, about twelve years older than me. I'd
just as soon have come out and asked her, but by then, too much
time had passed, and I didn't want her to think I'd been inordi-
nately concerned about the age gap between us. She did once mention that she'd been a regular on a 1970s children's program that
I was too young for but that my older siblings had watched with
devotion.

Her name was Dawn, and we'd met on campus during the
spring of my junior year. She seemed like a refreshing alternative
to my friends from the dorms. My best friend was a first-generation
Indian American girl from Sacramento with a penchant for alcohol
and theatrics. I loved her, but when I was being very honest with
myself, I had to admit that I found her exhausting. And while she
was my main confidante—we spent whole days and nights talking
to one another about what we did and thought and felt—she had
once made it explicitly clear to me that she had limited patience for
hearing me talk about my romantic exploits. "You sound almost
stupid when you're talking about your boyfriend," she'd once said.
And ever since, I'd tried very hard to keep most of that kind of
business to myself.

Dawn was black, which was one thing that had drawn me to

her. I had plenty of black friends, but not so many that I had ceased feeling excited about cultivating new ones. At first, I thought she was a student, but it turned out that she was on an extended leave from the university, having taken time off during her second or third year. Though older than me, she was sweet and innocent in a way I felt I'd only just left behind myself. As far as I was concerned, I'd grown up a lot in two years, a side effect of heartbreak, and as a result of having, at some point in the preceding years, learned to look at myself through more objective eyes, commanding, *Straighten up,* or *Grow up,* or *Wise up,* at times when the old me might have stood mute in shock or crumpled into despair. This is life, I learned to tell myself. These are the fleeting glories and their accompanying devastations: love and betrayal, unabashed pride and humiliation so poignant it requires you to lift your chin and stride out the door like a goddess.

When I met Dawn, I was dating a slightly older black guy I'd met at the campus film archive, where he worked. He wasn't a student, but he was a campus personality. I wanted the relationship to succeed, but I suspected that he was being somewhat cavalier with his affections. There seemed to be more than a few young black women with whom he was exceptionally familiar. Dawn didn't appear to know terribly much about him, and I took that to mean that they'd never dated or that he'd never flirted (successfully) with her and that striking up a friendship with her wouldn't later open me up to the mortification of discovering we had far too much in common.

In the spring of the previous year, after we had already looked at a few apartments together and my eagerness to leave the dorms had been mightily piqued, Dawn and I went for a coffee in Harvard Square. "Are we sure we should be moving in together?" she had asked, as if we were contemplating a far more serious commit-ment. I shot her a confused, half-betrayed look, and she attempted to clarify by saying that she was a Christian and that her values might seem unusual to me.

Her concern hit me like a rebuke from my own conscience. *For what fellowship hath righteousness with unrighteousness?* Instead of telling her that, like her, I was a Christian, I'd snarked back, "Well, if you're worried that we won't be 'equally yoked,' you can relax." Why was I trying to punish her for being transparent in her faith? And what was clouding my ability to be transparent in mine?

"Maybe I'm worried about living with someone who makes cheesy jokes about my religion," she'd replied, ruffled. But we went ahead with things anyway. It would have been far harder to find affordable one-bedroom apartments on our own. Like it or not, we had come to need one another.

Dawn and I were alike in certain ways. She seemed to come from a fairly sheltered middle-class black family with a handful of kids. But when she was my age, both of her parents were killed in a car crash. That was why she'd taken a leave of absence from school. Again, it was something I'd gathered, pieced together from our many day's-end conversations. The closest I'd come to asking Dawn to tell me her whole story from start to finish was simply listening to the bits and pieces that came tumbling out when we were relaxing together at home.

After we'd first moved in, we drove a U-Haul out to Roxbury to pick up some of her belongings from her brother's basement. The two of them had the same wide, spoon-shaped face and exquisite almond eyes. I could imagine the whole family was beautiful, in a gentle, almost surprising way. They'd been quiet together that afternoon, talking but not talking, not bothering with the kind of cheerful chatter we'd have made in my family: smiling our big smiles, volleying around jokes, and lobbing a slew of questions over to the outsider.

Dawn prayed before meals and woke up for church on Sundays (not Memorial Church but another in Cambridge). Sometimes, she brought people home from her church group, students who were my age mostly, from Harvard and the other nearby campuses. I always wondered if I'd bump into the Bible-study kids I'd met and embarrassed myself in front of that evening during my freshman fall, and for all intents and purposes, I did, over and over: the types were exactly the same, as was the feeling they incited in me, which was equal parts annoyance and shame, as if they were the flock and I the single sheep that succeeded in getting away.

Our apartment was large and sunny, but in winter it felt like a walk-in refrigerator. The number of tenants who had lived there before us seemed to bear a direct relationship to the layers of lino-leum curling up from the kitchen and bathroom floors. If you stood on the corner of Dane Street, where we lived, and Wash-ington, which led to campus, you could see the factory chimneys off in the distance. On cold days, their smoke hung motionless in the white sky. A block up, there was the bakery where I bought the (half-priced) day-old scone and cup of black currant tea that together helped take my mind off the wind rifling through the wool of my army surplus jacket (I had warmer coats, but that was the coolest one). As I set out from home each morning for campus, the cadence of my footfalls seemed to invite a new thought to take shape, and the twenty minutes it took for me to reach campus gave that thought the time to really get somewhere. Sometimes, it felt more like dreamtime, and I found that I'd worked my way through an idea or a memory it should have taken far longer to navigate.

The same held true on my treks back home at night, though the dark added an element of mystery and a sense of largeness to things that I never quite noticed when the sun was out.

I'm not sure how true it is to say that I thought a lot in those days about my mother. Sometimes I avoided thinking about her as a way of staving off worry. If we just left things as they were and didn't meddle with them, I'd tell myself, everything would be fine. When she and I spoke, she answered my questions with affirmations: *I'm feeling well. Everything here is just fine. Dad and I are keeping busy.* I couldn't ask the hard questions, the ones that would have pried into the space where certainty gave way. I couldn't even say a thing like, *But, Mom, how do you really feel? What are you thinking? Are you worried?* Because I couldn't bear to hear her peel away the strength and the assurance and show me where she was vulnerable or afraid. I was the youngest, after all, the kitten of the family, the baby, and in that role, I'd never had to learn to be strong for anyone else or to provide anyone else with necessary support.

For my part, I scrambled to show my mother how well I was doing, how pleased she should be with me, to rattle off the proof of how much I was in the process of achieving, because it had become impossible to tell her what was inside my heart. If I upset her, in her condition, what else might happen? There's a version of cancer, in the imagination, that is a monster we unleash upon ourselves and the people we love, something animated and augmented by stress and by anger. Wouldn't it tempt my mother's cancer to let her know how much a part of the world I had become—the world she'd warned me was fleeting, snared with moral pitfalls, a mere way station on our way to the hereafter?

My silence did nothing to mitigate my own worry. After I'd hang up from one of our calls, I'd imagine her sitting on the side of her bed near the phone, asking God for strength, for health, for more life. Underneath the prayers, I feared that she was afraid, no matter that she'd all my life told me the Lord took away fear, that she was serene in His promises. But what if the cancer wasn't content to stay gone? What if it decided to come back? Would she know? Would it speak to her in aches or a dull burn or a searing thunderbolt that flashed on and off through the day and night? I lay awake sometimes, worrying it might surprise her with the kind of pain that would cause her to say, "Oh," and have to lie back down on the bed in her clothes and her shoes and shut her eyes.

I'd started taking the late-night bus to Providence once a week so I could spend the night with my boyfriend, the one I suspected I shouldn't completely trust, who was by then enrolled in graduate school at Brown. I hadn't wanted to bring him home with me because Dawn would have disapproved, but she stopped me one morning as I was coming back into the apartment to collect my things for class.

"It's okay if you want to have your boyfriend stay here sometimes," she said.

"Oh, I don't mind going to him. I wouldn't want to make you feel uncomfortable."

"As a Christian, my choices are right for me," she said. "But they might not be right for you."

It was impossible for me to imagine the same words crossing back and forth between my mother and me. Did I think that by presenting a false or partial version of myself I could convince her she had been wrong, a few years back, when she'd wanted to pray for me with the ladies from church? Did it seem likely that hiding the facts of my day-to-day life would make her think her prayers, about me—and everything else—had been answered?

My mother. No matter how I'd willed my thoughts of her to behave, no matter how much I'd begged them not to conjure an image of her as sick or even vulnerable to sickness, as my senior year was just picking up momentum, her cancer came out of remission. At first, it was only Conrad's fiancée, Janet, a resident in emergency medicine at Boston Children's Hospital, in whom she confided. Janet came from an even more sprawling family than ours, and she fit in instantly with our heat and commotion. I suppose my mother felt more comfortable asking Janet for help with the dilemma of whether to seek treatment or whether, in place of fighting back against the disease, she should surrender the outcome to God. Asking Conrad would have been dumping her burden upon her son, though she must have known the news would reach him through his fiancée, anyway. Perhaps there was a part of her that wanted it so.

But by the time I was studying for my midterm exams, Mom had broken her silence. In any case, the cancer was no longer something she could hide. There were malignant growths on her liver, and her abdomen was swollen with a tumor so large it could be seen beneath her clothes—something that on a younger woman would have been mistaken for a pregnancy. She underwent the rounds of chemotherapy she'd initially resisted, which left her emphatically tired. She couldn't walk without help; she needed a wheelchair to get around most of the time. And there were new words used to describe the state of her condition, words terrifying in their intransigence. *Inoperable. Terminal.* Words that threw up their hands and said: *Go no further. End of the line.*

Some evenings, shivering under a blanket in my drafty apartment, I'd phone home. I missed Mom, feared for her, longed to hear her tell me she'd had a good day. "How are you feeling?" I'd say into the telephone receiver, and the voice that reached me was smaller, as if there were a distance greater than the breadth of the continent standing between us. "I'm okay, honey, just tired," she'd answer, sensing how much I wanted such a thing to be true, for it to be as simple as needing some rest, a bit of time off her feet. But everything I didn't ask—like what her doctors were saying or whether the tumors were shrinking or what God offered in answer to her prayers—was there listening in on our conversation, saying nothing but audible somehow in its silence.

Whenever Conrad, my physician-brother, the one person in our family with clinical, scientific understanding of cancer and what it meant, broached the topic of our mother's health, it was always gently, as if testing the waters of my knowledge. He could have sat me down and schooled me, shown me the textbook pictures the way he had years before when I was learning where babies came from. But instead his method was subtle, Socratic. "When was the last time you spoke to Mom?" he'd ask. Or, "How did she sound to you?" And always, I'd repeat back the same misinformation. That she sounded tired but otherwise the same. That she was hopeful about the chemo. That it would be great once we got past all of it and she was herself again. Conrad the cardiologist, whose head must have been filled with the painful truth of what my mother was actually going through and heading toward, listened, not pushing back, allowing me to take my own gradual steps into understanding. But by Thanksgiving, he told me that he and Janet had moved up the date of their wedding. "If we wait until spring, Mom may not be able to manage the trip." Shortly before the two of us flew out to California together for Christmas, he said, "You know, we might not have many more holidays like this with Mom." Just above his eyebrows, I could see the furrows that formed when he was serious. His eyes implored me to get it, to comprehend that this was real, that our mother was dying. Finally, the knowledge I'd been trying to evade closed in on me. It took no time at all. It had been there keeping pace with me all along.

I petitioned the dean to let me drop a literary theory class that I'd more or less stopped attending anyway, and when he asked for written explanation of my exceptional circumstances, I produced a short letter that included the statement "My mother is dying." It was as if I were entering into a contract with myself, signing my name to something I had finally come around to believing.

When we were at last all at home for the holidays, I housed a quiet fear. Mom was thinner. When I hugged her close, I could detect a faint chemical scent on her skin. Her hair was thinner, too; at night, she rested a small hairpiece on her dresser among the perfume bottles and brooches. When friends called to ask how she was feeling, sometimes she'd say, "I'm just waiting on my miracle!" And how faithless, how wicked I felt at those times for having surrendered to that terrible knowledge, the knowledge that had forced me to admit she was dying, that the odds of her surviving stage 4 colon cancer—which was how I had just recently begun to describe her condition, how Conrad and our mother (by way of her doctors) had finally explained it—were at best only about 15 percent.

Dad was home full-time with her by then. He'd retired after my sophomore year. They'd been traveling together, enjoying their leisure to the extent possible, though now their comings and goings were determined by the chemo schedule and by her checkups with her oncologist. Dad spent a lot of his free time working on the kinds of projects he'd undertaken when we were much younger, building bookcases and end tables, stirring up sawdust in his garage, sketching out the kinds of plans that had made him seem like a da Vinci when I was a little girl. Jean, who'd taken a leave from her job when Mom's cancer had returned, was living at home to help with all the things our father wasn't good at: fixing our mother's hair and makeup, getting her dressed and showered, and surprising her with colorful silk blouses and the little curios that made her happy. Jean, whose easy rapport with our mother sometimes unnerved me, if only because of the way it stood in contrast to all my own self-censoring. Jean, who over the years had been not just a daughter to our mother but also a confidante, a friend.

But more than to our father or Jean, Mom had given herself over to the care of her Lord, the one who any day now, if He saw fit, could still reward her with the miraculous healing she urged us to believe in and pray for.

When my mother talked about her miracle, I pushed myself to believe in it, too, but I found that wanting a thing to happen was not the same as believing it likely. Those times, I felt stricken with guilt. How could I be so pessimistic and hard-hearted? What if my belief in the harrowing statistics was all that stood in the way of her making it through everything alive?

How different would the process have been if I had remembered that we—my entire family and I—were going through it together, if I could have brought myself to say something simple and true to Jean or Michael or our father? But for some reason, I carried it around like a secret. Perhaps it was guilt at my own ability to have said a thing like "my mother is dying," to have put it in writing and signed my name to it and made it true. Shouldn't I have been telling people about the brave battle she was waging? Shouldn't I have been enlisting their support, making it clear how much I believed she had it in her to survive, to win?

Sometimes, I did try to imagine what it would be like if she made it, coming up with versions of the woman she'd have become by then. About a year after her first surgery, she and my father had taken a long road trip across the United States and into Canada. In North Carolina, they'd visited friends, and one evening at church, my mother had given her testimony to the congregation. Giving testimony happens a lot among Southern Baptists, who, as a whole, are eager to bear witness to the evidence of God in their lives. Most of the religious testimonies I've ever heard have followed a formula similar to the stories recovering addicts or alcoholics tell: of struggling with negative ways, hitting rock bottom, and then climbing back to a place of stability or prosperity with the help of a higher power. When my father told me with pride in his voice about how my mother had shared her salvation story at that North Carolina revival meeting, bragging that a video had been shot during the event, I'd said "That's great!" hoping I'd never be forced to view it. She'd probably told the crowd how, long ago, she'd been searching. Maybe she'd even found words to describe whatever it was she had once sought and how God had come to meet that need. But watching her tell that story to a roomful of strangers was something I instinctively shrank from. The Jesus-happy crowd, the naked faith that would have traveled along my mother's voice, the hand holding and head bowing—I couldn't fathom indulging the embarrassment, even before myself, of such raw, untempered, hardheaded believing.

But it wasn't just that. It also had to do with my own fear of claiming the faith I was born into, of owning it without concern for what it conjured in anybody else's imagination, without the anxiety of being likened to the Christians whose worlds were, by my estimation, too tiny, circumscribed by a few arcane commandments and deliberately impenetrable mysteries. The ones who voted against progress, who feared science, the ones who got married and lived tucked inside their houses. The ones for whom my distaste made me nothing better than a snob. It was because of them, or rather my fear of them, that I had refused to profess to the realness of God in my life. Wouldn't my mother's testimony implicate me in that reality as she understood it? Wasn't her voice still drifting out in every direction from that pulpit where she'd stood testifying, touching every inch of air on its way toward only it knew where? And when it found me, as one day it must, would it force me to choose between her world and mine? Would it mark me or claim me or simply slow for a moment, staring incredulously?

If only I could have sat beside her for a few hours and said, "This is my testimony," telling her every step I had taken on the path to that day, trusting that there was nothing I could say that she did not already know. If only I had known how to trust her with who I was. If only I had known how to ask her a thing like, *Where will we all be after everything that is happening has happened?*

V

ANOTHER DIALECT OF THE SOUL

*B*E IN THE WORLD BUT NOT OF THE WORLD. **HOW MANY TIMES** had those words traveled from her mouth to my ear? How many times had she implored me to pray for guidance, to give thanks, to claim the promise that *God did not give me a spirit of fear, but of power, and of love, and a sound mind?* All our life together, even before her diagnosis, she had been preparing us—not just my siblings and me, I now realize, but our father, too—to survive her. And not just to survive but to manifest the courage and the might her belief had always insisted we possess. *I can do all things through Christ who strengthens me.* She made me say it over and over again whenever I doubted. She made me say it to myself until it said itself, and once it did that, I didn't need to hear it anymore because I knew. Maybe that is the sum, the end-all of belief. Not a zealous adamancy but a quiet certainty.

My mother's language was always the language of the soul. But it grew clearer, more telegraphic, once the cancer began to accelerate her sense that she was on her way elsewhere. So much of the time, living with such knowledge, her mind must have been tuned to the idea of what awaited her: *I go to prepare a place for you. If it were not so, I would have told you.* In some strange way, the return to the soul state might simply be the answer to the prayer that sits behind every prayer: *Deliver me.* Is there another dialect of the soul, a way it speaks in those who don't possess the vocabulary of belief? A way it stirs and surges as if to say *Here I am,* something we don't hear but that we feel and, feeling, know.

I liked to sit in the leather armchairs facing the tall windows in Lamont Library. The windows looked out onto Mass Ave. at the intersection of Quincy Street, and when I'd glance up from my page, I'd see people I knew and people I didn't know moving back and forth along the axes of their lives. The reading room silence would obliterate all the outside traffic noises, and the daylight would baptize the pedestrians, it seemed to me, in a kind of transparent splendor, as if for the few moments they appeared in frame, they were resplendent in the inviolable promise we were all of us born into. It didn't matter if they were in a rush or a daze, if they coughed into their fists or if smoke streamed from their mouths. Each wore, for an instant if not more, a mantle of eminent belonging, as if the moment that held them was not a mistake, as if they were not lost or alone or under a heap of insurmountable dread. *Here I am,* something in them seemed to be saying to the pavement, the fallen leaves, to no one in particular.

I was taking a poetry workshop, my third so far at Harvard. In it, I had discovered that sitting down with an idea and letting it unfold in words and sounds offered me not just pleasure but an indescribable comfort. I wanted to write the kind of poetry that people read and remembered, that they lived by—the kinds of lines that I carried with me from moment to moment on a given day without even having chosen to. *Back out of all this now too much for us,* said Robert Frost, and when I heard his words in my ears, they gave weight and purpose to my footsteps, to the breath going in and out of my lungs; they gave me terms with which to consider bits and pieces of the things I otherwise didn't know how to acknowledge. Frost's voice telling me to retreat (at least that's part of what I heard in that line, hovering in space on its own, apart from the rest of the poem or even the rest of its sentence) emboldened me to admit that, yes, I was overwhelmed. My mother's cancer overwhelmed me. Her death, waiting out there in the distance, overwhelmed me. So did the loneliness I still sometimes felt, even amid the chatter and bustle of friends and classes.

Perhaps without realizing it, I, like my mother long before she belonged to me, had been seeking something. *I was searching.* Not for any one thing in particular, and not as a result of a single glaring lack, but seeking—scarching—nonetheless.

Poetry met my particular sense of need. Writing a poem, I sometimes felt like I was building a house from scratch, raising the walls, hanging the doors, laying out the rooms. It felt at times like backbreaking work. Other times, it seemed that what I was trying to evoke or encounter in a poem was already alive somewhere and that my job was merely to listen. The language of each of the poetry workshops I'd taken was built upon the assumption that there really was something else at play. My teachers talked about our poems as if they were sentient beings with plans and wishes of their own, wishes it was up to us to carry into language. "Your poem seems to be leading you in one direction, but you insist upon going in another." Or, "Try and cut out all this noise so you can hear what the poem is trying to tell you." It sounded quite nearly mystical, like we were playing at divination, but it also rang true. Wasn't it strange that a poem, written in my vocabulary and as a result of my own thoughts or observations, could, when it was finished, manage to show me something I hadn't already known? Sometimes, when I tried very hard to listen to what the poem I was writing was trying to tell me, I felt the way I imagined godly people felt when they were trying to discern God's will. "Write this," the poem would sometimes consent to say, and I'd revel in a joy to rival the saints' that Poetry—this mysterious presence I talked about and professed belief in—might truly be real.

Often, that spring, I found myself sitting in a reading room window with a book I ought to have been reading for class, but I also always had a black sketchbook into which I'd begun writing lines of my own. Sometimes, I wrote the same stanza over and over until something was unlocked and I could move forward. Once or twice, I'd stopped mid-poem, altogether stumped, and started a letter to myself in which I'd describe whatever it was I was having trouble getting into language: *What does it mean to slog through the weight of the everyday, to wake to anxiety, to spend the day straining to hear what they must be saying now that you're out of earshot, to have to put on the boots, though you're tired, always tired, and just keep going?* Sometimes all of the watching and listening and waiting finally gave way to a poem:

THE ORDINARY LIFE

To rise early, reconsider, rise again later
to papers and the news. To smoke a few if time
permits and, second-guessing the weather,

dress. Another day of what we bring to it—
matters unfinished from days before,
regret over matters we've finished poorly.

Just once you'd like to start out early,
free from memory and lighter for it.
Like Adam, on that first day: alone

but cheerful, no fear of the maker,
anything his for the naming; nothing
to shrink from, nothing to shirk,

no lot to carry that wasn't by choice.
And at night, no voice to keep him awake,
no hurry to rise, no hurry not to.

Sitting in the window thinking about language, threading my questions, worries, doubts, and fears into sentences, made me happy. As did the deep visceral longing that the voices of other poets awakened in me, a longing for the kind of momentary belonging that came from getting hold of an idea that had been waiting all along just for me. When I felt the presence of that other thing—the voice that seemed to be speaking to my hand as it moved across the page—I became clearheaded and steady, richer with something I hadn't known I possessed. Was that what my mother felt when she prayed? Was it what she quieted herself to hear so often during the days and nights, calling it *Lord*? Perhaps it was and is external, adrift, moving among the living like weather. Perhaps what it teaches, to each of us, no matter who we are, is our own necessary language, one that is both wholly new and yet familiar from a time that predates every other thing we recognize, even ourselves.

SOMETHING POWERFUL AT HER SIDE

I N APRIL, JUST AROUND THE TIME THAT SPRING WAS DECIDING
it futile to put off arriving any longer, I found myself once again
struggling with heartache. My boyfriend in Providence had been
seeing someone else, and the betrayal pressed down upon me constantly, from the time I drew the curtains and took my first glimpse
of the day—the wintry New England sky so often overcast, a blank
expansive white made up of flat, cold light—to the moment I lay
back down in the dark of my room at night. I carried it with me on
my walks to and from campus. It crept into the books I read, tam-
pering with characters' motivation, changing their faces and voices
to mine or his or hers. I squinted into the distance, mistaking any
number of innocent men for the one who had been careless with
my affection. I was angry, dogged by humiliation: why had I been
so stupid, so trusting? And, perhaps most vexingly, why was I still
lonely for the cad who had put me in such a mixed-up, wretched
state?

I should have been heartbroken about my mother, I reminded
myself one night. I should have been thinking only of her, preparing to go home to her in two months' time. Instead, I was breaking
myself apart over someone who wasn't worth my time. I was up
late trying to finish a paper, late enough that I felt alone, like the
sole person awake on our block, on our block and in the world. It
was a rare clear night, and the sky, for once cloudless, was glinting
with distant stars. *If our lives make sense*, I'd thought, *it must be a*

sense visible only from that great a distance. No matter that much of what watched from there had long since vanished, the light that was only just reaching me seemed alive with comprehension, compassion. *What would it tell us if it could speak?*

How many thoughts, how much longing and bargaining with who knows what had I wasted on someone who would eventually, I was sure of it, dwindle to just the faintest smudge of a memory? Where might I be if I had given that energy to something, anything else? And without having decided to, I was talking to the gathering of stars:

Please help me to let go of this story. Please help me to give my heart over to my mother.

If it was a prayer, it seemed to travel out into all that the night sky kept hidden.

I graduated. My mother made it to campus but slept in her hotel during the commencement ceremony. At one of the celebratory gatherings, Conrad's father-in-law leaned over to whisper to me that she did not look at all well. His words chipped through the stubborn veneer of my denial and nicked at my flesh.

I spent one last summer in Cambridge, saying goodbye to the site of my first real brush with independence. I spent a few nights in bed with a boy from my summer job, thinking I'd go back to being good, being chaste, in a few months' time.

In September, I moved back home to Fairfield. Despite my complete understanding of my mother's prognosis, I was still confounded by statements that suggested she wouldn't recover. It must be the very nature of denial not to assent until knowledge, which is abstract, has given way to incontrovertible fact.

At home, Jean was the one who knew how to minister to our mother's needs quickly and quietly, how to make sure she felt the dignity that her illness by that point seemed intent upon whittling away. Jean was the one who bathed our mother, who got her in and out of the bathroom, who emptied and cleaned the basin of the hospice toilet (like a lawn chair with a bucket lowered into its seat), who did all the other things I never even learned to do. And because it was Jean who knew how to lower her voice and speak quietly with my mother about the things that would make her most comfortable, it appeared to me, throughout the day and night, that the two of them were conspiring. I knew they weren't, but sometimes the sight of their heads close together, and the soft rumblings of their conversation, unsettled me: I was too far away, an outsider unable to anticipate what would be needed next, not wanting to be fully aware of how the things we were every day willing ourselves to accept would eventually play themselves out. I envied them that closeness, but I didn't begrudge it. For my part, I was most relieved by the companionable silence, punctuated by laughter, in which my mother and I sometimes sat watching old black-and-white movies on TV. That particular wordlessness always brought me back to my childhood, the time when she was everything to me. Laughing with her at something Katharine Hepburn or Rosalind Russell had just said or done, I could just about convince myself that I'd come full circle—that I'd gone off on my own and lived a life and then come back to her as if nothing else in the world could possibly matter.

What I was capable of doing well, it seemed, was cooking for my mother. She described some craving—old-fashioned buttery dumplings in chicken broth or fluffy tea cakes made with cinnamon and nutmeg—and though it had been years since I'd tasted or even thought of such things, I'd snap to it and make efficient use of the tools at my disposal in our kitchen. Even if it was just a plate of eggs and a cup of milky coffee, my mother beamed when I returned with a tray of the food she had convinced herself to want. "You're so good and so quick in the kitchen," she'd say, and I'd feel as though I was valuable after all, as though I were doing more than mucking around amid my own mess of feelings about what it was we were living through, more than merely indulging in thoughts of my own life and how it was on its way to becoming, I was certain, as weightless, silent, and inhospitable as a moonscape.

Between hospital visits, my father busied himself among his woodworking tools in the garage, or else he disappeared helping a neighbor hang drywall or lay a new floor, tasks that had always been a cinch for him and in which, I suspect, he could lose track of the larger reality riding him just as it rode the rest of us. Surely the clarity of such things, the indisputable right angles, the certainty of joint meeting joint, was preferable to the cloud of mystery that hung over our lives in those months. Still, why didn't he or I know how to stop, sit down, and begin the slow process of saying good-bye? Did anyone? Yes, we talked to one another. We hugged, reminisced, said "I love you" again and again, just like we always had. But what if goodbye sat deeper than any of those things? What if goodbye was about dragging the depths and finding new words, words capable of saying something much bigger and much more permanent? Were those the things that Jean and my mother were saying when their heads were close together and their voices barely a whisper?

"Your father has always had a hard time with goodbyes," my mother said one afternoon, after Jean or I had made a comment about how Dad always seemed to be chasing after some or another chore to do. "Well, when his parents were dying, he couldn't deal with it and found ways of running away."

When she said the word *dying*, it struck me that she knew very well what was happening, had come to understand where all of this was pointing. Of course she had. Hadn't the doctors, hadn't even her own son the doctor, made it clear what could and could no longer be done? Still, no one wanted to talk about it, not even her. She was fifty-nine years old, after all. Death should have had no business with her.

It occurred to me then that I was angry with my father. I was infuriated by his inability to respond to the death leaning toward us from just out of frame. I should have been angry at myself for the same reasons, but I chose to direct the anger outwardly instead. Through my own stress-addled reasoning, my father became the source for everything we were going through: my mother's going away from this life was really her going away from him and whatever pain I had come to believe—to be very certain—he had caused her. Maybe it was the result of all the time she had been made to spend alone, waiting for him to come home—all the time he'd been away from her in the military or in his apartment in Silicon Valley. Maybe that longing had planted the first seed of the cancer. If not that, then surely he'd done something else. He was a man, after all; wasn't that crime enough? Don't all men lie to women at some point, hurt and betray them? Hadn't men been responsible for the only pain I'd known up until that point, a pain that had, at times, felt capable of making me turn against myself in mind and body? I desperately needed a target for the anger my grief had launched, and so I convinced myself that, in simply being the man to whom she was married, my father had fostered the cancer and taught it to thrive.

One night, I was so desperate to let out some of what had begun to eat me up that I found a reason to scream at him. "This is your fault!" I cried, standing halfway between the living room and kitchen, shouting loudly enough that my mother must have heard. And when he was surprised, taken aback rather than shamed, I turned up the volume. "You're the one who's doing this! You're fucking killing her!"

I could see him flash on. He looked at me as though he were Moses and I the Israelites who had proven themselves incapable, yet again, of keeping God's law. And he was that big, it seemed to me then, a man on that everlasting scale, a man built from first fire, from unbreakable stone. His mouth tightened, but the words came out quietly. "Watch your language when you are in my house," he told me. And, remembering that it was still in his power to say so and that I was still his child to punish, he added, "Go to your room."

Some nights during the daze of that autumn, while my mother drifted in and out of sleep with the half dreams and hallucinations of narcotic medications, I'd lie on the floor at the foot of her bed. Jean would lie down on the floor to her side. We kept blankets and pillows there in her room just for that, a precaution we'd begun taking once our father's presence in the bed had begun to cause her discomfort and he'd moved into the small bedroom across the hall. I'm sure he, too, must have felt discomfort, knowing how delicate she had become, how much the physical reality of his wife had already begun to elude him. He stood back in deference to Jean and to the hospice nurse who came by each day. From the outside, it seemed that his knowledge of his wife's body had been erased. When he lifted my mother from her wheelchair, it was with a nervous caution. When he wheeled her around the neighborhood for a little fresh air, he seemed so much more awkward, so much more tentative than he did, say, wheeling a barrow full of stones or dirt, things I'd seen him handle with a confident, offhanded ease. It was as if he was struggling to attend to this person who was already only partly of this place, almost no longer his.

I wondered if he felt lonely or banished in the twin bed in the room across the hall or if that little bit of distance kept him from feeling that his presence—not the physical one but the real one, the sum of who he was and who he had been, with and to and in response to her—wouldn't wound her, if ever it had. I was drawing from my relatively new knowledge of what happens to people who have become intimate with one another, how you can be devastated by someone's actions and feelings, even as you hold him near and breathe in the close smell your bodies create together.

I had been home six weeks, and the necessity of that time made everything that had come before feel remote, not only far away but vague, only half-remembered, as if nothing but that new Now was real. One night, my mother began talking to someone in a low voice. Though I knew the medications caused this, it always startled me, as if she could see through this world to the next, to the places where ghosts and angels sit and walk and gesture unseen among us. Very calmly, as if she were speaking to someone seated beside her on the bed, she said, "Yes, I know she will, if that's what she wants to do." My eyes filled with tears. I felt instinctively that she was talking about me.

"Who is there with you?" I asked.

Usually, she'd laugh and say a thing like, "Oh, this medicine has me confused." But this time she said, very clearly and now very much awake, "There are two angels sitting here, Tracy, and one of them just told me you're going to become a writer."

Jean and I must have asked her what they looked like, what else they'd said, but all I remember is the ensuing silence, the feeling that something powerful was there at her side. Did it mean she might live after all? Could the angels, or whoever had sent them, see to that? Or had they come to usher her away, to orient her to a new and altogether foreign realm?

I was afraid. Suddenly, she seemed far from us, more spirit than flesh. We were a whole lifetime away from those nights when, still a child, I'd lie in bed beside her, talking and then saying my prayers before sleep. *Dear Lord, thank you for a good day. Please give us a good night's rest and watch over us. Please bless . . .* Nights when I'd inhale the scent of her, pace my breathing to hers, and sometimes toss my arm up around her side or warm her back with mine. It was simple then, a kind of perfection. There was a perfection even to the times when I struggled with fear, when my eyes played strange tricks on me, and everything would appear as though it were very, very small and at a much greater distance from me than it ought to have been. As if the house around us had become a toy house. I felt like a ghost, stranded at an infuriating distance from the things and people I loved and needed, or a giant, too big to make use of the place where I thought I belonged. "Everything is fine," she always assured me, and then I'd squeeze my eyes shut and lean against her until morning.

But now, she was the one who was larger than all of us, the one who no longer belonged here in the world that felt, all of a sudden, so small. Finally, I could accept that she was going. She was already partway gone. What I felt, inescapably just then, was earthbound: anchored to this world, caught inside a merciless finitude. Then I heard her breathing the steady, slow, ragged-sounding breaths we listened for so closely in those, her final weeks.

If I were Jean, I'd have known what to do with my emotions, the self-pity and the fury and the fear of what it would feel like when what we were waiting for had finally happened. If I were Jean, I'd remember that, no matter how shipwrecked I felt, no matter how lost and deprived of air, it was our mother who came first. Jean had always known that, had lived by the fact. Jean, who'd been present for every medical appointment. Jean, who'd learned to counter our father's nervous energy and his distress-induced impatience with gentle nurturing. Mother, my grandmother, who was living with my aunts in New York by then, didn't have the faintest idea what was happening to her oldest daughter. She was lost in the recesses of her own mind, in a labyrinth of memories she no longer possessed the words to describe. And so it was Jean who became for our mother the one thing anyone who cannot care for herself longs to have: a mother of her own.

I wish I could have looked what was happening in the face and stood my ground, not as some version of myself amped up on misguided rage, but as me, the Tracy my mother saw in her mind when she called my name and waited for me to appear. I wish I could have said to myself, *Your mother will be gone soon,* and known to take in that truth without rushing to hide it behind some other, smaller truth. I wish I'd been adult enough to let what was happening reach me in its totality, rather than just thinking of it in bits and pieces when I was alone, away from a witness or potential companion in my fear. It was my mother, after all, the woman I was born to, built from, the one I turned to for every morsel of truth I hungered for as a child.

In November, having been told by her doctor and hospice nurse and by our own sense of her ups and downs at that stage in the cancer's progression that she was at the very end, everyone came back home. My brothers brought their wives with them and moved into the upstairs guest rooms. Wanda reclaimed her old bed. For a stretch of days and nights that dark late autumn, we all found ourselves sitting vigil around our mother's bed, watching her and talking to one another in quiet voices while she slept. Pastor Gainey, who had been coming by the house to pray with us, but also, I came to understand, just to spend time with his sick friend, was often with us in her room, basking in her presence, which still felt palpable despite the fact that she was, by then, rarely awake.

"Sometimes, I think if I can just come over and touch Kathy's foot, I'll feel good. It's a kind of blessing," a longtime neighbor said, laying a hand on her blanket. And I didn't mind the comment or the gesture, could understand the urge to see her as slightly more than human. She *was* becoming more than human, letting go of a body riddled with signs of its own mortality.

But mostly we were silent, listening to her breath as it rode in and out past the fluids that had built up in her chest and throat. That burbling sound that pained us but that we were on edge to hear.

There was a long silence during which her chest didn't seem to move. It felt like the moment of stasis after an object tossed in the air has reached its apex and before it begins its fall. Was that how it would happen? Was that what we were gathered there for, what we had been dreading and perhaps also hoping might come to release her and us from the grip of such grim anticipation?

Before I could react, Pastor Gainey took my father's hand and my brother's, starting a chain reaction that linked all of us together around her bed. And he began to sing, in a voice I'd grown up with but that I seemed to be hearing just then for the first time:

> *While I draw this fleeting breath,*
> *when mine eyes shall close in death,*
> *when I soar to worlds unknown,*
> *see Thee on Thy judgment throne,*
> *Rock of Ages, cleft for me,*
> *let me hide myself in Thee.*

Tears streaked my face as I struggled to accept that she could go without waking, without even signaling goodbye, without hearing our last words to her, words I had at last begun to rehearse to myself.

But her eyes flicked open, like a doll's eyes, wide and round and surprised at the group of us. She was still there, still alive, still one of us. She opened her mouth to smile a child's wide smile. "Hi," she said. It was a long, lilting salutation, as if we had arrived with a cake on her birthday.

A STRANGE AFTER

I BELIEVE SHE WANTED TO KEEP LIVING, BUT SHE WASN'T HUNG up on it. It makes sense now, the way she'd said that God *could* heal her. Meaning it was within His power, up to Him. Just as He could choose not to and instead to call her home, to let her live in the ever after she always believed was beyond this one. Having her there made it real, not the frivolous cartoon place I'd tried to convince my cousin Nina of when we were kids, the one with gold-paved streets and block after block of identical mansions, but someplace with purpose. A place where my mother's faith and her goodwill might be reunited with her spirit's original amplitude so that she was large, larger than all of us who grieved her. Larger than the world as she had known to imagine it or the God in whom she had trusted, who was larger and stranger than she'd known to imagine Him.

In the days preceding her funeral, the house was full, and we moved through the blur of actions that always fills in the space between someone's death and our ritual for saying goodbye. I was surprised at what it felt like, surprised enough that I wondered if what I was feeling was really what I felt: an empty, groggy disbelief coupled with an unexpected relief. As if the long buildup to letting go was almost worse than the silent free fall of afterward. That wasn't it, exactly. But at least, finally, there was a name for what I felt—grief—a shape to try to fit it into. There were words, sanctioned words I might offer or collect like the dull, heavy coins of that new realm.

There were times, lots of them, when someone would offer to pray with me. I never said no. I possessed no inclination to take God to task for my mother's death, didn't find it difficult to think of her death as something that had happened to her rather than me, some twist or fold in her destiny that had only just brushed against mine.

My mother had been so adamant about the afterlife that she'd forbidden us from making a shrine of her grave. "Bury me in a simple pine box, and don't visit my body in the ground. I won't be there." She'd said it almost happily, triumphantly, as if doing such things might constitute proof that Heaven is real. And we came as close to doing what she'd asked as the funeral industry would allow, eschewing the brushed titanium Cadillac of coffins and choosing, instead, the plainest oak.

At the burial, we stood around the gravesite in our dark mourning clothes. Pastor Gainey spoke, I'm sure, movingly, powerfully, but my mind would not stay still. *Is she with us now, or has she already gone? And if she goes, can she ever come back?* I thought of her watching our flimsy bodies, our bowed heads and put-upon shoulders, with a tenderness and a clarity beyond our ability to grasp. How miniature our lives must have looked from there and how utterly bereft we must have seemed, standing over the hole in the earth that would never contain her.

Look up, I imagined her saying. *Look up and see how much distance waits beyond this life! Be happy for me! Be glad!* In the first moments after her death, when it was clear that she was gone, I looked up at the ceiling above where her body lay. I had been thinking about what people say happens when a person dies, how the spirit hovers in the room awhile, watching from above, taking in the fact that it has come free of the body that was once its anchor. November 14, 1994. A rainy Monday night. I wanted her to see my face as she floated off toward whatever awaited her, as if that gesture might serve as a signal that I believed she was on her way to that else-where, the tunnel and the light, the other side. But I hadn't given any thought to what it would feel like to me, staring up at what my eyes told me was nothing at all.

The memorial service was at First Baptist after the funeral. Conrad and our father and I each spoke (the others had feared it might be impossible to keep their emotions under control long enough to say anything), and then we listened to the other con-gregants as they made their tributes and offered their goodbyes. One of my mother's church acquaintances was a young man I'd never met before, my own age or perhaps a bit younger. When her health had taken a swerve for the worse, he'd begun coming by the house to sing for her. He stood up and sang one of her favorite hymns—I wish I could remember which—and though my heart buckled each time his voice went off-key, I was touched and peevishly jealous, that the two of them had shared something so intimate, so quietly profound. How many more lives would we find, if we only knew how to seek them, within the life we recog-nized as hers?

A woman we'd known for a long time, who had been living with an illness of her own for several years, rose and described a vision she'd had the evening of my mother's death. As she began to speak, I tried to remember what had plagued her health. Was it epi-lepsy? Mental illness? After years of hearing her name, I realized I had only the vaguest sense of who she was. She had always seemed somewhat rattled to me, as if her sickness or the medication facilitating her recovery had taken her a little ways away from perfect clarity. But this woman—Sharon, that was her name—spoke in earnest.

"I saw Kathy being ushered up to Heaven," she said, gesturing with her arms so that her rings caught the pulpit light and her bangles clanked against one another. Her makeup had been applied with a heavy hand, Southern Baptist–style, like Tammy Faye Bakker, so her eyes seemed fixed in place, dark spots on her otherwise powdery face. "And I saw all the many angels who were there to welcome her." At that point, she stretched out her arms and fluttered her hands like a singer waving to fans from a spotlit stage. "They were curious about this person, this blessed person who was coming into their midst."

It was the kind of church talk that usually caused me to glaze over. The fluffy clouds and white robes, the harps and heavens, the unsettling depictions of Christ as a spaced-out blond naïf. But Sharon was talking about my mother. And if she had information—even a medication-driven intuition—about where my mother had gone to and about how I might attempt to imagine her—well, I wanted it, wanted to add it to my stable of versions, the ones I flipped through before sleep when the stars all seemed to be facing elsewhere.

A reception was held in the room just behind the sanctuary, a room where I'd sat for years in putty-colored folding chairs listening to Sunday school lessons. A room that, because of its multiple functions, also bore the faint Jesus-smell of stale coffee. Tables of food had been set up along the wall by the church ladies who had succeeded the ones I remembered from my childhood. Some of them weren't much older than me. The meal was homespun potluck fare, and it was offered in love, but again, I was irrationally angry, just as I'd been with my father weeks earlier, unleashing upon him a rage that was merely a symptom of my own impending grief. Nevertheless, I found myself despising that church meal. It was hodgepodge, mismatched. Nothing like what my mother would have put together for company.

I'd baked an Alabama lemon cheese layer cake and a black-and-white checkerboard square cake, which my mother had made only on special occasions, and while the others of us were sitting in the memorial service, one of those well-meaning ladies had hacked them into tiny cubes and skewered the bits with wooden toothpicks. A handwritten note sat between them reading: *Kathy's daughter has baked cakes using her mother's special recipes.* I crumpled it in my hand and tossed it in the trash. No matter that she was already gone, and no matter that the ladies who orchestrated this gathering had just as much right to grieve her as we did, I was rankled.

The other girl I knew in high school who'd lost her mother to cancer, the one who drove the old burgundy Saab, was there. She read about the service in the obituary we had placed and came to pay her respects. We were alike in our loss. I didn't know how I ought to behave in light of such a fact. We walked outside and talked about mundane things, smiling those pained smiles that meant there was something we were aware of not knowing how to say.

In the weeks following the funeral, after all the distant family had left and routine began to reassert itself, I found it surprising that there was space for so many of my ordinary moods, stretches of any given day when everything, or almost everything, felt normal, or almost normal. But then I'd catch myself thinking of my mother as if she were there, just a room away, and the reality of her death crept back in like the mortar between bricks, holding everything in place in a strange After that no longer included her.

Back when I was in grade school and fascinated by anything old-fashioned, I'd convinced my mother to buy me a few kerosene lamps. I liked to read by them, even though their light was flickering. It made me feel like I could step inside history and live there awhile, not my same self but not quite a stranger either. My mother derived nostalgic satisfaction from sharing those things with me, things she remembered from her rural childhood in the 1940s, beautiful obsolete things that almost seemed to delineate the borders of a place where child versions of the two of us might be able to meet.

One dark winter afternoon when one of the kerosene lamps was burning in the living room, I put down my book and wandered into the next room where my mother was blocking together pieces for a quilt. *The Phil Donahue Show* was on the television, with the sound turned down low. "Go back and check on that lamp," she'd said after a few minutes.

"Okay," I'd replied, but the TV caught my attention, and I didn't go.

"Is that lamp all right?" she'd asked after another minute.

And, certain that it was, I'd told her, "Yes, it's fine."

A minute later, something told me to get up and go check. It was a quiet but urgent feeling, and I jumped up to make sure everything was in order. When I got to the living room, I saw a column of flame licking the ceiling. My mother had the presence of mind to cap the top of the lamp with a dish resting on the same table, and luckily the flame consented to being snuffed out, though it left a dark, sooty ring on the ceiling. It took a long time for the spot to fade.

Sometimes after Mom had died, I'd be going along as if everything were fine, as if the day were any ordinary day. And then the fact of her death—no, not simply the fact of her death but rather the facts of her death and her life; her presence in this world and the presence her absence made; the whole of what I remembered or lacked; everything she gave and left and what, in leaving, she took—the fact of all that, like a column of threat and promise and light, would flare bright and hot in my mind.

ABIDE

ROUND THE NEW YEAR, MY FATHER BEGAN SEEING SOME-
one. She was a family friend, a widow whose husband had
died the year before my mother, also of cancer. My father and this
widow had so much in common, simply in terms of what they'd
lost, that their bond must have felt destined, possibly even ordained.
My father took to preening, taking stock of what he looked like.
He went out in the evenings. Some nights, he didn't bother coming
home. After a time, when his relationship no longer seemed to be
simply a means of compensating for the loss of my mother but a
source of happiness in and of itself, I began to feel threatened. Not
for myself. I felt threatened because this new woman, a perfectly
kind, respectable, loving woman, had managed to find a place of
primacy in my father's heart—the place I'd wanted him to guard,
at least a season longer, for my mother.

I dreamt over and over, in countless variations, that my mother
stood facing my father and his new companion. Finally, understanding that she'd been replaced, she retreated, returned to wherever it was she had been. No—first, she'd linger a moment, joining
Jean and me in wordless commiseration. Then she would go. She
was always silent, watching with such a calm understanding that
the dream felt unbearable. Waking, I began to pose foolish riddles
to myself: what would my father do if she did come back? Whose
side would he choose? What would he prefer, given the choice:

the old life or the new? I knew this was not a choice in which I was directly implicated, yet when I allowed myself to suspect that, on occasions, he did seem more inclined toward this new life, I was made to suffer. Perhaps because I was a product of the old life, every indication that the new life mattered felt like an indictment. I stewed over these musings, understanding perfectly well that the logic fueling them was flawed. Jean must have felt the same way because she and I bickered with our father frequently about how quickly he had shifted his focus from our mother and her house and the two of us there in it to this new woman who commanded so much of his attention.

Sometimes my father and I would pass from this bickering to a heated debate. We'd yell, then pause for air, then hurl our feelings at one another, urging, daring the other to respond. Sometimes, these arguments would go on for long stretches, until the anger would dissipate and we'd find ourselves just talking, or talking and crying. Jean would sit there silently, uncomfortable with the mess of our feelings, angry at both of us for letting things go so far, though those were precisely the times I felt that my father and I were for the first time in my life breaking down the barriers to a more genuine knowledge of one another.

I'd never spoken so freely or so honestly with my mother. I'd never had the occasion, having hidden from her everything that would have brought our most starkly differing viewpoints into contact. I hadn't known how to do anything else. The idea of debate—of vehement disagreement that gives way to understanding—was something it had taken college, and all the theories I'd thrown myself behind as a way of testing out my beliefs and the power of my intellect, to acquaint me with. Before that, I always shrank away from disputes, not understanding what they were good for. Whenever my brothers had argued politics with my father, the exchanges had always deadlocked, with nobody shifting from where they'd started. The room had filled up with an ugly heat that the parties in question had eventually fled. When my parents had debated with the Mormons and Jehovah's Witnesses who sometimes came knocking, they'd done so with the belief that they were defending the one true God against false idols and that everything rode upon not changing viewpoints, not backing down. My parents had stood firmly on our side of the threshold and the proselytizers had stood firmly out there on the porch, and eventually someone had conceded that the conversation had run its course. In contrast to all those stagnant arguments I'd grown up watching, living out what felt like a genuinely dialectical approach to conflict made me proud—not just of myself but also of my father, as though he and I were learning the terms of a language we could share. Those times, I'd harbor a satisfaction: *I am an adult now,* I'd think. *I was a child when she died.* Now I realize what was really going on: that, bit by bit, fighting with my father helped me forgive him for needing to go on living his life among the living. And it helped me to forgive myself for having been too young, too inexperienced at life, to have opened myself up with a similar honesty with my mother.

I wonder if my father felt similarly liberated, if he was at all relieved by this chance to show his children who he was or needed to be. I don't know how to describe the deep visceral jolt—the queasy mix of shock, shame, and dread—that swallowed Jean and me when he held up the gauzy negligee he had purchased as a Valentine's Day gift for his girlfriend. It mortified me, but it also, very quietly, reminded me that I could finally just be myself with my father, who had, after so many years of working to be more, finally let himself become an ordinary human man. That same mix of feelings, felt all at once like a cold blast—shock, shame, and dread, followed immediately by something like permission to become more fully and unabashedly myself—arose one winter afternoon when, going through the garage pantry in pursuit of the last jars of our mother's homemade preserves, Jean and I happened upon the place where my father had chosen to store his supply of condoms.

Before winter gave out, I decided to throw a party. There had been too much sorrow in our home, too many gatherings fueled by loss. I invited my college friends who'd landed in the Bay Area and the high school friends I'd reconnected with since my return. I wanted a total convergence, and not just of my own worlds. Conrad had by then taken a position in Pittsburgh, and Wanda had moved back to LA, but my father had agreed to be there, and so had Jean and Michael and his family. I'd wanted to cook and drink and play music in the house in a way that brought some of the life back to it. I remember sketching out menus in the days leading up to the party, just like my mother would have done. When the night of the party arrived, we stood talking in darkened rooms, the dim lights an uncanny testament to the spirit of that time, when we were still running on empty, trying to replenish something we'd eventually have to learn to live without. A couple of high school friends had brought a bottle of cream tequila with them, and I recall the timbre of my own forced cheer, trying to get everyone to join me, to drink and eat and dance so I'd have a reason, once they all left, to fall into a deep, blank sleep.

Nobody had said much about my mother. I suppose enough time had passed so that everything had already been said, or been written in cards and sent, or else left awkwardly unsaid. I'm sure someone must have offered a word or several of condolence, which I'd tried to smooth over or rush along, out of my own exhaustion with the rituals of grief. One guest whom I'd never liked much at college—she was unceasingly competitive and blunt-minded with a slightly bullying personality—had spent most of the night talking about her upcoming wedding (I wasn't invited; I'd never even met her fiancé), though she had found time to get in a jab about the Super Kmart she'd driven past on her way to our house. Perhaps the night was simply an attempt to pull myself back into the world everyone else still dwelled in.

I had other friends who knew what it felt like to live without a mother. Too many others. The girl whose mother had driven the burgundy Saab. And Qiana, with whom I'd walked the two blocks to high school until it became clear that waiting for her each morning would invariably make me late. Her mother had died within weeks of my mom, from an illness that had plagued her quietly for perhaps the same length of time as my mother's cancer. And there was a girl I'd been close to briefly in the fifth grade, whose mother was there and then all of a sudden was not. And another whose father was a pilot and whose mother had once let us drink a bottle of champagne at a sleepover on New Year's Eve. And Rose, who wasn't a girl but a woman and who was like a sister to my sisters. They all knew what it felt like to have a dead mother. How did they describe it to themselves, this state? I barely knew. Once, I spent the evening with two of them out at the ranch that one girl's father, the pilot, had inherited upon his wife's death. It had been in the family for a long time, and someone needed to take it on, so he'd left his suburban tract neighborhood and moved into the big house at the end of a long row of mammoth cypresses, the same trees as grow in graveyards. The three of us motherless girls had decided to take a walk in the orchard, and because the stars were out, or because we were all three together for the first time since everything had changed, we'd started talking about our mothers.

"I think she's there and here at the same time," someone said, tipping her head up toward the sky—a sky the trees seemed to push farther back so that the distance we looked up toward was even less fathomable, less within our grasp.

The words came out of my mouth before I even knew I'd wanted to speak. "I know she wanted it to be exactly like the Bible says, but I think it has to be different." How far off everything felt. Not just my mother and not just the answers to the questions her death had set into motion. I felt remote even from a clear sense of what I myself believed. A breeze moved through the trees. "There's just so much out there . . ." I trailed off.

We tried talking our way to a sense of what we believed. We tried talking in a way that might make us feel both looked after and utterly free. Standing there, with our shoes sinking into the ground and the wind rifling the orchard leaves, with the smells of fruit and rot and the sounds of nocturnal animals going about their nocturnal rituals, we tried to say some of what we thought or felt or wondered. We tried, but it was too soon, or else the dark had rendered foreign all we thought we knew, and so we didn't ever manage to speak of how irremediably broken we all were. Perhaps we didn't need to.

In our silence, the darkness began to close in. I felt it all at once, like a presence that knew more than I wanted it to know and pushed up against me with the heft of that knowing. I wanted to run back through the muddy orchard rows not just to the bright, ordinary light of the house, but to a time and place when someone would be awake in a different room, calling out to us now and again, saying, *Isn't it time you girls were getting to sleep?*

CLEARANCES

ALONE IN MY ROOM, BY MY WINDOW OVERLOOKING THE ROOF-tops and the low hills that were wet and green in the distance, reading poems to myself became a kind of ritual. The slim volumes of poetry I'd brought home with me from college offered a sense of continuity between the life I'd begun to lead on my own and the life I'd been drawn back into upon returning home. Every time I set foot in my room, it was as though I were chasing the handful of writers I'd come to know while I was away—chasing because I didn't want to let them get away, didn't want them to veer out of my grasp (I was certain they'd want to escape, given how little I knew how to say, and how little there was there to command their attention). Those winter afternoons spent upstairs with the pack of my most necessary poets—Seamus Heaney, Elizabeth Bishop, Philip Larkin, Yusef Komunyakaa, William Matthews—were teaching me about what it felt like to try to regard the totality of something I'd only known in part. A life, they told me, is made of what happens and what is lost. Looking back, we learn to name those things, to see and understand them. We hold them for a minute, looking first with innocent, untrained eyes, but if we hang there for a while longer, we can step into a different kind of gaze, one capable of seeing what is absent, longed for, what has been willed away or simply forgotten.

The heartbreak I'd felt once my romance with my high school

teacher had been shut down marked one of my losses, as had the
debilitating ache of losing love after that, again and again. I thought
about those earlier losses and realized how far they'd receded not
just into the past but into the distance, where feelings no longer
reached. Had I willed them away, or had they simply run their
course? But the loss death brought refused to recede. Death was
like an indelible error no one could correct. It did not relinquish
its hold on the present tense. It left a shape so deep and intricate it
made no sense whatsoever to try to fill it. No, the only thing to do,
I suspected, would be to move over and learn to live beside the gulf
left in my mother's wake, peering down into it at times out of need
but making every effort not to topple over and fall in.

There's a sonnet sequence called "Clearances" in Heaney's
book *The Haw Lantern* that I found myself returning to again and
again. It is an elegy for the poet's mother. I had a visceral love of
one particular sonnet about the two of them peeling potatoes in
silence while the other family members were away at Sunday Mass.
I suppose it reminded me of all the days when I was my mother's
tiny satellite, accompanying her everywhere, happy at her side. But
the poem that resonated most mysteriously for me was the sonnet
that closed the sequence:

> *I thought of walking round and round a space*
> *Utterly empty, utterly a source*
> *Where the decked chestnut tree had lost its place*
> *In our front hedge above the wallflowers.*
> *The white chips jumped and jumped and skited high.*
> *I heard the hatchet's differentiated*
> *Accurate cut, the crack, the sigh*
> *And collapse of what luxuriated*

Through the shocked tips and wreckage of it all.
Deep-planted and long gone, my coeval
Chestnut from a jam jar in a hole,
Its heft and hush become a bright nowhere,
A soul ramifying and forever
Silent, beyond silence listened for.

What did it mean to be both empty and a source? Was there something I housed or might one day house? Something the loss of my mother would enable me to give? Or was it her loss that was the source of something? Would something worth having eventually spring from it?

I sometimes thought of how I'd chosen to look up in the first moments after her death. I had made a pact with myself that I would, wanting to show her my face, to tell her I believed she was on her way, as she'd assured us she would be. I'd turned my face up to that nowhere, wanting to feel what it housed, wanting to show that I knew it housed not just something, but my mother, my source. What hurt so much in those months after her death was exactly what Heaney's poem knew how to name: that my gaze in those moments had been pointed up toward a place beyond my discerning, a place I'd never hear or reach or understand for as long as I was myself.

But the poem didn't just lament that aspect of loss; it created a conundrum of presence and largeness, a realness more real than the absolutes we live by: *A soul ramifying and forever / Silent, beyond silence listened for.* Such language consoled me, and it beckoned me to the page, pushed me to test whether I might be capable of writing truths like that into being, truths that would prove better than the ones that eluded or exhausted me from moment to moment in my new life.

Reading at the dark oak desk in my room, the same desk where I'd once written letter after letter to my teacher, I felt close to something. Not my mother. I'd taken her too much at her word to believe she might still be there in the house, living beside us like a ghost. But I did feel, just at those times, a certainty that eluded me throughout the entire rest of the day. It was what I'd felt back at school, sitting in the library armchairs and scribbling poems into my sketchbook, the soul language that seemed to genuinely answer back when I called to it. Sometimes, the clarity with which I heard or felt it was undeniable. It was then, and not without trepidation, that I let myself imagine that poetry might be a means of getting from this portion of my life to the next.

The day to day of my life was not unpleasant. Jean and I had become so close, so candid with one another, and so much like genuine girlfriends that the twelve-year age difference separating us seemed almost to have vanished. She, my father, and I had finally reached a kind of peace, living together in the house that had belonged to my mother more than anyone else. When Dad was there with us and not at his girlfriend's, the three of us ate meals together on the dishes that were my mother's, set the table with linens that were hers, and moved in and out of rooms where objects that had been more hers than ours leaned out from every crevice. We were happy. As happy as we could or ought to have been, anyway, eating our meals, drinking our wine, and watching our movies together, or else going out, each alone, into his or her own private version of the night. Sometimes, Jean and I spent evenings with our father and his girlfriend, evenings where the four of us were content, laughing at the stories that emerged from the new life our father was living. Together we accepted the terrible, immovable fact that our mother would not, could not ever, come back. It wasn't a grim peace. It was simply our lives picking up again after the standstill of shock. The way a train that has sat stalled on the tracks, its lights dimmed and its engine dawdling and a restless impatience or an angry helplessness gripping the passengers waiting in their seats, suddenly lights up and moves forward again toward its destination.

One afternoon, Pastor Gainey came by to check on us and found me home alone reading a Jane Austen novel. I had baked a lemon-cornmeal cake, and the kitchen sent that smell all through the house. It was long enough after the funeral that we both felt free to be smiling and cheerful. I had just taken a job as a substitute teacher, and the fact of having someplace to be most days gave me confidence. Though the visit didn't warrant such a show of formality, I set out my mother's silver coffee service.

"Someone's going to snap you up one of these days and marry you," Pastor Gainey said, chuckling.

I could tell he meant it as a kindness. It made me feel all of the sudden like one of Austen's heroines, like I might be inching my way toward my own plotline, and I felt a shiver of anticipation. I still didn't have any clear plans. I hadn't felt capable, in my final months at college, of making any. While my classmates had been applying to graduate schools and internships or setting up jobs in journalism or finance, all I'd been able to do was tell myself I was going home to be with my mother. It was a decision no one had asked me to make; it had made itself. I was going home to my mother. I was going home. That was as much of the future as I could bear to see. But that was already months ago. Now, my mother was gone and I was still at home, still uncertain whether I had the wherewithal to pick up and move forward. In that state of mind, Pastor Gainey's comment teased me into imagining, for just a split instant, that the vague, faceless force of the future might all along have held something in store for me. Yet as the thought spooled forward, I started to feel afraid of what it would mean to stay there in my hometown for too long and to get snapped up and married just the way that I was: dreaming of doing things (of writing books, to be specific) but having done (and written) next to nothing. It also made me mindful that living in my childhood home was saddling me to the different selves I'd been in that house through the years: the obedient schoolgirl, the surly adolescent, the adult in whom something critical had been stamped out by grief. The longer I thought on it, the more Pastor Gainey's remark struck me as a warning.

In the weeks just before Mom had died, I'd sent off a slapdash application to the creative writing program at Brown. It was the only writing program I was even remotely familiar with, from my visits to Providence before my boyfriend and I had broken up. I'd done a hasty job, as if sending the thing off quickly might diminish the guilt that had come from plotting out my own future in the midst of such an all-consuming present, a present during which nothing but my mother's dwindling life should have mattered. How odd that fewer than three months sat between where I had just been and where I now found myself. It was January. A new year. There was still time to do things properly, to choose another program and put together a solid application that might serve as the bridge to carry me forward and away.

One of the last bits of advice my mother had offered me was to go to grad school. "Further your education. Nobody can ever take that away from you." She said it one afternoon while we sat together on her bed, though we seldom spoke, in those days, about what I should do with my life. For my part, I was afraid to make reference to the time when she would be gone. It was too painful a reality to try to peer into, let alone speak of. But she was being practical. She wanted me to understand that I'd have to look after myself at some point, to climb back onto the day-to-day world I'd been yanked from by her illness.

"Mom wants you to think about applying to law school," Conrad mentioned, a day or two later, when he and I were alone. The prospect of studying law chilled me, but I decided that taking half of her advice and going back to school would be one way of honoring her wishes.

My mother. There were things that had worked their way out of hiding after she died. A notebook dug up from a drawer, in which she had written, *Maybe I can publish my cookbook!* A paperback, covered in a sheet of Sunday comics and barricaded behind wigs and handbags in the top of her closet, that turned out to be a modest sex manual entitled *Nice Girls Do*; it struck me as so innocent that I'd felt a wave of almost maternal compassion for her. But these things were finite. They only pointed me to the woman I had known, when what I wanted and needed were things that might give me a sense of my mother as someone I might still come to know.

Sometimes, when my aunts called from New York to check in on us, I'd ask them to tell me stories about my mother, about what she was like before my siblings and I were born, before she fell in love with my father, when she was still just a girl.

"When we were little, Kathy loved to play 'hospital.' She'd lie down and make us cover her with a quilt and tell us to go get her a handful of raisins. She'd pretend that was her medicine." "Before Kathy met your father, there was a boy she used to talk to named Napoleon, and another boy named Willie James." Tidbits, anecdotes that felt like stolen glances of my mother. The phone calls with my aunts—conversations that were friendly, jovial, not quite motherly but nurturing in a different way—also helped flesh out my idea of who my mother's sisters were, not just in relation to my mother but as people, women, characters in the stories of their own lives: Ursula, who taught kindergarten in Harlem; Evelyn, whom my mother, I suspected, had been closest to; Lucille and June, who lived together in a house just north of the city and who were sisters in the way twins are sisters—two halves of an apparent whole—though they weren't twins and probably didn't think of themselves that way; Carla, right around Jean's age and still marveling herself at the spectacles and the plenitude the city had to offer, who'd driven me on a tour of Harlem at night; and Gladys, who had flown to California to shepherd Mother back to New York and who once looked at a pair of pointy-toed boots I was wearing and said, "You could put your foot dead up someone's ass in those shoes." My aunts held facets of my mother in their voices and their stories and in their very bearing. They were women in whom I might catch glimpses of my mother—and to whom I might reveal myself with the courage and honesty I lacked when my mother, their sister, was alive.

I decided to apply to Columbia. Every chance I got, I tinkered with my essay. It wasn't a personal statement in which I was asked to tell about myself and my relationship to poetry. The application asked for a brief commentary upon a book of contemporary poetry. I chose *Dock Leaves*, a slim volume by a British poet named Hugo Williams. It was dedicated to his mother, who'd died the year before mine, a fact that had disposed me toward a feeling of kinship with the poet—or gratitude that I might get to tag along as his poems did the work of grief and commemoration. I turned to the essay eagerly during quiet moments—and, to be sure, I had nothing but time. By the time it was done, and I sealed everything into the big white envelope, the gesture felt not so much like a wish or a shot in the dark as a prayer.

Months later, not long after a terse form letter of regret from Brown reached me, I received word that I had been admitted to Columbia. Holding the envelope in my hand, I convinced myself to trust that the angels my mother saw that night in her room had been right. I convinced myself to trust that they had been speaking to me through her. At the time, the thought of them there in the room with us, in their perfection so thorough it could only sit outside of this human plane, had cowed me. Now, needing them to be right, not knowing what I'd do if they were wrong, I submitted to them, took them at their word. I claimed them as my angels, imploring them to give a piece of my mother back, to show me that she was still available to me—not locked in the past tense, but rather eternal and ongoing. *A soul ramifying and forever / Silent, beyond silence listened for.*

EPILOGUE: DEAR GOD

WHEN I FIRST BROUGHT MY NEWBORN DAUGHTER HOME, it felt as if I were setting foot into a house where someone had died. There was that same unsettling sense of connection to an unknowable elsewhere, to the vast and mysterious place that threatens us at least as much as it makes us feel eager and whole. There was that same awe, exactly that: wonder and terror. That same sense of being helplessly small in the face of something infinitely powerful and unsettlingly near. It was that way again when my sons were born. Wonderful and terrible. Is that what my mother met each time another of us arrived, tugging her world in a new and as-yet-unnamed direction?

Those first hazy newborn weeks, in the half-light of feedings, and in the sleepless whirl of everything else, I discovered another version of my own urge toward the divine: the desire to pray. *Dear God, protect her.* At first, that was all. And then, *Dear God, please allow me to give her everything she deserves.* And then, *Dear God, let me live long enough to help her along whatever path she chooses.* I prayed this way for my daughter and again for my sons. I spoke these prayers aloud. They came out of me with urgency, a fervency that did not strike me as quite me. It was all I could do, all that the deep and abiding need would permit—the need to believe that not even death would put an end to the bond I feel with my children. I still do not really know what led my mother to God with the kind of vigor she seemed to possess for the idea of that particular here-after, but I wonder, now that I have become a mother myself, if her faith was born of something fundamentally very simple. I wonder if gazing into each newborn face—at each little being who seemed at once ancient and utterly new, fragile and yet, by turns, possessed of an almost discomfiting poise—had put my mother (as it did me) in search of anything that would permit her, quite simply, to last. *Dear God, please let me keep her in my life even after I no longer have a life. Please let me always, always be her mother.*

Is God each of the many different things we seek in the course of a life? Family for a short time, and then unfettered independence, and then love? Is God what animates the body, drawing us into a deeper, more primal sense of our physical selves? And then, when that appetite is calmed, does God move out of the body and into wherever it is that tenderness or compassion reside? Does God become an armament we leverage for the ones we love, the ones we have committed to nurture and protect? I don't know what I think. I know that the God I was taught to see as a child, the one who watched over me like an omnipotent father, is still one piece of the God I call upon now. But I feel myself most alive, most elec-tric with faith, breath, and courage, when I think of God as a cur-rent that runs through all that is. Not by will or by choice. Not as a benediction but because there are laws that even God must obey.

When I think of the shape God made in my mother's mind, even as she faced illness and death, I now believe that what I am seeing is the shape, from my own incomplete vantage point, of my mother's mind.

My mother. In the now I belong to, she has been gone so long it's almost as though she must only have been a dream that felt real but wasn't. She has been gone so many years, the moment is

approaching when she will have been gone longer than she was
with me, and perhaps then it will turn out that I can only struggle
to remember her the way one does a dream. So many years during
which, at times, I have felt relieved not to have had to see her take
in my mistakes. Years that have granted me permission—at least
I've taken it as permission—to remember her in any way I choose.
Though today, when I try to put her back together in my mind, it
is because I am searching for the real her, the woman she would
have shown herself to be; the woman who could sit me down and
tell me exactly what to do, how to mother my children so that they
will feel safe being children, how to be playful and patient and for-
giving, the way she somehow always managed to be; the woman
who would cast every one of my memories and fantasies of her as
uniquely wrong.

I am searching. It has taken the writing and reliving of all of this
to convince me that this is what I am doing and that my search
must have at its core not just my mother and whatever answers she
could provide for the questions I never learned how to ask. I'm also
searching for a glimpse of the person I could have been alongside
her but chose not to be: the confidante, the fearless interlocutor,
the daughter eager to share how it feels to take her first resolute
steps into the onrush of experience. What shape would God have
taken on inside that version of my mind?

There was a moment in writing this book when I thought that
I would watch the videotape that was made, in 1991 or '92, of my
mother giving testimony at that North Carolina church meeting.
I thought that sitting down and listening to what she was saying,
hearing the words in her voice, and watching her face, her body,
the ways that she communicated herself and her faith, might help
me to finish saying what I had set out to say. I thought that sitting

down and watching her give testimony might allow me to finally live out and release the adolescent feelings of embarrassment that had prevented me from watching the video in the first place. And I thought that listening to her describe her own need for God and the faith that she had embraced might allow me to claim a piece of whatever it was she once testified to. It would have been so easy to let her have that last word and to convince myself that she was speaking for both of us. I was ready to give that much to her, to cede that much.

But I discovered that the video is gone. Just like the life we all once shared in that house, the video disappeared in the years after our mother's death—boxed up, carted off, mislabeled or mistaken for less than it was. If she is to speak now, it will be in a voice I command myself to hear, a voice I must remember or imagine into being.

I AM THREE, RESTING MY HEAD ON MY MOTHER'S HIP, TUCKING my body into the crook of her knees as she lies on her side on the couch. She doesn't speak. It is early afternoon and we are alone together in the house. I can hear the quiet mewling of her stomach, digesting the lunch she's just eaten. I have eaten the same thing, but my body is silent. The only sound I make is my breathing. We are napping together, but I am awake, wedged into the space between my mother and the cushions of the couch. There is nothing I currently want. There is nothing I must do. I feel the fabric of her pant leg against my cheek and smell her perfume. Her body seems to bob or sway, but only slightly, as she breathes. My mother seems like a mystery because she is larger than me.

"Mommy?" I'll say, finally, knowing she is there, that it is her body my small body has burrowed into, but wanting to know that she knows I am there, too. "Mommy?"

"Yes, Tracy?" she'll ask, calmly, once I have punctured her sleep with my need to hear her voice, to feel it rise through her and hum against my ear.

"Oh, nothing," I'll answer. "Nothing."

ACKNOWLEDGMENTS

This book would not have been written without a number of happy coincidences.

Princeton University, which has been my professional home since 2005, has brought me into conversation with some of the most remarkable writers of our time and facilitates the stability that has allowed me to invest my energy and focus upon my writing. My colleagues there inspire me to want to grow, develop, produce, and contribute to the conversation their voices make in the world.

The Rolex Mentor and Protégé Arts Initiative, in its generous commitment to young artists and to the conversation across genres and generations, provided me with the opportunity to work closely with eminent writer and cultural critic Hans Magnus Enzensberger. His guidance, his example, and his friendship have forever changed my sense of myself as a writer and a citizen. He gently but honestly pushed me to find my voice in prose, to invest in characters, and to invite the world beyond myself into this story.

My agent, Markus Hoffmann, helped me to hone the core of this book. I remain indebted to him as the reader whose interest urged me on when it would have been very easy to stall or stop.

My editor, Robin Desser, became the reader for whom I committed to push into the most difficult regions of the story I had set out to tell. Her compassion, insight, and belief calmed and consoled me. And her wisdom and intelligence taught me how prose is built. It would have been quite nearly enough just to share this work with her, but I am immensely grateful that she has helped me to turn my own private material into a book.

Continued and ongoing thanks go to Tina Chang, for her faith, insight, and friendship through these many years.

It is one thing to excavate one's own private material and another thing altogether to share it with the world, having discovered, along the way, how much other people's lives and stories are integral to it. I wish to thank my family for trusting me to tell my story, which has brought elements of their stories to light. And I wish to ask forgiveness for anything they would have remembered differently or anything they'd have preferred to forget.

I conceived of this as a book from a mother to her daughter. My luminous Naomi has been in my mind and heart throughout the writing of every line of this story. And now that her brothers, Sterling and Atticus, have arrived, perhaps this book will give them access to their mother and her people that will be important to them as sons and one day as men.

My most urgent, exultant, profound, and loving thanks go to my husband, Raphael Allison. My first reader. My best friend and soul mate. This (and everything else, always) is also for him.